The LAUREL & HARDY DIGEST

A COCKTAIL OF LORE, LOVE AND HISSES
SERVED BY WILLIE McINTYRE

The Laurel & Hardy Digest

© Willie McIntyre 1998

First published 1998

ISBN 0 9532958 0 X

Published by:
Willie McIntyre,
39 Bankhouse Avenue,
Largs,
Ayrshire,
Scotland,
KA30 9PF.

Printed by:
Cordsfall Ltd
0141 332 4640

CONTENTS

Chapter 1: Factfile 7
Chapter 2: Testimonials 9
Chapter 3: Stan Laurel 15
Chapter 4: Oliver Hardy 21
Chapter 5: Movie Milestones 27
Chapter 6: Trivia Allsorts 37
Chapter 7: Fandom 43
Chapter 8: Props and Clothes 47
Chapter 9: Leave 'Em Laughing 49
Chapter 10: Recollections 51
Chapter 11: Star Quotes 57
Chapter 12: Sightings and Citings in Print 59
Chapter 13: Music 63
Chapter 14: Plays and Musicals 67
Chapter 15: Four Giants 69
Chapter 16: Movie Melting Pot 73
Chapter 17: The Rogue Song 81
Chapter 18: Deletions and Variations 83
Chapter 19: Slips 87
Chapter 20: The Later Films in Perspective 97
Chapter 21: Mixed Reviews 101
Chapter 22: Pressbooks 105
Chapter 23: Laurel and Hardy in Colour 113
Chapter 24: Cartoon Films 115
Chapter 25: Film Collecting 119
Chapter 26: Film 107 and Beyond 123
Chapter 27: Supporting Players 125
Chapter 28: Laurel Without Hardy 139
Chapter 29: Hardy Without Laurel 143
Chapter 30: Apocryphal Anecdotes? 147
Chapter 31: On Television 151
Chapter 32: Film Fun 157
Chapter 33: Ulverston and the Museum 159
Chapter 34: Sons of the Desert 161
Chapter 35: Bonnie Scotland 167
Chapter 36: Influences and Connections 169
Chapter 37: On Tour 173
Chapter 38: Epilogue 183
Appendix 1: Chronological Listing of Films 185
Appendix 2: Laurel and Hardy's Foreign Films 187
Appendix 3: Recommended Reading 188
Index 189

FOREWORD AND ACKNOWLEDGEMENTS

"Nobody liked them except the public," said Laurel and Hardy's introduction in the 1960 compilation film *When Comedy Was King*. Happily, however, their brilliance is now recognised by critics and public alike.

My own awareness of Laurel and Hardy goes back to when I was four years old. I fell in love with Stan and Ollie then and remained hooked ever since. For many years I have hoarded titbits of Laurel and Hardy lore. Some I have published, some not – until now.

This book started as a collection of trivia aimed to amuse. Gradually it grew to something more and it was difficult to know what to omit. For completeness some old ground is covered for newcomers to the world of Laurel and Hardy, but the emphasis is on lesser-known aspects and I hope that readers will smile as well as study.

Many, many helpers need credit. Most of the book's content has been written for me by Laurel and Hardy enthusiasts worldwide; all I have done is reproduce their observations and tributes. Thanks go to the following for their contributions and support:

Johan Amssoms, Paul Aungiers, Tony Bagley, Stephen Barlow, David Bartlett, Dave Beecroft, Steve Bolton, Barry Boyd, Adrian Brailsford, Lee Brimilow, John Bromfield, Leo Brooks, John Broom, Dougie Brown, Kevin Brown, Mark Burns, John Burton, Douglas Cairns, Dean Howard Carroll, Brian Clarry, Chris Coffey, Robert Collins, Roy Cooke, John Cowell, Robbie Crawford, Bill Crouch, Rab Cruickshank, Bill Cubin, Gordon Davie, David de Kort, Gino Dercola, Trevor Dorman, Ron Dunn, Philip Ellis, Alan Ellsworth, Wendy Fairie, Robert Fallis, Geoff Fielding, Barrie Finney, Andy Furkins, Tony Gears, Wes Gehring, Alexander Gleason, Alison Grimmer, Paul Harding, Jonathan Hayward, Kevin Hepplestone, Harry Hoppe, Harry Ingle, Mike Jones, Del Kempster, Barry Kendall, Barry Knowles, Marshall Korby, John Land, Andrew Leathley, Brian Macdonald, Les Macdonald, Glynne MacDonald, David Macleod, Janice MacNicol, A J Marriot, Jimmy Marshall, John McCabe, Melvin McFadden, Rab McKellar, Graham McKenna, Donald McLeish, Peter Mikkelsen, Glenn Mitchell, Grahame Morris, Peter Morris, Steve Mullin, Stephen Neale, David Newton, Robert Noks, Ken Owst, David Oyston, Howard Parker, Jill Passmore, Sally Passmore, Stan Patterson, Walter Plinge, Steve Randisi, Laurence Reardon, Juggie Reid, Bram Reijnhoudt, Glyn Roberts, Roger Robinson, Simon Robinson, Alessandro Rossini, Chris Seguin, Ian Self, Andrew Sharpe, Phil Sheard, Randy Skretvedt, Dwain Smith, Perry Smith, Henry Sorenson, Anthony Stubenrauch, Frank Sugden, Joyce Sugden, Michael Tate, Jack Taylor, Fred Terris, Medici Tiziano, Paul Tragelles, John Ullah, Dave Walker, Larry Walker, Roy Walton, Paul Ward, Nancy Wardell, Bob Watters, Darren White, Guy Wigmore, Philip Martin Williams, Eric Willoughby, Joe Wilson, Eric Woods and David Wyatt.

Bob Spiller gave much appreciated encouragement and support when I needed it most and was a great help in putting the book together.

My wife, Pat, also deserves a bouquet for patiently supporting me throughout the book's development.

John Stewart worked wonders with the layout and printing.

There will be people whom I have failed to acknowledge. To them I offer apologies and no less thanks.

As great care has been taken to check

factual information, I can only plead that any errors are not due to want of trying. However, it has to be said that what contributors claim is sometimes suspect, not always verifiable and may even be contradicted by other sources. With truth an elusive commodity, the reader needs to keep an open mind, particularly where opinions are expressed.

Above all, though, I ask that you simply enjoy this book and share in the widespread affection which made it possible.

Part of the sale price of this book includes donations to the Laurel and Hardy Statue Appeal and the Laurel and Hardy Charity Fund.

The book is dedicated to all people who love Laurel and Hardy.

Willie McIntyre

CHAPTER 1: FACTFILE

LAUREL, STAN

* Real name Arthur Stanley Jefferson. Born in Ulverston, England on June 16th, 1890.

* Auburn hair, blue eyes. Height 5ft 9in. Weight 10st 10lb (in 1933).

* Educated at King James Grammar School, Bishop Auckland.

* Following stage appearances in England as a comedian, toured America in Fred Karno's Company in 1910. Became producer for a short time. Successful comedy roles on screen since around 1917.

* Married to four women: 1926-35 Lois Neilson, 1935-37 and 1941-46 Virginia Ruth Rogers, 1938-40 Vera Ivanova Shuvalova ("Illeana") and 1946-65 Ida Kitaeva Raphael, who survived him. Mae Charlotte Dahlberg was his common-law wife from 1918 till 1925.

* Legally changed his name to Stan Laurel in 1931, preferring "Stan" to "Stanley".

* Two children, Lois and Stanley Robert, who lived only a few weeks.

* According to his wife Ruth, Stan could dance and yodel and believed in reincarnation.

* Died on 23rd February, 1965.

HARDY, OLIVER

* Real name Norvell Hardy. Born in Harlem, Georgia, USA on January 18th, 1892.

* Black hair, brown eyes. Height 6ft 2in.

* At his heaviest, weighed 25st.

* Long and varied experience on the stage and screen.

* Married three times: 1913-1920 Madelyn Saloshin, 1921-1937 Myrtle Lee Reeves, 1940-1957 Virginia Lucille Jones.

* No children.

* Had a leaf-shaped tattoo on the inside of his right forearm.

* Won more than thirty-five trophies, including two gold medals, for his ability on the golf course.

* Never legally added "Oliver" to his name.

* Died on August 7th, 1957.

Their Christmas pudding may have been a failure, but Laurel and Hardy warmed many a heart

CHAPTER 2: TESTIMONIALS

✳ Marshal Tito had a large collection of Laurel and Hardy films. Josef Stalin, Winston Churchill and Franklin Roosevelt all had regular private showings of their films, though not under the same roof!

✳ Former US President Ronald Reagan spent an evening in Italy along with the First Lady watching Laurel and Hardy films prior to participating in an Economic Summit the next day.

✳ Buster Keaton said, "Don't let anyone fool you, Chaplin wasn't the greatest, I wasn't the greatest. It was Stan Laurel."

✳ Bob Hope calls Laurel and Hardy, "The Mount Rushmore of Comedy."

✳ Film critic Leslie Halliwell realised that the majority of the public preferred Stan and Ollie to Chaplin, Keaton and Lloyd and confirmed this by entering most of their silent shorts and every one of their sound shorts in his highly esteemed *Film Guide*.

✳ In 1938 Basil Wright wrote in the magazine *World Film News*, "Let us hope that a fund will be immediately forthcoming to buy and preserve all Laurel and Hardy films, and institute a cinema, with a constant repertory of their work. For, apart from the nostalgia of old times, it is a shocking thought that a younger generation might have to grow up without the beneficial assistance of their ripe philosophy."

✳ In a compilation of Jimmy Tarbuck's ten best comedians, drawn from his twenty-five years (in 1990) as an entertainer he included Laurel and Hardy. Tarby went on to say, "I saw Laurel and Hardy live and if they say that Charlie Chaplin was a genius, where do you place Laurel and Hardy?"

✳ Cliff Hanley, writing in Glasgow's *Evening Times* in 1989 observed, "Chaplin was concerned with social questions. Laurel and Hardy with the total nonsensicality of the human race. Social problems go out of date. Nonsense never does. Chaplin actually took himself seriously. Stan and Ollie knew the truth, that seriousness is for bores."

✳ In a Master Class, Laurel and Hardy biographer John McCabe reminded his audience that stupidity was a universal source of humour and that in Laurel and Hardy we are really looking at ourselves.

✳ Greta Garbo was an admirer of Stan and Ollie and had kittens called "Laurel" and "Hardy".

✳ Even our Royal Family are addicted. In 1991 it was reported that Princess Diana loved to go on secret bargain-hunting trips and her favourite alias was "Mrs Hardy". She and Prince Charles, a professed Laurel and Hardy fan, also used the name "Hardy" to make secret travel arrangements.

✳ Robert De Niro's first heroes were Laurel and Hardy, according to *Today* in 1995.

✳ Kurt Vonnegut dedicated his novel *Slapstick* to Stan and Ollie. The book, published in 1976, opens with the caricature below and notes, "The fundamental joke with Laurel and Hardy, it seems to me, was that they did their best with every test. They never failed to bargain in good faith with their destinies and were screamingly adorable and funny on that account."

✳ "Stan was a great, great comedian," said Marcel Marceau.

✳ The Blake Edwards epic film *The Great Race* (1965) with Jack Lemmon and Tony Curtis carried the dedicatory credit "For Mr Laurel and Mr Hardy" and is noted for its spectacular pie fight near the end.

✳ J B Priestley was an enthusiast for Laurel and Hardy's work. He compared his leading characters in *Out of Town* to Laurel and Hardy and made reference to Stan Laurel's music-hall days in *Lost Empires*.

＊ Jimmy Murphy, Stan Laurel's real-life valet, explained that he only went with Stan to the theatres or movie shows. "We travelled all over America and we were like buddy-buddy pals. He'd get up every morning and wake me up and give me my breakfast. Not many bosses do that." Murphy never referred to Stan Laurel as "Stan" – it was always "Mr Laurel" and his eyes would fill with tears at the very name.

＊ In an article about director Denys Arcand and his controversial film *Jesus of Montreal* Arcand said, "It's totally eclectic the way my mind works – to me Laurel and Hardy and Ingmar Bergman are equally good. I enjoy them both just as much. So I try to put that in films."

＊ The following was in an old *Boys and Girls Cinema Book*:

> Laurel and Hardy have, naturally, made several records in film making, apart from their long time together as a team. They were the first comedians, for example, to play their parts at normal speed. Before this, comics on the screen had dashed about at break-neck speed, much of the fun being lost as a result. They were also the first comedians to use their own names in pictures, and this they have done ever since. Much of their success lies in the fact that, generally, they speak little. They rely upon mime, or pantomime, to get their laughs. This is one of the reasons why they are popular comedians right round the world.

＊ Rosina Lawrence, who can be seen in Hal Roach films including *Way Out West*, *Pick a Star* and *On the Wrong Trek*, was asked, "How do Laurel and Hardy compare with other comedians of the period?" She replied, "I prefer them to all other comedians and, of course, I prefer their type of comedy to the comedy of today. It had a childlike innocence to it." When asked, "What was it like working with Laurel and Hardy in *Way Out West*?" Rosina said, "Oh, they were great. I think they are the greatest comedians I have ever known. And not only that – they were kind and sweet and gentlemen. I loved it."

Stan and Ollie with Rosina as "Mary Roberts" in Way Out West

＊ Anita Garvin, another of Laurel and Hardy's supporting stars, said, "I first met Stan Laurel while working for Joe Rock. On the screen Stan's character changed between his early solo films and his later Laurel and Hardy films, but not his temperament. I just adored him. He was wonderful. I liked Oliver Hardy too, but he seemed to be the quiet one of the team. Hardy didn't seem to care about thinking of comedy. Stan was very clever. . . . The director was never cognizant of the fact that he was not doing all the directing. In all the years that I worked with Laurel and Hardy, I never heard either of them use a dirty word. I know it sounds corny, but they were really what you would call perfect gentlemen. In show business that's rare. Babe[1] Hardy never tried to make people laugh when he was between takes. Stan Laurel, on the other hand, was always trying to make people laugh. I think he enjoyed that more than anything. I kept in touch with him until he died."

＊ The following was part of a feature article by Peter Tory in the *Daily Express* in 1993:

> If I were to advise the young on what comedy they should view from early black and white cinema, I would suggest Laurel and Hardy. The comic interplay between the nervous, stupid, blank-featured Stan Laurel and the fat and endlessly exasperated Oliver Hardy offered an appeal which was universal and timeless.

---

[1] Hardy's nickname "Babe" is discussed in Chapter 4.

✳ Richard Wilson (television's Victor Meldrew) was quoted as being a devotee of Laurel and Hardy. Next time you watch *Way Out West* note the phrase used by Ollie following his soaking in the river – he said he had "one foot in the grave". Did this inspire the title of Wilson's TV series? In one episode of *One Foot in the Grave*, Victor is buried in his own backyard with only his head above ground. This scene closely resembles an ordeal for Ollie in *Way Out West*, when only his head is visible above ground level, protruding through a hole in a trap-door.

✳ In a series of *Dr Who* novels published in 1993 the doctor's travelling companion was an avid follower of Laurel and Hardy and often referred to an old friend, Arthur Jefferson, whom he met once in Ulverton (Ulverston miss-spelled!).

✳ Actor Nigel Planer's son Stanley was named after Stan Laurel.

✳ Andy Gray played Hardy in Tom McGrath's play[2] when it appeared in Perth in 1994. He said, "I always wanted to do the play. Anyone who does any kind of acting at all would want to be involved. We had videos running almost non-stop during rehearsals and the more you watched the more you realised that Hardy was a great actor while Laurel was a genius."

---

[2] See Chapter 14.

✳ A "Top Ten" of people who appeared in films with Stan and Ollie (but not necessarily on screen at the same time as them): Jack Benny (*Hollywood Revue of 1929*), Lou Costello (uncredited in *Battle of the Century*), Peter Cushing (*A Chump at Oxford*), Margaret Dumont (*The Dancing Masters*), Jimmy Durante (*Hollywood Party*), Jean Harlow (*Liberty, Double Whoopee* and *Bacon Grabbers*), Boris Karloff (French version of *Pardon Us*), Buster Keaton (*Hollywood Revue of 1929* and *The Stolen Jools*), Alan Ladd (*Great Guns*) and Robert Mitchum (*The Dancing Masters*).

✳ Paul Merton was once a civil servant. He said that he knew that if he stayed in that job he, "would just end up as a very sad figure, able to recite every Laurel and Hardy film ever made, but not able to do an awful lot else." *Paul Merton's Life of Comedy* on television in 1995 had a photograph of Laurel and Hardy in the background when Paul was talking of his own mirthful world.

✳ An exhibitor at the Linton Theatre in Linton, USA wrote in 1929, "Just played Laurel-Hardy comedy and wish to state MGM deserves great praise in making comedies of this calibre. We had a big feature on the bill and truthfully cannot say which was bigger draw."

✳ Cardiff and Wales scrum-half Rob Howley was nicknamed Stan Laurel.

The men (or rather "the Boys") in the white suits

As in Beau Hunks, Hardy didn't just smash pianos – he could play them too!

✱ The artist David Hockney featured in *You* magazine in 1996 and a photograph of his home showed a portrait of the Boys.[3]

✱ Anthony Newley was pleased to hand over his subscription fee to become a member of the Sons of the Desert, the Laurel and Hardy appreciation society. Tony said, "I've always loved the Boys."

✱ A picture of footballers Paul Gascoyne and Chris Waddle dressed as Laurel and Hardy was in the *Daily Mirror* in 1995.

✱ Frank Skinner said, "You remember the Laurel and Hardy films in which Ollie got married and Stan would always be turning up with a jigsaw or something? I think that's how we [himself and fellow comic David Baddiel] will end up." In another interview he said, "If I could look like any bloke, I think it would be Elvis in 1958. If I buy myself anything, I think, 'Would Elvis have worn that?' Unfortunately I end up looking like Stan Laurel." Frank is a member of the Busy Bodies Tent of the Sons of the Desert in the Midlands.

---

[3] Laurel and Hardy are often affectionately referred to simply as "the Boys".

✱ When asked why he was such an ardent fan of Laurel and Hardy, Eddie Large said, "Because their comedy was simple, yet it was perfection. There will never be two like them again."

✱ Charles (Dr Rock) White, rock writer, lecturer, broadcaster and official biographer of Little Richard says he has "a chronic addiction" to Laurel and Hardy.

✱ Darren Day, star of stage shows *Joseph and His Amazing Technicolor Dreamcoat* and *Summer Holiday* and host of *You Bet!* on television, says his all-time heroes are Laurel and Hardy.

✱ In the Barbra Streisand biography *Streisand – Her Life* by James Spada, Barbra recalls a time when a neighbour used to baby sit her during the afternoon. "We used to watch Laurel and Hardy every day . . . on a tiny little television with a big magnifying glass."

✱ Many pubs throughout the world have been dedicated to the Boys. UK examples are the "Laurel and Hardy" in London E11, the "Laurel and Hardy" Wine Bar/Coffee Lounge at High Street, Hoddesdon, the "Laurel" in Brierley Hill in the Midlands, the "Hardy" in Oldbury in the West Country and the "Stan Laurel" in Ulverston.

* Roy Hudd gave this advice on presenting pantomimes: "Don't put in any blue material. My yardstick is to ask if Laurel and Hardy would have done it."

* Ventriloquist Ray Alan appeared on the same bill as the Boys during their British tours. His fondest memory of those days is an occasion when Hardy climbed a long staircase, despite trouble with his legs, to ask for Ray's autograph. Ray is a member of the London Sons of the Desert and Lord Charles shares Ray's membership!

* Norman Wisdom is also a member. While Norman was appearing in a show in Belgium, he had a visit from the Boys. Stan was very keen to clown on stage with him but, because Stan and Babe were due to appear the following week, the management put a stop to it.

* Ken Dodd joined the You're Darn Tootin' Tent of Teeside and Bella Emberg is a member of the Call of the Cuckoos Tent on the Clyde Coast.

* Add to the names of Laurel and Hardy admirers some more whose admiration has been expressed in the media: Russ Abbott, Brian Conley, Adrian Edmonson, Peter Goodright, The Grumbleweeds, Noddy Holder (former lead singer of Slade), Jeffrey Holland, Joe Longthorne, Rik Mayall, Stanley Unwin and Gary Wilmot.

* Jean Parker, who starred with Laurel and Hardy in *The Flying Deuces*, said, "Hardy was just precious! He loved to play the piano. On the set they had a small piano on the side, and, between takes, he would go 'rattling away' on it."

* "Les voir suffit, même s'ils ne font rien[4]", a comment from Pierre Etaix, sums up their screen presence beautifully.

---

4 "To see them is sufficient, even if they do nothing."

With friends on the studio backlot

Drawing by Tony Bagley

CHAPTER 3: STAN LAUREL

* Despite suggestions that Madge Metcalfe's parents (Stan Laurel's grandparents) were averse to a music hall comedian as a son-in-law, Stan told his daughter Lois that his parents were so much in love and his dad had such a brilliant reputation as a theatre impresario[5] that they gave their permission for Arthur Jefferson and Madge (Stan's parents) to be married in the Holy Trinity Church in 1884. Madge's parents attended the wedding.

* Arthur Jefferson and Thomas Thorne took over the Theatre Royal in Bishop Auckland for the autumn season of 1889. The joint venture lasted only one year, but Arthur Jefferson stayed. Early in June 1890 Madge left Bishop Auckland to have a baby at her parents' home in Ulverston. Madge, an actress in her own right, had to return to Bishop Auckland for the opening of the new season and left the fragile baby, Arthur Stanley Jefferson, in the care of Grandma Metcalfe.

* The Jeffersons thrived in Bishop Auckland and on December 16th, 1894 Madge had a baby girl, called Beatrice Olga. Stanley was once more reunited with his parents. Arthur became manager of the Theatre Royal in North Shields and the family left Bishop Auckland for North Shields in July 1896.

* The name "Stanley" was once common as a surname and means, "from a stony field".

* At King James I Grammar School in Bishop Auckland there was no doubt that Arthur Stanley Jefferson – who was much later to become Stan Laurel – was a laughter maker. In later years Stan recalled that his master, Mr Bates, would call him to his study to entertain him and the other masters while relaxing after school. But Stan's father was not happy with his academic progress and enrolled him at the age of ten at the Academy in Gainford.

* The Academy was a much stricter establishment and the move was quite a jolt for the young boy. He was later to recall how he missed "those happy days in Bishop Auckland".

* Stan's father took over the Metropole Theatre in Glasgow in 1901 and the Jeffersons moved to Glasgow in 1905.

* Some accounts tell us that Stan Laurel was schooled in English music halls and never knew a real home, living in trunks, dressing rooms, railroad stations and theatres and travelling with his parents while they toured with various troupes of performers. Stan's education, we are told, was a hit and miss affair, his mother teaching him when conditions permitted.

* It was on the stage of the Panopticon Theatre in Glasgow that young Stan gave his first public performance, in 1906. "The act was awful," Stan admitted later. Above the door of the theatre was a sign prophetically reading, "Mind the step." It was a joke – there was no step!

* After he left school there were many struggling years in vaudeville ahead for Stan. He appeared in Dudley in 1908 at the Royal Opera House in the pantomime *The Sleeping Beauty*. He was back in Dudley in 1909 in another pantomime, *The House that Jack Built*.

* Also recorded is an appearance at the Hippodrome in Todmorden in 1909, in the play *Alone in the World*. When interviewed in later years, he would remember only that he had a part as an American hobo angler, who, after speaking one line, threw down his fishing rod and walked off – never to be seen again. Stan's memory, however, did him a disservice, for he had a second role, the impact of which was certainly not forgettable to the reviewer from the *Todmorden Herald*, who recorded, "The humorous element is very pronounced. Mr Stanley Jefferson, as PC Stoney Broke, is a first rate comedian and dancer and his eccentricities create roars of laughter."

---

[5] Music hall was not considered "legit" and Arthur Jefferson was far from being a "theatre impresario" at that time.

Sartorial elegance without the bowler

* There are stories of a stay in Holland: Stan, a mere kid, stood in shop doorways through long, wet nights with odours from bakery basements aggravating his gnawing emptiness. The lad remembered his vision became blurred. Then he collapsed. He came back to consciousness in a hospital. As food restored his strength, Stan discovered the Dutch authorities intended to deport him. Knowing that this move would return him to paternal custody, he fled.

* Back in England Laurel (still called Stan Jefferson) toured with the Fred Karno troupe in *The Mumming Birds*, which Karno eventually took to the USA (with Charlie Chaplin) in 1910 under the new title *A Night in an English Music Hall*. Young Jefferson returned to England because of Karno's low pay, but Karno recalled him, at a higher salary, and he returned to America in 1912 and later changed his surname to Laurel.

* For nearly four years the Karno troupe toured America and when it eventually separated, Stan went on the vaudeville stage again. Later he was offered screen work with Universal Studios and he divided his time between the stage and screen, preferring the former. At no time during this period did he command much attention and it was not until he joined the Hal Roach studios in 1923 that he clicked in a big way.

* Controversially, researcher Leo Brooks says, "Forget what you have read about Mae Dahlberg being the one who held Stan back for years. Stan had no ambition, no drive, to be a star. As long as he had his bottle and steady bookings coming in he was satisfied. He was on the stage, where he wanted to be. It did not matter that he was on a tread-mill to nowhere."

* In a number of interviews given by the Boys in 1929 and 1930, they were asked, "Who thinks of the gags?" Stan would reply, "We both do." Laurel recalled, "Leo McCarey would write the skeleton story and bring it to the set, where I, Babe and the writers would go into a huddle and come up with the finished script."

* When McCarey left Roach in 1929, Stan began to take over more and more of the responsibility for the Boys' films. By then the Boys' roles had been shaped and they were stars. With their success assured, Hardy began to fade into the background and left the creative end to Stan.

* Stan Laurel summed up Laurel and Hardy's aim: "We are doing a very simple thing, giving some people some laughs." They still are!

* Ruth Laurel said, "Stan thought that Oliver Hardy was the funniest man that ever lived."

Stan Laurel stated that Putting Pants on Philip *was his favourite film with Ollie*

* In 1933 Stan was quoted by *Photoplay* as saying that he had never been inside a Hollywood night club. "Oliver and I have lived apart from the rest of the movie colony, because the hardships of those lean years made too deep an impression on us to let us be wastrels now."

* Stan Laurel never lost his passion for the simple, visual fun of his Karno days. His California home, Fort Laurel, had windows fitted by studio special-effects men so that the weather could alternate from rain to blizzards at the touch of a button, to the consternation of guests. The unwary were also startled by the Laurel patent lavatory, which had an unnerving habit of sinking to the floor whenever anyone sat upon it. Visitors who emerged, ruffled but tight-lipped, could expect more surprises in the course of the evening. Above the bar there was a life-size portrait of the great man himself, with eyes which could be discreetly removed from a secret room behind it. Stan dispensed drinks generously and, as soon as a guest showed signs of having had one too many, he would make an excuse and slip away to stand behind the painting. Alone at the bar, they would have the unsettling experience of watching the eyes in the portrait roll around and wink at them.[6]

* Stan's working class roots endowed him with a rebellious streak which he could not resist exercising when among the affluent. At more than one Hollywood dinner party he concealed a small rubber hot water bottle, filled with vegetable soup, inside the armpit of his jacket. Half-way through a meal he would finger his collar and, on the point of apparent collapse, mumble weakly that something was wrong with the food. Then he would suddenly double up and "vomit" on his place, squeezing out the hidden soup. In the stunned silence which followed, Stan would suddenly revitalise and, picking up a soup spoon, politely began eating the disgusting mess on his plate. The laughter by those who had seen him do the trick before repulsed even more those who had not.

[6] *When the World Was Young* by Graham Nown.

Wno? Me? Rebellious?

* Professor Wes Gehring wrote in *Bowler Dessert* in 1990:

> One should be aware of Laurel's disruptive personal life (he married four women a total of eight times), but the period viewer often saw a performer worlds apart from his inspiredly dimwitted, asexual screen persona, though both indulged in battles of the sexes. This disparity, or more precisely the messy real life problems that accented it, possibly hastened the team's decline, which is rarely touched upon in Laurel and Hardy literature. At the very least, with the dominant creative partner often saddled with such a volatile lifestyle, it severely handicapped the duo's ability to find independent production money in their declining film years (1940s).

* Stan's Russian wife Ida always wanted to be a journalist from the time when, as a secretary, she earned extra money with a few hours' writing every day. But the family had to flee to China, where a stranger "discovered" Ida's voice and she trained for opera. Her road led to Hollywood and films. Ida called her Stan "Stanischka".

✳ Stan had a high wall built around his small estate. Asked why, he replied, "My ex-wives keep taking it by storm. So I am turning this place into a fort, to be known henceforth as Fort Laurel. All attacking blondes will be repelled on sight." He even had a "Fort Laurel" sign hanging over the driveway entrance.

✳ Asked why he had gone through so many marriage ceremonies to the same women Stan said, "It's one way of throwing a party."

✳ Lois Laurel said of her father, "A womaniser? Quite the opposite. He was frightfully Victorian, which is why he got married so many times. As soon as he fell in love he married, because he thought that was the proper thing to do. And he was never unfaithful to his wives."

A posed photo from Stan's silent short
Monsieur Don't Care *(1924)*
mirrored matrimonial experiences in real life!

✳ On Laurel and Hardy's 1952 British tour, during a backstage reunion in Leeds, Stan Laurel was asked by one of his former schoolmates why Laurel and Hardy had come over to England. Stan said it was because he was being pressured to renounce his British nationality and become an American citizen. This could have been during the Executive Session of the "House Committee on Un-American Activities", held in September 1951, in Los Angeles, California. Having been told that if he refused he would be banned from making any more films in America, Stan retorted that he and Hardy would go to England and make films there. At this point in the Leeds conversation, Stan said emphatically, "I was born British and I'm going to die British. No-one will ever take that from me." The case against Chaplin was obviously fired by deep rooted, manipulative intentions. Chaplin was later, justifiably, cleared of all charges, but there was no accusation levelled at Chaplin which could not have been equally aimed at Laurel. Laurel's circumstances were almost identical to Chaplin's.

"It's been a great life and I'm happy that I have made people forget some of their sorrows"

✻ Stan was a fisherman and was proud of his Tuna Club lapel badge and his yachtman's cap.

✻ In a letter to a fan, Stan wrote, "Interesting to note you are fond of music. I have no talent in this field whatsoever. Actually I never had much interest in this department. Never did appeal to me." It would appear that a combination of modesty and filtered memory were at work here.

✻ In the early 1960s Jerry Lewis asked Stan Laurel to work for him. He offered Stan a position as technical adviser with his company at $150,000 a year. Stan turned it down. Says Lewis, "He wouldn't believe I really needed him. There was no way I could convince him it wasn't charity."

✻ Stan was invited to comment on scripts for a proposed television cartoon series based on Stan and Ollie's adventures. He expressed the desire that the cartoons should not repeat earlier Stan and Ollie stories.

✻ Stan used to wear a beret when out shopping in Santa Monica so that he was seldom recognised.

✻ According to a report published in *Intro* in 1961, Stan Laurel moved from Malibu because television reception became too weak in that area.

✻ When they were old men, Mack Sennett invited Harold Lloyd, Stan Laurel, Buster Keaton and Jacques Tati for afternoon tea. When it was time for the old men to go home, Keaton and Tati helped Stan Laurel, whose left leg was partly paralysed. In walking he threw it forward with difficulty. People in the street recognised him and gathered round to smile at him. He pretended to them that he was trying out a funny walk as part of a new act.

✻ Who has first claim on Stan Laurel? His birthplace in Ulverston or the fishing village of North Shields, where he lived for four years until the age of eleven? Stan returned three times to the North-East after he became world-famous and each time he declared that his heart belonged to Tyneside. In 1932, during a civic luncheon at North Shields Town Hall, he said, "I just feel I belong here." He later tried to make a nostalgic return to Dockwray Square. "I reached my old home, but couldn't get inside because of the crowd." When Stan returned to Tyneside for the last time, at the age of sixty-two, he said, "Ee, hinney. It's just like gannin' hyem again!"

✻ In his last years Laurel said, "It would have been nice to have made a little money along the way." He was especially upset by not receiving television residual monies for showings of the team's old films.

✻ Laurel died on February 23rd, 1965 following a heart attack. He is buried with Ida in the George Washington section of the Forest Lawn Hollywood Hills Cemetery in Burbank, USA.

✻ Poignant words were delivered at Stan Laurel's funeral:

> What else had they been born for – it was their chance. With gay hearts they gave their greatest gift and with a smile to think that, after all, they had something to give which was of value. One by one death challenged them; one by one they smiled at his grim visage and refused to be dismayed. They found the path that led them home and when at last they laid their lives at the feet of the Good Shepherd, what could he do, but smile?

Drawing by Tony Bagley

CHAPTER 4: OLIVER HARDY

* Oliver Hardy said to his biographer John McCabe, "There is very little to write about me."

* In the late sixteenth or early seventeenth century, the Norvell family were forced to flee from Scotland to England and became part of the early group that settled the colony of Virginia in the New World. The Norvell plantation in Virginia was burned by the British and after the Civil War they moved to Georgia to make a new start, settling near Atlanta.

* Families with the name Hardy were mostly landed gentry and yeomanry of England and were held in high esteem by the monarchy. Oliver Hardy's line has been traced back to Michael Hardy, a well-to-do landowner who lived in Yorkshire in the latter half of the sixteenth century. In 1733 the colony of Georgia was founded by James Oglethorpe, who was accompanied by Jesse Hardy, whose descendants prospered and owned plantations and slaves. Oliver Norvell Hardy's father, Oliver, was an American Civil War veteran who later worked on the Georgia Southern Railroad as a line foreman.

* "Babe" Hardy was the youngest of five children.

* The name "Oliver" comes from the Old French, meaning "olive tree."

* Oliver Hardy's mother, Emily, was once told by a fortune-teller that her son's name would one day be known throughout the world.

* E R Moak recorded in *Photoplay* in June 1933:

    When Oliver was five years old, life handed him his first severe jolt. His [widowed] mother had always made her children believe that Santa Claus was a most generous soul, for up to then she had been able to decorate their Christmas tree with several gifts for each. But the sugar bowl bank was empty. Now she was forced to tell them the dream-blasting truth! "Mother did what she thought

was the square thing," Oliver sadly reminisced, "but we were so young to be disillusioned – and there were so many blows awaiting us later on." The incident stands out to Hardy, the man, as vividly as it did to Oliver, the child. It accounts for the loads of presents he now sends to Los Angeles orphanages every Christmas!

* Hardy's fine singing voice is known to us through his occasional tonsil quiverings on the screen. In his youth he was part of a quartet named The Twentieth Century Four. Their combined bulk was recognised in their alternative name of Half a Ton of Harmony.

* On the *This Is Your Life* American television show, Alcia Horne recalled of Oliver Hardy, "I remember him as a very brave boy. He went into the Oconee River to save his brother, Stan, from drowning. He pulled him out and applied artificial respiration, but it was too late. He had been in the water too long."

* During his early film career, Hardy battled through a blizzard from a studio to save a fare. He caught a cold and in his spartan bedroom fought off delirium as he grew weaker. He was afraid to call for help lest his landlady would demand his overdue rent. His temperature rose rapidly, his parched throat craving water that was not to be had. He fell unconscious and pneumonia almost claimed him.

* Of Hardy's nickname "Babe", John McCabe wrote, "He knew we don't choose our own nickname as a rule and he was stuck with his. 'Babe', indeed, was the name his wife, Lucille, always called him in public because 'Oliver' was too formal. 'Ollie' was someone else and his baptismal name 'Norvell' was used only by his mother and his siblings." The fact that he did not like "Babe" may come as a surprise to those who assumed that its widespread use since his early film career implied a stamp of approval. This information was contained in an early thirties magazine article, but in the intervening years does not seem to have been widely known.

* At various times Hardy claimed to have opened the first film theatre in Milledgeville, Georgia, and sold it when he left for Florida. Other times he just claimed he managed the theatre. Leo Brooks established that the truth is that he was a projectionist and cleaned the place.

* Most books and articles on Babe list two Mrs Hardys – Myrtle and Lucille. The first mention of an earlier Mrs Hardy appeared in the book *Stan – The Life of Stan Laurel* by Fred Guiles. According to Guiles, Babe met a pianist and singer named Madelyn Saloshin in 1913 at Jacksonville, Florida. Later research substantiated this and revealed that Babe and Madelyn took out a marriage licence on November 7th, 1913 and were married the same day in Macon, Bibb County, Georgia.

* An alternative scenario is that Hardy met Madelyn while she was working in Milledgeville, possibly at the Electric Theatre. It is very doubtful that Hardy's mother would have approved of the marriage. This probably explains why they were married in Macon (thirty miles from Milledgeville, where Babe and his mother lived). Madelyn supported them both by playing and singing popular tunes at the local night spots in Jacksonville. Through her connections, she was able to secure Babe small roles in films at the Lubin Film Studio.

* Hardy had a moderately successful movie career as an actor (often as a "heavy"), but his real success came when he joined the Hal Roach studios in 1925.

* Charley Chase, the star on the lot at that time, could trace his friendship with Hardy back to 1918, when he both directed and appeared in films with Hardy. Chase had long wanted Hardy as a foil in his films, so Hardy was among friends and admirers when he joined Roach.

* Oliver Hardy said, "Nothing is funny unless people can believe it could have happened. That's why impossible things like a comedian coming along and eating doorknobs isn't funny. Nobody eats doorknobs."

* Hardy also said, "I think no comedian should wear clothes that are funnier than he is. It's all right to emphasise eccentricities, but never make them outside reasonable experience. The situation should be funny, not the man. We try to be careful of mannerisms, for merely repeating a gesture that once brought a laugh is no way to get more laughs."

Clothes OK?

* Margaret Chute wrote in *Royal Pictorial Magazine* in the early 1930s, "In Hardy's opinion the best actress in Hollywood is Marlene Dietrich. He admires her tremendously and thinks she is both beautiful and clever."

* Stan Laurel remained a British subject all his days. John McCabe observed, "You know the marked British flavour in much of his creativity. What you may not know, but have probably intuited, is that Babe Hardy had a similar sense of humour, in no small measure (I'm sure) seasoned by the strong British strain in him."

* His screen mannerism of twiddling his tie, accompanied by a nervous laugh, was designed to cover embarrassment. This childlike gesture became one of Ollie's most endearing mannerisms.

✳ Laity often quote Ollie's famous catch-phrase as "another fine mess". Aficionados will tell you that Ollie never said, "another fine mess", but exclaimed, "another *nice* mess" at Stan's incompetence. However, in a Laurel and Hardy radio show, known variously as *The Wedding Party*, *The Marriage of Stan Laurel* and *The Wedding Night*, Ollie does indeed say, "Here's another *fine* mess."

✳ Oliver Hardy's favourite film is sometimes stated to have been *Fra Diavolo* or *Swiss Miss*. Lucille Hardy told Leo Brooks that his top five favourite films of his career were:
1. *Way Out West* (Roach)
2. *The Wizard of Oz* (Semon)
3. *No Man's Law* (Roach)
4. *Jitterbugs* (Fox)
5. *The Fighting Kentuckian* (Republic)

✳ At the time of filming *Our Relations*, Hardy is supposed to have asked Iris Adrian if she would go to dinner with him. Then, according to Iris, later that day he phoned her and cancelled, using the excuse, "I am an old fat fellow, and you wouldn't like me." However, in 1936 he was only forty-four years old and was not fat. In *Our Relations* he was lighter than in his previous film, *The Bohemian Girl*. Hardy was a ladies' man; women were attracted to him. He was also in complete command of his career. What likely happened was that when Hardy arrived home, reality set in. He was being sued for separate maintenance by his second wife, Myrtle. One of her charges was that he had been seeing other women. To have been seen in public with Iris at this time would have helped support Myrtle's case. Hardy was a private person and he had seen how the media played up Laurel's problems with women and Hardy certainly wanted nothing like that.[7]

---

[7] Leo Brooks writing in *Bowler Dessert* (1992).

Hardy favourite

❋ A letter sent by Lucille Hardy to Frans Stijnis appeared in the Dutch magazine *Blotto*. Part of it read as follows:

What was Babe like? . . . He was a most kind, thoughtful, gentle and sensitive man – sensitive to other people's feelings, extremely so. A gentleman in every sense of the word – a truly "gentle man". He was not at all the blustering know-it-all, overpowering person he portrayed on the screen. In fact, just the opposite. He was easy to get on with and always tried to see the other side of a question and so make allowances for a difference of opinion. However, at rare times he was quick tempered but just as quick to get over it. He was always helpful and considerate of others and I never knew him to refuse anyone who was in trouble and needed help. In fact both Babe and Stan were always most helpful to members of both cast and crew working on their pictures and helped many young performers get their start in show business. It seems I am always being asked, "Was he as funny at home as he was in his films?" The answer is, "No, he was not." He had a great sense of humour, yes, but at heart was a very quiet and serious person – at times even timid.

❋ When he was asked his weight, he would occasionally plead ignorance. "I don't know – my scales only go up to three hundred pounds." Once Laurel added to the joke by suggesting, "Why not use two scales? Put one foot on each and add them."

"Neither of us ever knew quite what made us funny," said Hardy once. "I guess it was because we were so completely unalike in every way. But, like bacon and eggs, we seemed to be about perfect together – but not so good apart."

✳ In the BBC's 1974 *Cuckoo* programme from their television series *Omnibus* Lucille Hardy said of her husband, "Babe loved his home life. He did carpentry work around the house. He made most of our garden furniture and made little things for me like my dressing table, vanity chair and things of that kind." She also said, "He never considered himself a comedian. He thought he was a straight man for Stan and it always amazed him when anyone thought he was a comedian."

✳ It is said that on the set Hardy was often impatient to go off to the golf course and that sometimes Laurel would delay filming Ollie's irritated looks until the end of the day, when Hardy really was irritated.

✳ Kirk Alyn, the original Superman, recalled, "Every so often Babe would hold a dinner party at his place in California. He had a small theatre in which he would show old Laurel and Hardy comedies. After the films, Babe would have a large buffet dinner set up for us. Then we would all take turns entertaining on a small stage in front of the screen."

✳ Ruth Laurel said, "Stan taught Babe to dance."

✳ Ellen Corby (Grandma in *The Waltons*) claimed to have introduced Lucille to Hardy. Ellen and Lucille had both worked together as script supervisors.

✳ Babe's brother, Baldy Hardy, appeared in some of Laurel and Hardy's films, as did the Sage sisters of Atlanta, Babe's nieces.

✳ During the second World War, when domestic help was not available, Hardy gave up golf so that he could personally tend his large garden and swimming pool.

✳ Towards the end of Hardy's life, he had a stroke, which rendered him unable to speak. A touching story recalls that Stan went to visit his pal and was left alone with Babe for a few minutes. Lucille was inquisitive when she noticed that no sound was emerging from the room and looked in to check that all was well. Stan and Babe were having a lively conversation without words, using pantomime learned from their early careers.

✳ Hardy died on August 7th, 1957, having been severely disabled for months. His ashes were buried in the Masonic section of the Garden of Valhalla Memorial Park in North Hollywood.

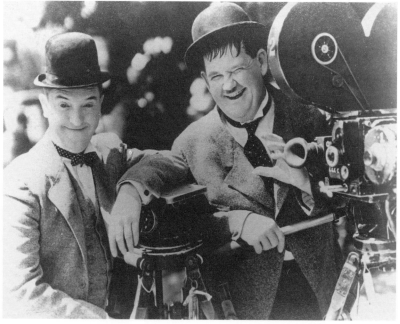

*The Boys with the
tools of their trade*

CHAPTER 5: MOVIE MILESTONES

* The currently favoured assessment for the number of films in which Laurel and Hardy appeared together between 1920 and 1951 now stands at 106 and constitutes Appendix 1. While filmography compilers love precision, perhaps (as Chapter 26 suggests) this figure should be regarded as fluid, not definitive. This chapter features selected milestones.

* *Why Girls Love Sailors* (1927)
This film defies attempts to classify it with any other Laurel and Hardy film. It has a parallel only with *That's My Wife* (1929) in that Stan's performance is partially transvestite though in totally different style; he was a demure wife to impress an uncle in *That's My Wife* and here was a vamp to seduce the ship's captain. The freak ending is startling.

* *Hats Off* (1927)
A huge success at the box office, this has not been seen in the UK or USA since 1928. Rumours circulated for years about the existence of a 9.5mm[8] copy in Europe. During one researcher's long search for this "lost" film, he found evidence of it being shown at a film festival in Denmark in the late 1970s. He managed to trace the film to West Germany and corresponded with a film collector there, about either buying the film or obtaining a video copy of it. At this point a fellow collector, for attempted personal gain, tipped off a representative of the Roach studio of the find and they scared off the contact. *Hats Off* remains *"Hats Lost"*.

* *Do Detectives Think?* (1927)
The first appearance of Laurel and Hardy in their familiar bowler hats was unremarkable in itself as detectives usually wore them in that era.

---

8 9.5mm is an early film gauge once popular in home cinemas, but now rarely seen.

* *Putting Pants on Philip* (1927)
This is noteworthy in that Stan Laurel (as Philip) shows what a good actor he was, as well as being a very funny man. The scenes in the tailor's shop are poignant and touching as he battles in vain against his uncle and the tailor, who strive to replace Philip's kilt with more conventional attire. The highlight of the film is when Philip emerges from the dressing room, dishevelled and shamed. His eyes seem truly tear-filled as he adjusts his tie and cap, realising he has lost the battle for his dignity. But he rebels again!

* *The Battle of the Century* (1927)
Laurel called the team's innovatively slower pacing "slow-slapstick". To him, the key example was the duo's epic pie fight in this film. Laurel's recollections were:
We went at it, strange as it may sound, psychologically. We made every one of the pies count. A well-dressed man strolling casually down the avenue, struck squarely in the face by a large pastry, would not proceed at once to gnash his teeth, wave his arms in the air and leap up and down. His first reaction would be one of numb disbelief, then embarrassment and a quick survey of the damage done to the person. Then indignation and the desire for revenge would possess him. If he saw another pie close at hand, still unspoiled, he would grab it and let fly.

* *From Soup to Nuts* (1928)
In the hands of two inept waiters, Laurel and Hardy, *nouveau riche* hostess (Anita Garvin) throws a party which degenerates into a farce, punctuated by a virtuoso performance by Anita as she chases a recalcitrant cherry round a plate.

The tit-for-tat is well underway, leading to . . .

✳ Big Business (1929)

Stan Laurel said that the idea behind this film was that Stan and Ollie would go from door to door, selling Christmas trees, with a series of incidents at each door, but that the business at James Finlayson's house developed so that they ended up making the remainder of the film right there. Thus was born what most scholars agree was one of Laurel and Hardy's best films.

✳ Double Whoopee (1929)

This silent also exists in a "vocalised version". Though the voice impersonation for both Stan and Babe is off-beam, this experimental pilot film was considered by some as an acceptable alternative version. No further titles were "sonorised" however.

✳ Unaccustomed As We Are (1929)

"Slow slapstick" anticipated the more realistic needs of sound film production, allowing Laurel and Hardy to make the smoothest transition to "talkies" of all silent comedians. Proof is in their first sound film.

✳ Perfect Day (1929)

The mudhole used for the finale had been excavated and filled with water in one of the Hal Roach studio streets. It measured eight feet deep, twenty feet long and twelve feet wide. Pulleys were used so that the Boys' car could be lowered to the bottom without accident.

✳ Night Owls (1930)

Leo Brooks enlightens us:

Stan explained in an interview in the *Los Angeles Times* that he was forced to edit out much of the best material in order to trim the film to two reels and that he would have liked to have released their films in whatever length that suited him, the problem being that MGM and the theatres could only use two-reelers. Here Stan loses credibility. He never expected us to know that what he had to edit out of the films was very boring material in the first reel and also a gag that failed to come off in the second reel. How do we know this? This was the first film Laurel and Hardy made with extra foreign versions. The Spanish version, *Ladrones*, still exists. Hal Roach would not let Stan have anything to do with these foreign versions and *Ladrones* contains the footage that Stan edited out of the English version.

. . . the wrecking of Stan and Ollie's car
in Big Business

✳ *Blotto* (1930)

With a drunken theme, the keynote song is *The Curse Of An Aching Heart*. A pressbook suggested, "Oliver Hardy's whiskey tenor would make a confirmed drunkard tear at his hair with envy and Stan Laurel's ditto alto would be the pride of a Limehouse rummy. And the wonder is they do it all on iced tea!"

✳ *Brats* (1930)

The sets were painstakingly constructed (a claim not always appropriate to the Laurel and Hardy shorts), giving a fascinatingly convincing scale to the diminutive Stan and Ollie. A special gag to look for is the photograph of Jean Harlow on the mantelpiece, an "in-joke" reused the following year in *Beau Hunks*, but with a different photo, more in keeping with the wayward character of Jeanie Weenie.

"Loved by everyone" applies to the Boys as well as Jeanie Weenie

✳ *Below Zero* (1930)

Stan and Ollie are street musicians. In one scene Ollie is addressed as "Mr Whiteman". Paul Whiteman, the "King of Jazz," was a dead ringer for Oliver Hardy, hence another "in-joke".[9]

---

[9]   Whiteman is caricatured in the Walt Disney Silly Symphony cartoon *Musicland* (1935), in which he has been mistaken for Ollie.

✳ *The Stolen Jools* (1931)

This novelty film, with guest appearances of dozens of prominent stars including Norma Shearer, Wallace Beery and Edward G Robinson, was once thought lost. Laurel and Hardy's names are prominent in publicity material and the film was released in Britain as *The Slippery Pearls*.

✳ *Our Wife* (1931)

Babe London, the bride in *Our Wife*, said:

Of all the comedians that I've worked with, I enjoyed playing with Laurel and Hardy most. To me they were priceless. They followed the script pretty closely. Stan did most of the directing. He explained the scene to me and we would play it. Of course, you would play it in your own style, but there wasn't much improvisation as far as I was concerned. Stan really was the brains of the two and they were such a wonderful team. They worked together so beautifully, but in their private lives they both went their own ways.

✳ *Come Clean* (1931)

A pressbook said, "Laurel and Hardy have the hard luck of rescuing a woman from the river and this woman rewards them by forcing herself on them. The Boys have a hard time keeping their little secret when the woman hides herself in the Hardy bedroom and the two wives converse in the room beyond." The pressbook somehow failed to capture the flavour of this archetypal film.

A pity this instrumental mishap is not actually seen in Below Zero

✳ *One Good Turn* (1931)
Lois Laurel recalled, "Whenever I went to the studio to watch my father working, I would see this big, fat man beating him up and making him look terribly silly. I thought Babe was utterly horrid." She told her father and his response was immediate. "He wrote a film in which he got the best of Babe. He got to kick him, thump him, and bop him over the head. That film was written especially for me. And, after I saw it, I was all right and grew to love my Uncle Babe."

✳ *Any Old Port* (1932)
Publicity material stated that a real boxer asked Stan for the shorts he had worn in the film. Wearing them, he won his next three fights by a knockout!

✳ *The Music Box* (1932)
If a Martian arrived on Earth and we wanted to show it what human life is really all about what would we choose? Perhaps the best choice of all would be this most straightforward of thirty-minute film comedies. It is sublimely simple and deservedly won the duo a special Oscar.

✳ *County Hospital* (1932)
Stunt man Yakima Canutt said that the planned "rear driving" climax was abandoned because it would have cost too much as a stunt and rear projection was used, but Taxi Boys two-reelers made the same year had elaborate driving stunts, all shot for real around the streets of Culver City. A very good short is therefore less than perfect. Stan was very upset when it was not approved as he wanted.

✳ *Towed in a Hole* (1932)
Stan wanted to end the film with a wild routine of the two of them on the boat they had been refurbishing, as it ploughs through heavy street traffic in the style of the Keystone Kops.

✳ *Twice Two* (1933)
In the words of a pressbook, "Wedded bliss is given a real test by Laurel and Hardy. They decide to celebrate their wedding anniversary on the spur of the moment. They are married to each other's sister. Laurel and Hardy also play the roles of the smiling brides."

✳ *Oliver the Eighth* (1934)
A subtlety: though the Boys own a barber's shop, Stan goes down the road for a shave!

✳ *Thicker Than Water* (1935)
Over to a pressbook again: "*Thicker Than Water* marks *finis* to what was probably the most successful series of two-reel comedies ever produced since the advent of motion pictures. For more than seven years Laurel and Hardy have romped through two-reel pictures, only occasionally appearing in films of greater length. Now the demand is so great for comedies of greater length as vehicles for the famous fun duo that Hal Roach has decided to grant the public's request and in the future there will be no more two-reelers with this stellar combination."

✳ *On the Wrong Trek* (1936)
Stan and Ollie made a guest appearance in this Charley Chase short. Charley's mother-in-law says, "That's another fine mess you've gotten us into," showing that, as early as 1936, Ollie's catch-phrase was being misquoted.

Connoisseurs are divided over Twice Two, *some feeling uneasy about the "gender-bending"*

✳ *The Rogue Song* (1930)
Hal Roach's assertion that Stan and Ollie were belatedly brought in as comic relief to salvage a picture that for its time was experimental finds an echo in a reviewer's comment: "Its comedy moments, which thrust into the story with scant regard for their suitability, succeed in delighting the audience." Reading between the lines of contemporary reaction to the film, however, suggests that despite MGM's misgivings and the reservations of some critics, *The Rogue Song* was able to succeed on its own merits – the novelty of an opera singer in the dashing personality of Lawrence Tibbett, a dramatic, romantic tale, good sound reproduction and the use of full colour.

✳ *Pardon Us* (1931)
The first Laurel and Hardy feature, this prison film, based on *The Big House*, has a mixed reputation. Lacking in structure, it is nevertheless one of the most entertaining features and the release on video of "extra" scenes (from foreign releases and deleted scenes) has acquired it new cult status.

✳ *Pack Up Your Troubles* (1932)
It was Hardy who suggested Laurel take over the bedtime story telling scene with Jacquie Lyn. It would otherwise have been a Hardy solo scene.

✳ *Beau Hunks* (1931)
This four-reeler (known in Britain as *Beau Chumps*) was first shown in Britain in 1932 paired with the MGM feature *The Guardsman*. When it reached some cinemas later, however, it was paired with the same feature but enjoyed top billing.

✳ *Fra Diavolo* (1933)
Fra Diavolo, otherwise known as *The Devil's Brother*, was so good that close to thirty minutes of the musical and dramatic scenes had to be edited out of the film to shrink it to the desired length. Commercially this was the most successful film Laurel and Hardy ever made.

✳ *Sons of the Desert* (1933)
William Seiter completed filming of *Sons of the Desert* in sixteen working days. It used to take longer than that to do one of their shorts. What is even more amazing is that Seiter had to shoot around Stan on several occasions because of his drinking. Luckily for Stan he and Seiter were old friends and he could depend on Seiter to cover for him.

Babes in Toyland *was also released as* March of the Wooden Soldiers

✳ *Hollywood Party* (1934)
The trailer promised "906 new reasons for laughter."

✳ *Babes in Toyland* (1934)
A London newspaper review of 1934 said:
It is difficult to define exactly wherein the picture fails to be as good as its predecessors, but possibly it is because to some extent the inimitable pair of comedians are losing their novelty. It is easy to see what is going to happen next – what act of foolishness will be committed by Laurel and what expression of indignation and scorn will be made by Hardy. The rest of the characters – Little Bo Peep, Tom the Piper, the Old Woman who Lived in a Shoe, Mother Goose and Silas Barnaby, the meanest man in the world, not to mention the Three Little Pigs, get on with the business of telling a straightforward pantomime tale.

✳ *Bonnie Scotland* (1935)
This feature was in part a parody of *The Lives of a Bengal Lancer*, having the same technical adviser (Colonel W E Wynn who had served with the Seventh Bengal Lancers). On the set of *Bonnie Scotland* Stan said, "When it comes to making a film, I'm so near to the darned thing I can neither see nor feel it. Everybody tells me it is going to be the best we've made. All I know, by this time, is that I want to get it finished as quickly as possible. By the time we're nearly through with a film I never seem able to make up my mind whether it is a howling success or a crying shame."

✳ *The Bohemian Girl* (1936)
Stan said, "We have found that good music is an ideal background for comedy. The contrast of fine singing voices and classical instrumental numbers with carefully chosen humorous situations is ideal 'theatre'. It is just startling enough to be entertaining when the various elements are properly blended."

✳ *Our Relations* (1936)
There is a subtle twist to
add to the complicated
and clever story line.
When Mrs Hardy and Mrs
Laurel bail out whom they
think are their husbands,
but who are actually their
sailor twins, the sailors
prefer the wrong wives.
Bert Hardy likes the look
of the blonde Mrs Laurel,
while Alfie Laurel thinks
that the little Mrs Hardy is
"not so bad".

✳ *Way Out West* (1937)
The scenes of the Boys
crossing the stream at the
opening and ending of
Way Out West were shot in
Sherwood Forest, north of
Hollywood. There are no
rivers in that area, so
Roach rented a steam
shovel and dug out a
stream bed. They poured
over 25,000 gallons of
water into the bed, from a
nearby lake. This waste of
precious water in water-
short Southern California
created an uproar.

✳ *Swiss Miss* (1938)
Swiss Cheese (the working title for *Swiss
Miss*) was planned as one of Hal Roach's
"A" feature musical comedies. Roach
wanted the Boys to provide the comedy
relief, as part of the "second plot". This was
never planned as a standard Laurel and
Hardy film.

*Whoever heard of mousetrap merchants
in a musical?*

✳ *Block-Heads* (1938)
World Film News said:
The blow has fallen; a final announcement from MGM confirms the permanent break-up of the Laurel and Hardy team. It is hardly worthwhile imagining what disagreements have caused the tragedy; one can only with bowed head accept the fact. Even the news that Harry Langdon – a great comedian if there ever was one – is taking Laurel's place is but cold comfort.
It was widely expected to be their last film with Roach, but, happily, more followed.

✳ *The Flying Deuces* (1939)
The cast was cosmopolitan: Oliver Hardy hailed from Harlem, Georgia, Stan Laurel from Ulverston, England, Reginald Gardiner from Wimbledon, England, James Finlayson from Larbert, Scotland, Jean Del Val from Reims, France and Michael Visaroff from Kiev, Russia. Producer Boris Morros was born in Russia.[10]

---

[10] His real name was Boris Milhailovitch and he was later revealed to be an American agent. His autobiography *Ten Years a Counterspy* was filmed in 1960 under the title *Man on a String*, with Ernest Borgnine playing the role of Morros.

✳ *A Chump at Oxford* (1940)
The bank in the film is called the Finlayson National Bank in recognition of Stan and Ollie's number one foil, James Finlayson. Another in-joke.

✳ *Great Guns* (1941)
When the Boys moved over to the big studios, Stan complained, "We had no say in those films and it sure looked like it." Stan and Ollie appear as characters within their own movie as opposed to being the subject of it and the plot is over-complicated.

✳ *Air Raid Wardens* (1943)
This was a smash hit, one of their biggest all time money winners. Even *Variety* gave them rave reviews. It may have been far from vintage Laurel and Hardy, but it was what the public wanted to see. Over a shot of a mountain, a title in the trailer read, "Down from Olympian heights in a cascading torrent of sheer magnificence . . . the Quixotic adventures of the two greatest romanticists of the modern era!"

Wartime heroics: the Boys prepare to enter the "hide-in" of the Nazi spies in Air Raid Wardens

✳ *The Big Noise* (1944)

The love interest is kept in check until the last couple of reels and there is quite a lot of business with the Boys. The closing shot of the dancing fish with Stan and Ollie grinning broadly is a classic. Certainly not the best film they made, but by no means the worst, as is sometimes claimed.

✳ *The Bullfighters* (1945)

Highlights are the tit-for-tat exchange in the hotel lobby and the macabre, almost symbolic, freak ending with Laurel and Hardy reduced to skeletons.

✳ *Atoll K* (1951)

An abiding mystery: cinema projectionists have independently recalled screening this in colour; one described the film as "shot in the most atrocious colour". The version was probably not under the title *Atoll K*, but they all remember it as Laurel and Hardy's last film. It was also released as *Utopia*.

Laughing Gravy with Stan and Ollie on the roof in Laughing Gravy

Laurel and Hardy pose for a spot "on the air"

CHAPTER 6: TRIVIA ALLSORTS

✱ The first unwritten law of physics: For every Stan there is an Ollie.

✱ A film called *Here Comes a Sailor* starred Snub Pollard and Marvin Loback, a comedy "thin and fat man" team in the silent films of the late 1920s. Pollard and Loback are waiters. One of the waiters is asked to serve the salad undressed, and does so. One of the guests chases her cherry around her plate in the same fashion as Anita Garvin in *From Soup to Nuts*. They made other films which resembled the early Laurel and Hardy films very closely. Parallel gags and storylines are to be found in: *Sock and Run* and *Putting Pants on Philip*; *Once Over* and *The Finishing Touch* as well as *The Battle of the Century*; *Double Trouble* and *Bacon Grabbers*; *Men About Town* and *Should Married Men Go Home?* The big surprise is that it is pretty certain that these Pollard/Loback films were made first, before the Laurel and Hardy films which they appear to imitate. Borrowing and reworking would seem to have taken place quite substantially.

✱ Laurel and Hardy are revered in China, where their physical characteristics represent ancient Chinese icons.

✱ An American on *TV-AM* stated that he had cured himself of cancer by laughing at Laurel and Hardy films.

✱ A Laurel and Hardy CD ROM was released in 1996. Reviews and biographies are in German, but the film clips are in English, including the titles. There are photographs of the Hal Roach studio, twenty video clips, the complete *We Faw Down* and around a thousand stills.

✱ In the genus game of Trivial Pursuit is the "Entertainments" question, "What were the 3,000 projectiles used in Laurel and Hardy's *Battle of the Century*? Answer: custard pies." The question was a little inaccurate, but laudable is the mention of the Boys in yet another modern medium.

✱ Roy Rogers's first horse – a present from his dad – was named "Babe".

✱ Racehorses named after Laurel and Hardy films include *Laughing Gravy*, *Below Zero* and *Hollywood Party*. There was also a horse named Oliver Hardy and one called Stan and Ollie.

✱ The most successful Grand National jockey of all time was called George Stevens, who won the race five times. He is not to be confused with the Roach studio's cameraman of the same name.

✱ According to *The Fishmonger Clarion*, forty-five animals have been counted in thirty-two films.

✱ A filmography of Laughing Gravy, the dog best remembered for its role in the film with its name, tells us that it also appeared in *Pardon Us* as a pet of one of the plantation workers' children, in the scene when the workers are singing *South Bound Passenger Train*. And Laughing Gravy wandered around Ollie's trailer in the gypsy camp in *The Bohemian Girl* and slept in a snow-covered wagon with Stan and Ollie.

✱ On Christmas Eve, 1934, Nola Luxford, New Zealand actress and broadcaster in Hollywood, crammed into a studio a hundred and sixty people, including Laurel and Hardy, to make an hour-long broadcast to New Zealand.

✱ A recording exists of a pilot show for a projected Laurel and Hardy half-hour radio series, made for NBC in the late 1930s or early 1940s.[11] Moderately funny, the show was never broadcast.

✱ Derann Films were presented with the Music Retailers Association Award for the Best Spoken Word Release of 1990. The recording which brought them this honour was *Laurel and Hardy on the Air* on compact disc and audio cassette, which included the half-hour radio show.

---

[11] The actual date is a matter of debate. The recording is the one mentioned on page 23.

✳ Stan Laurel's grin was chosen by the Royal Mail to put a smile on UK letters as part of a package of ten 20p first class greetings stamps which went on sale in 1990.

✳ In 1991 the US Postal Service issued a $5.00 booklet of stamps depicting Laurel and Hardy and other comedians, all five stamps being the work of caricaturist Al Hirschfeld.

✳ At least seven other postage stamps have been issued with Laurel and Hardy's image: 1972 Fujeira, 1986 Republic of Maldives, 1989 The Gambia, 1991 Guyana, 1992 Republic of Equatorial Guinea, 1995 Burkina Faso and 1996 Norway.

✳ Laurel and Hardy impersonators who have performed the "asking the time/spilling the drink" gag from *Great Guns* include Dick Van Dyke and Henry Calvin, Lucille Ball and Gale Gordon and Harry Secombe and Roy Castle.

✳ According to valet Jimmy Murphy, Stan used to stage pantomimes at Christmas for the neighbourhood children.

✳ The *Daily Record* dated July 21st, 1934, reported, "Efforts are being made to persuade Laurel and Hardy to appear in this year's pantomime at Drury Lane. It is doubtful if the two favourite screen comedians will see their way to oblige. They might enjoy pantomime work well enough for a change, but Hollywood is not likely to let them go." It didn't!

✳ Laurel and Hardy despaired over a surprise appearance on American television's *This Is Your Life* in 1954. Laurel called it "a staggering experience . . . we certainly never intended to start out [on television] on an unrehearsed network show!" Back in 1929 Laurel had stated,

"The reason we avoid all public appearances [is because] people expect us to be funny all the time. We are like everyone else with a regular business. Comedy is our business." Hardy added that improvisation did not allow for quality control. They could not always live up to their high comedy standards.

✳ Proceeds from activities celebrating Red Cross Day in 1940 were given to the war relief fund. There was this announcement:
  By special proclamation of Acting Mayor Warren Shannon, Stan Laurel, film comedian, has been appointed Acting Mayor of Treasure Island for the day and his running mate, Oliver Hardy, will be acting Chief of Police. From Hollywood will come celebrities of the stage and screen for a special benefit performance. Laurel and Hardy will present a comedy skit.
According to one report, Laurel and Hardy auctioned the props used in *The Driver's Licence Sketch*, in aid of the fund.

✳ Of all the traits that endear us to Laurel and Hardy, their good manners most set them aside from others. The ultimate in good manners in their films is when Ollie so painstakingly introduces himself and Stan. He places as much emphasis on introducing Stan as himself. It is pleasing to consider that the courtesy and gentle manners of the Stan and Ollie characters reflect the personalities of the real Laurel and Hardy.

✳ Jean Harlow said, "There was a friendliness and camaraderie about that small [Roach] studio that was vastly different from the impersonality of the larger studios. No one was too busy to help or advise. Stan and Babe realised my ignorance and did everything in their power to make me feel at ease."

✳ Leo Brooks sees a contradiction: "We have on the one hand some who worked on the lot, especially the women, telling us how sweet and kind the Boys were at all times and on the other hand men who had worked on the lot at the same time saying the tension got so thick you could almost cut it with a knife."

✳ At the time of the release of *Thicker Than Water*, Laurel and Hardy face masks were on sale for only $15.00 per thousand.

✳ In 1997 there was a spate of Laurel and Hardy life-sized statues, made of wood and resin. One dealer reported, "We have been amazed at the demand." It was amazing indeed as prices ran as high as £399 each and had poor facial resemblance.

✳ Thieves stole the index and middle fingers from a waxwork statue of Stan Laurel at a tourism exhibition in Blackpool.

✳ A statue of Stan Laurel stands at Laurel Court (formerly Dockray Square and renamed after Stan), North Shields, Tyne and Wear. A collection is underway to fund the making and erecting of a Laurel and Hardy statue in Ulverston.

✳ A diary notes that on 7th November, 1936 Prime Minister Stanley Baldwin went to see Queen Mary about the abdication of Edward VIII. The Queen may have shared King George V's liking for the Boys because the diary records, "The Queen enchanted him by the sentence with which she greeted him: 'This is a nice kettle of fish, isn't it?'" If the Queen had called the Prime Minister by his first name it would have been even funnier!

✳ *Random Edition* (Radio 4, 9.9.95.) looked at the year 1937. In anticipation of King George VI, there was expression of a wish that their new monarch would have the looks of Clark Gable, but disappointment in that he looked more like Stan Laurel.

✳ One day Stan was irritable over a money matter. Later, in a fit of remorse, Stan personally decorated a barren tree on his front lawn with hundreds of dollar bills. Good-naturedly he jested over the greenery, "See it does grow on trees after all."

✳ On stage Laurel's voice was often lower in pitch than in the movies and Hardy's was a little higher.

✳ In 1929 Laurel observed, "People like to laugh at the misfortune of others. It's human nature. So we merely exaggerate those misfortunes. We multiply everything, making humour in the very fact of repetition."

✳ Stan Laurel told the following story: "I suppose you know that in England hotel guests leave their shoes outside the door when they retire so that the porter can give them a polish during the night. I did that as a matter of course the first night we landed in the States in our New York hotel. The next morning I got up, went to the door, looked out – and no shoes. I went down to the desk clerk, mad as hell, and demanded to know what had become of my shoes. When I had explained where I had put them, the man wanted to know why in the hell I had done *that*. I explained but it didn't do any good. My shoes were stolen – and, because of my financial situation at the time, they were the only shoes that I owned! So – and this is true – I actually walked over to the theatre fully dressed, wearing my slippers."

✳ As a child Stan Laurel had a love for Beers Treacle Toffees.

✳ The Roscoe "Fatty" Arbuckle trial for manslaughter over seventy years ago was one of Hollywood's most infamous scandals. Despite his acquittal, Arbuckle's cinema career was ruined and his attempted return to stardom was never to succeed. Laurel and Hardy were amongst those who tried to help Arbuckle to regain his place among the Hollywood greats.

Fatty Arbuckle

✳ In Blackpool (in 1947) Hardy opined, "In a place like Hollywood, the curtain is always up. Everybody knows everything about you and if they don't, they invent it. There's nothing sacred to the gossip columnists." He recalled Clark Gable telling him that on one occasion, when there was a rumour afoot of Gable's romance with Carole Lombard, he went home one night to find a gossip columnist under his bed!

✳ Added Laurel, "Ollie and I have been fortunate. We're not glamorous. We never gave wild parties. We tried to be respectable, law-abiding citizens in a community that lives with one ear to the phone and the other to the ground!"

✳ Eric Campbell, the twenty-stone "heavy" in eleven Charlie Chaplin films, worked with Stan Laurel in UK music halls. Like Laurel and Chaplin, Campbell emigrated to the USA and became one of the earliest silent film stars. Billy West (one of Chaplin's most successful impersonators) hired Oliver Hardy as a Campbell equivalent in several films. Eric Campbell died young in an automobile accident. Stan Laurel said, "Eric was a mountain of a man. I think he would have been a great success in the movies when sound came because he had a beautiful, big voice. The odd thing was that he was really a very shy man – like Charlie in that respect."

✳ Babe Hardy took a Roach cameraman with him to the golf course to film a few of his swings. Playing the film over and over, Babe noticed that his biggest fault was in lifting his head too early when striking the ball. On subsequent visits to the golf course he disciplined himself to keep his head looking down at the position where the ball was before he hit it, until it was approximately a quarter of the distance on its way. This innovative film investigation is a credit to Hardy's dedication and expertise and preceded by half a century computer and video analysis of the action of golfers and other sports individuals.

✳ Did you know that there is a cabaret star in Ireland known as Hal Roach? No newcomer this chap, in 1992 he completed a 25 year cabaret engagement.

✳ Members of staff confirmed that Stan Laurel appeared, unannounced, at Queen's Park School Sports at Netherpollok in June 1947. He handed out sweets to some of the younger children there – Stan remembered his school days in Glasgow over forty years on! Following a fire in 1996 part of the school was demolished.

✳ Stan Laurel was partly responsible for the "discovery" of Marcel Marceau. While Laurel and Hardy were in France, making *Atoll K*, Stan saw Marceau's act and organised some publicity for the up-and-coming mime star.

✳ In 1952 a Mr and Mrs Short sent a pair of white carnations to Laurel and Hardy, who were playing at a theatre in Nottingham. Laurel and Hardy were touched by this gesture and the following year they invited the Shorts to meet them backstage at the Newcastle Empire Theatre. "To have met such men," Mrs Short said, "was the highlight of my life." Although the meeting lasted just five minutes it led to a correspondence which lasted for thirteen years. In 1973 the Shorts generously donated the Stan Laurel letters, over twenty in all, to the Newcastle Central Library so that other people could receive pleasure from reading them.

✳ Admirers of Laurel and Hardy's number one supporting actress Mae Busch might like to note that there is an area in Southampton called Maybush!

✳ The pavements (or sidewalks) of both sides of Hollywood Boulevard are covered with "stars" of famous people from the entertainment world. Laurel and Hardy have stars as do the following celebrities who worked with Laurel and Hardy: Billie Burke, Mae Busch, Charley Chase, Joyce Compton, Billy Gilbert, Alan Hale, Jean Harlow, Patsy Kelly, Edgar Kennedy, Harry Langdon, George Marshall, Robert Mitchum, Eugene Pallette, Jean Parker, ZaSu Pitts, Snub Pollard, Herbert Rawlinson, Hal Roach, William Seiter, George Stevens, Lawrence Tibbett, Thelma Todd, Ben Turpin, Lupe Velez, John Wayne and Chill Wills. Dick Van Dyke's star is next to Stan's.

✳ The most impressive group of stars ever brought together was in 1942 for the Hollywood Victory Caravan, which went on a tour in aid of funds for the US Navy. The stars included Charles Boyer, James Cagney, Claudette Colbert, Bing Crosby, Cary Grant, Bob Hope and Laurel and Hardy.

✳ There are three tenuous links between the Boys and Will Hay. . . . In Hay's biography *Good Morning Boys* he relates that his parents moved to Ulverston for a short time, a couple of years before Will's birth. He was yet another British comic to work for Fred Karno, after Stan had left. And he made a film called *Hey! Hey! USA* in 1938 with Laurel and Hardy co-star Edgar Kennedy.

✳ There are several people in the USA with the name of Laurel Hardy.

✳ Jelly Belly beans have been placed into mosaic patterns to form portraits of famous people ranging from Abraham Lincoln to Princess Diana. The Goelitz Collection of Jelly Belly Art includes Laurel and Hardy.

✳ Hallmark Entertainment currently owns the Hal Roach library for the western hemisphere. Beta Taurus, based in Munich, owns it for the eastern hemisphere.

✳ Traffic lights which play tunes from Laurel and Hardy movies are to be found on street crossings in Ploesti, Romania, to help blind people to cross the road.

✳ Admitting that it was only a brief still and a promotional prologue to the main programme, Laurel and Hardy appeared on Europe's largest screen, at the National Museum of Photography, Film and Television in Bradford. Was this the biggest ever Laurel and Hardy?

This is believed to be the only surviving poster billing a theatrical appearance of both of Stan Laurel's parents, Arthur Jefferson and Madge Metcalfe. The "Benefit Night" was AJ's apology for neglecting Bishop Auckland audiences the previous autumn season. He had reopened the Theatre Royal, Blyth in September 1893 and had been too busy to arrange a programme of the standard Bishop Auckland theatregoers had come to expect. Bishop Auckland forgave him.

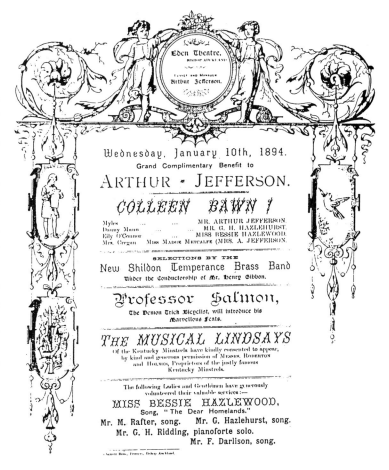

Paolo Peruzzo, Emilio Isca and Giorgio Cavazzano were three of fifty artists from all over Italy who had drawings of Stan and Ollie in an exhibition in Acquaviva in 1997

CHAPTER 7: FANDOM

* Fans in Manchester produced their first batch of Laurel Light Ale to coincide with Stan's centenary in 1990. The ale was a taste of things to come and was followed by Hardy Heavy which was – wait for it – a stout! The Stanley Arms in Southport had two very special draught beers – Stanley's Mild and Ollie's Mild. On Babe's hundredth birthday there was Ollie's Centenary Special Ale. Laurel and Hardy's supporting stars were also remembered – James Finlayson was celebrated with Fin's Beady Eye Bitter. There was even a beer called Lucky Dog.

1890 - 1990

* In the Tuschinski Theatre in Holland in 1992 Bram Reijnhoudt staged a celebration for Babe's centenary; the theatre was filled with twelve hundred people. The theatre had another packed house the following Saturday for virtually the same programme. In a separate programme at the nearby Film Museum, Hardy's solo films attracted an audience of three hundred.

* At the Los Angeles Movie Palace in 1995 two thousand people watched Chuck McCann and Jim McGeorge perform a live act as Laurel and Hardy and a 35mm screening of *Brats* and *Sons of the Desert*.

* In Harlem, Georgia, Oliver Hardy's birthplace, each year there is an Oliver Hardy Festival, which is attended by about twenty thousand people.

* Sean Connery's actor son, Jason, bought a dog from the Battersea Dogs' Home and said, "I'm calling him Ollie, because he's a bit fat and reminds me of Oliver Hardy."

* The late Les Macdonald estimated that he had seen *County Hospital* one hundred and fifty times.

* Albert Kirby has a big picture of Stan and Ollie over his telephone so that if any conversation becomes tedious he can look at it for relief!

* Dougie Brown (Stranraer) and Harry Hoppe (Düsseldorf) both have pet cockatiels which can whistle *The Dance of the Cuckoos* and *The Trail of the Lonesome Pine*. In the summer of 1995 another cockatiel that whistled Laurel and Hardy's theme tune flew off from an RSPCA worker's home in Bradford. *The Sun* and Martin Kelner's morning show on Radio 2 resulted in the cockatiel being found.

* Les Goldsbrough recalled his days as a cinema projectionist in Middlesbrough when he would arrive at work early to run the latest Laurel and Hardy film for the cleaners as they prepared for the Saturday morning children's show.

* The *Sunday Post* in 1994 had columnist Bob Miller telling of premium bond winnings totalling £1,500 amassed by him and a bunch of his fellow golfers. They had always dreamed of a golfing holiday in Portugal or Spain. But they spent the money on an extravagant weekend at the Sheraton Hotel in Edinburgh, with a dinner dance, cocktail party and Laurel and Hardy show.

* In the mid 1980s Ethel the Chimp (from the film *The Chimp*) was revived in the guise of Michael Tate, the purveyor of fun telegrams to the inhabitants of Merseyside, with his "Ethel the Dancing Chimp Grams".

Consistently popular: Way Out West

✳ At their 1984 International Convention in Ulverston, Sons of the Desert met the author Leslie Halliwell, who was conducting interviews for a television documentary. Leslie had just completed his latest book *Seats in all Parts*. The book recalls many of the famous films and stars over the years and Stan and Ollie are often referred to in more ways than one. Philip Martin Williams tells us, "I first spoke to Leslie Halliwell about his love of Laurel and Hardy back in 1978. He must have had a remarkable memory for films for when I spoke to him he could take me virtually scene for scene through *Sons of the Desert*. Yet it was with the shorts that his heart belonged and he laughed loudly just talking about *Laughing Gravy*."

✳ What is your favourite Laurel and Hardy film? Polls consistently nominate *Way Out West* as a clear winner. Which is your least favourite Laurel and Hardy film? The clear failure is *Atoll K*. *Way Out West* is sometimes reported to have been Stan's favourite whereas the bad reputation of *Atoll K* and Stan's very poor opinion of it probably helped to assure its position at the bottom. Other favourites consistently nominated are *Sons of the Desert*, *The Music Box*, *Towed in a Hole*, *Helpmates* and *Them Thar Hills*.

✳ When Roy Castle's widow Fiona donated some of Roy's possessions to help promote the charity he set up, there were found to be bowler hats, biographies of Laurel and Hardy and pictures of Roy at the Laurel and Hardy Museum in Ulverston.

✳ In addition to a filing cabinet full of research material, Randy Skretvedt owns nearly 500 statues and toys, almost 100 films and about 1,200 photographs, including Oliver Hardy's scrapbooks and photo collection up to 1937.

✳ Bargain souvenirs are hard to find but Bill Winfield bought a 7x5 inch photograph, signed by Laurel and Hardy, for £12.00, in the mid-1990s!

✳ *The Big Reel* in 1995 advertised Laurel and Hardy signed photographs starting at $550. A 10x8 inch photograph with a slight smear and some silvering was offered for "only $990".

✳ The next year the same magazine had a page of autographs for sale. At $1,000 for a signed photograph, the Boys were outclassed in price only by Humphrey Bogart and Hattie McDaniel.

✳ In 1995 a three-sheet colour poster for *March of the Wooden Soldiers*, in near mint condition, was offered for sale in the USA for $1,200.

✳ A check sold in the *Collector's Showcase* monthly Los Angeles auction for $665.00. The amount of the check was $25.00, the date was November 30th, 1930 and the signatory was Stan Laurel. What put it in a special category was the fact that he signed it to Oliver Hardy. It seems that Laurel and Hardy were playing poker between takes on the set, and the check was payment for what Laurel lost to Hardy. Hardy's endorsement was on the back.

✳ In 1994 a postcard which had been signed by Laurel and Hardy was donated by Ronnie Barker for auction for charity. It raised £300.

✳ Towards the end of 1995 Royal Doulton advertised a pair of limited edition mugs of Laurel and Hardy, exclusively available from Lawleys by Post, at £99.50.

✳ Stan Laurel's nephew, Huntley Jefferson Woods, added a street sign to his memorabilia collection! Jefferson Street in Blyth was named after Stan's father AJ, and the street was knocked down as part of the town centre redevelopment. On hearing the news, Huntley contacted Councillor Deidre Campbell, requesting permission to add the street sign to his collection. Said the Councillor, "It seemed a nice idea for the family to retain this link between the town and Stan Laurel." The sign was salvaged and presented to Huntley, who said, "My grandfather, Arthur Jefferson, put a lot into Blyth and I was keen to have the street sign as a memento of the family connection with the town."

✳ Laurel and Hardy cigarette cards are quoted as being among those which attract the highest prices. Cards which cost around £15 in Britain attract prices at auction in the USA as high as £430. According to *The Times* in 1995, "The reason prices have remained reasonable over here is that people can remember when they were given away. Some even resent paying £1."

✳ An item from the *Daily Star* in 1989 read, "A bundle of fifty-one letters written by film comedian Stan Laurel and a doll he sent to a young fan fetched £5,600 yesterday. They were bought by a mystery London buyer at the Nottingham auction."

Drawing by Tony Bagley

CHAPTER 8: PROPS AND CLOTHES

✻ *Pratfall* (Volume 1 Number 6, 1971) said, "You know those crazy cars from the Laurel and Hardy films? The ones that were mashed in at the sides like an accordion, or the ones that were scrunched down? The cars might have been crazy, but their inventor sure wasn't. His name – Dale Schrum; his game – creating those hilarious monstrosities and renting them to the Roach studios for $500 per day. Mr Schrum also insisted that no one but himself drive the cars. He always built a small compartment somewhere inside the cars so that he could sit there, unseen, and drive from underneath while peering through a well placed peep hole."

✻ Sigmund Freud refused to have a piano in his house so perhaps the deeper significance of *The Music Box* has escaped us. And if you laugh at a piano destroying a wall and a car in *Call of the Cuckoos*, perhaps it is just a Freudian reflex.

✻ The mantelpiece clock which comes under Stan's shovel in *Dirty Work* seems to be the same clock that appears in *Our Wife*, *Their First Mistake*, *Oliver the Eighth*, *Bonnie Scotland* and probably many more.

✻ For films Stan accentuated his lugubrious walk by cutting the heals off his shoes.

Stan's suit was expensive

✻ At a film memorabilia sale at Bonhams in London in 1996 a sailor's suit, worn by Stan Laurel in *Men o' War* and signed by Laurel and Hardy, sold for £1,265.

✻ Paradoxically, the ill-fitting, seemingly cheap suits worn by Laurel and Hardy were the work of top tailors. Their coats and trousers were carefully made from expensive material, to exaggerated shapes and sizes. Publicity explained that cheap cloth would not withstand the rough treatment the Boys' clothes were subjected to and in order to attain the correct degree of bagginess and tightness essential to their respective suits, the comedians were carefully measured for their fittings. At the beginning of each year, Laurel and Hardy placed an order with their tailor for ten suits each, it was claimed, each suit costing sixty dollars.

✻ Stan Laurel said, "The bowler hat to me has always seemed to be a part of a comic's make-up for as far back as I can remember. I'm sure that's why Charlie [Chaplin] wore one. Most of the comics we saw as boys wore them."

✻ Stan usually wore his bowler back-to-front.

✻ English landowner William Coke ordered the first bowler hat in 1849 to protect his head from low branches while shooting on his Norfolk estate. He tested it in a shop of the London hatters, Lock's, by stamping on it twice. It was undamaged and Coke bought it for twelve shillings. The hat was named after Thomas Bowler who made it to Lock's orders. In the USA the same design is known as a derby, because Lord Derby was the first person to popularise it there.

* In the *Sunday Mail* in 1937 was an advertisement for insuring one's bowler hat! "Should your 'Dormie' meet disaster either at the theatre or football match, it won't spoil your fun. By bringing the remains to Dormie House you will have it replaced free of charge." New, all fur, bowlers could be bought for as little as 10/- (50p).

* Christies reportedly sold Laurel and Hardy's hats for £10,000 at an auction in London in 1989. Another pair, this time worn in *Swiss Miss*, was sold by Christies for £11,000 in 1993. The buyer was James Oliver, a 24-year old student from Wiltshire, who bought the hats for his dad. According to *Best* magazine, in the same year a pair of bowler hats, worn by the team in *Hats Off*, came under the auctioneer's hammer at Christies in London and were sold for a cool £16,000!

* The Bradford and Bingley Building Society's logo is two men in bowler hats. In 1996 one of the directors bought a bowler hat from a London auction for £2,000. The hat headband was signed by Stan Laurel with the message, "Thanks, Harry," and was originally part of the collection of the late Harry Brown, stage doorman at various London theatres between 1930 and 1960. Stan gave it to him during Laurel and Hardy's 1947 tour of the UK.

* In 1990 a bowler hat autographed by Stan Laurel was bought for £8,500 by film actor William Forbes-Hamilton, of horror fame, who was starting a museum of entertainers' props in Newquay, Cornwall.

* An original fez from the film *Sons of the Desert* fetched £3,570.

* A Laurel and Hardy quiz dared to ask, "For five points each, can you name the thirty-two items made from wood products which the Boys were told about in the film *The Tree in a Test Tube?*"

"Never mind the fez – how much for the Yellow Rose of Texas"

CHAPTER 9: LEAVE 'EM LAUGHING

٭ If we ever needed proof of just how much fun was to be had on the set of a Laurel and Hardy film, ample evidence is to be found in the films themselves, where not all laughter was intentional.

٭ Even in 1915 it would seem that the presence of only half the duo was enough to trigger off mirth from the "leading lady". In *Something In Her Eye*, at a moment of supposed drama on emerging from the house with her father, she is laughing uncontrollably.

٭ In Stan's solo film days too, mirth appeared unannounced. In *Just Rambling Along* (1918), keep your eye on him when he's tasting all the food at the counter at Bud Jamison's urging. With his mouth full for the third time, Stan is unable to suppress a laugh.

Not all jocularity was planned

٭ In *From Soup to Nuts* Edna Marian's signs of mirth appear after Stan has entered the kitchen, knocking Oliver's bowler hat into what looks like mayonnaise. This is a perfectly natural response, of course!

٭ *Berth Marks* was only the second talkie Laurel and Hardy made and working with the new technology caused some unforeseen problems. Filming on location at the Santa Fe Depot attracted large crowds who watched and giggled at the antics of the stars. During the silent era this posed no problem, but the sound equipment picked up each laugh and retakes were needed for nearly every scene. Unwanted laughter afflicted poor cameraman Len Powers, too, who ruined more than one shot when he broke up over a particularly funny *ad lib*.

٭ In *Chickens Come Home*, when Stan is caught bending down outside the door of Ollie's office, watch for the fleeting smile on the face of the girl telephonist.

٭ In *Towed in a Hole*, Ollie tells Stan that he doesn't want to talk to him. Stan closes the roof of the cabin, causing Ollie to slide down the mast, covering himself with paint. At this stage if you turn up the volume you can hear somebody having a short laugh, presumably one of the film crew.

٭ In *Sons of the Desert*, in the Chicago night club scene in which Laurel and Hardy meet practical-joking Charley Chase, they so convulsed the production team members that numerous retakes were necessary. Laurel's expression during one part of this action proved so funny that it completely upset the equanimity of Hardy and it was several minutes before the latter was able to regain his composure.

٭ "Kewpie" Morgan, the hefty 300 pound actor who plays King Cole in *Babes in Toyland* actually laughed himself sick from over-exertion in his laugh scene in the picture!

٭ When the new drafts in *Bonnie Scotland* disembark from the ship and march past onlookers, Ollie's disgust at Stan's attempts to march in time gives way to a broad grin of amusement a few frames before he disappears out of shot. Who can blame him?

٭ Della Lind experienced similar difficulties in restraining laughter in *Swiss Miss*. In the sequence where Stan and Ollie come up to collect the piano, there is a shot so framed that the Boys occupy the foreground and the viewer's attention is immediately drawn to their actions. Next time you view the film, resist this tendency and focus on the background where you will see Della Lind scarcely concealing a smile at their antics. Again the reaction is perfectly natural.

* The laughter from the younger sisters of Della Lind when they visited the set of *Swiss Miss* meant that the shooting schedule had to be delayed until they had departed!

"Smile, please"

* Minna Gombell played Mrs Hardy in *Block-Heads*. She said, "It was almost impossible for me to keep from laughing at the comedy antics."

No time for levity

* In *Saps at Sea*, when Fin (as James Finlayson is now often affectionately called) puts on the head-mirror and prepares to apply his "own invention", Stan is munching a banana, but on seeing Fin put on the mirror, he looks up at Fin and allows a quick smile to escape, just as Ollie asks, "What's that?" It is a really quick smile, swiftly mastered as Stan looks interested in Fin's medical wizardry.

* Twentieth Century Fox took advantage of a similar situation for some publicity under the heading "Hilarity rules on the set of *A-Haunting We Will Go*". There is a scene in the film that has Dante, the magician, performing one of his feats with Stan and Ollie as his foils. Dante is about to invoke the magic words and the Boys, clad in ample Oriental costumes, are pantomiming. Everyone is set for the cameras to roll, we are told – everyone except Sheila, who appears as Dante's assistant. This take, it seems, is too much for her and she roars out with laughter, to the consternation of the director. After trying three times to shoot the scene and failing, he solved the problem by having the laughing lass face away from the Boys during the whole scene.

A comical sight in any language

* In *The Big Noise* an old routine proves to be irresistibly funny. Outside the gate of 32 Elm Road, about nine minutes into the film, Bobby Blake blows the Boys' hats off and they reprise their hat-swapping routine. After the third attempt to get the right hats, listen carefully to the soundtrack and you'll clearly hear a member of the crew laughing.

* "You know this business of being funny is a lot of fun," Laurel said. "I get a great kick out of it. Many times I'll start some piece of comedy business and the sheer buffoonery of it will strike me so hard that I'll have all I can do to keep from laughing at my own antics. In fact, sometimes I'm unable to withhold a chuckle and that generally means a retake."

CHAPTER 10: RECOLLECTIONS

✳ A Mrs Chisholm was at school with Stan Laurel at Stonelaw High School in Rutherglen. She remembered attending a dancing class at the school. The boys all wore white gloves and she recalled that Stan played tricks with his hands by making the gloves into funny shapes.

✳ Georgie Harris, best remembered for his "stooge" appearances with Leslie Fuller in many a British comedy of the thirties, said, "Stan first came to my attention in 1910, when I joined a firm called Levy and Cardwell, playing in the pantomime *The House That Jack Built*. We had a boy called Jack Harrison, who was playing Idle Jack, and all I could hear at the rehearsal was Mrs Levy and Mr Levy saying to Jack Harrison, 'Look, Stanley Jefferson used to do it this way. . . .' I did not realise until years later, when I was in Hollywood, that the Stanley Jefferson they were talking about became Stan Laurel. . . ."

✳ " . . . A gentleman by the name of Oliver Hardy came to me, little Georgie Harris, on the Fox lot and asked me if there was anything doing for him in my pictures. He would very much like to play something in one. I talked to my director, Benny Stoloff. He knew Babe very well indeed, but we had nothing at that time for Mr Hardy."

✳ Georgie Harris surmised, "They were two of the greatest exponents of spacing and timing. The beauty of Laurel and Hardy was their teamwork. Many of the things that got their biggest laughs weren't in the scripts." During *The Masquers Revels*, at the Philharmonic Auditorium in Los Angeles, Harris did a sketch with Laurel and Hardy. Georgie was supposed to come into a little store and be served. He had to jump off a counter towards Babe. "He had these old trousers on and as he saw me dive he lifted his trousers up and I went into his trousers. It wasn't rehearsed. It stopped the show."

✳ Effects man Roy Seawright said, "Hal Roach was stubborn as a Missouri mule. Roach had been a truck driver and he ran the studio like he used to drive trucks – hell for leather. Once he decided on a course of action, no-one or nothing could ever make him change his mind, come hell or high water. Roach was from the old school. He figured that the man who paid the bills should be the one to call the shots."

✳ In *Hello* magazine in 1992 Lois Laurel was asked whether she appeared in any Laurel and Hardy films. She said, "When they did *Pack Up Your Troubles*, they considered me, but by the time they wrote the script and got ready to shoot, I was too old, so they used somebody else. But I danced in *Swiss Miss* and did a voice-over in *The Chimp* – at least I laughed when I wasn't supposed to in a certain scene and they left it in."

✳ Reminiscences from those who were employed at the Hal Roach studios emphasise what pleasure was to be had from working on the set with Stan and Ollie. Minna Gombell said, "On the stage I have been everything but the end man in a minstrel show and on the screen I've been rich and poor, a lady and a guttersnipe, but the greatest experience of my entire career has been playing in *Block-Heads* with Laurel and Hardy. At first I was reluctant to accept the offer because of the difference in medium. To me Laurel and Hardy are the kings of absurdity and accomplished artists in pantomime. I doubted whether my experience had been the proper preparation. Any apprehension I may have had dispelled after two days on the set. The spirit of that comedy unit is marvellous. Everyone works so hard and at the same time has such a good time. I could not kick Stan as the script required. 'Kick higher and harder,' he would demand and I would try again. Finally we got through the scene somehow, but I felt that Stan's shins must have been black and blue before the director approved that bit of action."

✳ Margaret Chute wrote in *Royal Pictorial Magazine* in the early 1930s, "Their sets are like a large schoolroom, where everyone seems intent on having a good time. Their work runs along on oiled wheels; they work hard, but they are playing most of the time as well. That is why their comedy is so spontaneous. I have seen a bunch of blasé, bridge-playing, gossip-whispering extras put down their cards and stop their gossiping in order to watch Laurel and Hardy and laugh at them."

The "oiled wheels" of fortune turned in Laurel and Hardy's direction

✳ G W Thompson wrote, "I remember sometime just after the war, when Laurel and Hardy did a tour of England. I was only a lad at the time and my brother and I, passing the Clarendon Hotel in Leamington Spa, on our way home from school, happened to glance in the revolving door and noticed a portly gentleman sitting on a sofa in the foyer. The gentleman was none other than Ollie. We drew his attention to our little bit of mime, the one with the top of the thumb being removed from the left hand. (The left thumb bent at the joint, the right also bent, put the two together, then conceal the join with the right index finger, then pull apart.) On seeing this he was greatly amused and repeated the movement back to us." [12]

---

[12] This trick comes from *The Bohemian Girl.*

✳ Anita Garvin said in 1990, "After he'd shot a scene, Babe would like to sit in his chair and strum his ukelele and sing, whereas Stan would be thinking, thinking. 'What do I do next? What's funny?' That was Stan. I remember only one picture I made with James Finlayson. He was fun to work with and he always had something amusing to say." [13]

✳ Although Peter Cushing was little more than an "extra" in *A Chump at Oxford*, he was able to observe at close quarters "the professionalism and sheer hard work it demanded to create Laurel and Hardy's perfection." According to Cushing, Hardy was a great key-chain swinger and he would stroll around the studio thus occupied, humming a little tune as he went. "He had a plentiful supply of doughnuts constantly within reach, which he would eat most delicately and once he confided to me that they were to 'keep his weight up'! About six o'clock one evening, after a particularly busy day, the director, Alfred Goulding, told Laurel and Hardy they could go home. He had only one more shot to do – a bird's-eye view of the maze – and he would use their doubles. When the 'rushes' were shown the following day, the two stars insisted upon reshooting the scene themselves, because the doubles had tried to be funny, instead of thinking of the situation and reacting naturally. Their thought for others was exemplified when several undergraduates had to fall, fully clothed, into a swimming pool. They made sure that blankets and brandy were available after each ducking, to sustain the actors, quivering with cold while waiting between 'takes'."

---

[13] The film was *With Love and Hisses*. Anita and Fin also appeared in *Hats Off*, but not in the same scene.

✳ Ronnie Ronald was a popular singer and whistler during the 1940s and '50s. When he appeared on the same bill as Laurel and Hardy during one of their British tours, Babe asked Ronnie to teach him how to whistle. He paints an image of Babe, sitting in his dressing room, fingers in mouth, being very frustrated because he couldn't master the whistling technique – just as Ollie did in the movies when trying to master finger-wiggle and kneesie-earsie-nosie. [14]

✳ Captain Robert Harry Arnott wrote in *Captain of the Queen* in 1982, "[In 1947] I was off-duty through the daytime, and called in [to the officers' wardroom]. A deep, melodious voice from the doorway flowed over the three or four of us sitting inside. I looked up at the man whose absurd antics had sent me limp with laughter twenty years earlier as I sat in the children's half-price seats at our local cinema. 'Do have a chair, Mr Hardy,' I said. 'Isn't Stanley with you today?' 'No, he isn't, son,' answered Oliver Hardy. 'With my bulk those chairs really won't do. Mind if I take the settee?' 'Please do,' I told the great funny man. 'Er, would you like a drink?' I asked him. His face relaxed into a smile. 'Why, yes. May I join you in a cup of tea?' Sipping his tea with his little finger outstretched, Oliver Hardy told me that he and Stan Laurel had been on the British music hall circuit. 'How did it go?' I asked innocently. Mr Hardy's chubby cheeks darkened. 'Not at all well, I can tell you. Can you imagine Stan and myself as stand-up comics?' 'Well,' I said, 'you could always make me laugh.' 'Ah, yes, dear boy, but that was in our film situation routines. Neither of us is a Bob Hope.' Mr Hardy finished his tea, thanked the steward and raised himself carefully from the settee; he didn't seem any taller than my own 6ft 1in, but his beam was enormous. Much older, much sadder than the funny man of my boyhood, Ollie rolled towards the door. I half-expected him to twiddle his tie as he turned to say, 'Cheerio, chaps, and thanks for the tea.' But he didn't and in another instant was gone. What a shame, I thought, that great comics have to grow old."

---

[14] These bits of fun come from *Fra Diavolo*. See also page 162.

✱ In *Yours* magazine in 1991 former newspaper editor George Cregeen wrote, "The year was 1952. The venue, the Hotel Normandy, in the stylish resort of Deauville. I was there to report on the inauguration of a daily air service. After an evening of enjoying the best wines that the hotel could offer we retired – full of song – to our accommodation. We were still in full voice when there was a rap on the doors which separated us from the adjoining suite. They were not locked and we opened them to find . . . Laurel and Hardy! 'I wonder if you would oblige us by being a little quieter?' asked Ollie, then that bright smile came to his face – 'or may we come in and join you?' Come in they did. Never again has there been such a melodious rendering of *The Trail of the Lonesome Pine*."

✱ Audrey Harmon from North Shields remembered that Stan Laurel, "Had brilliant orange hair. We all remember him as a very nice person, very homely, who laughed and joked all the time."

Homely?

✱ Founder of the Merseyside Sons of the Desert, Les Macdonald said, "My prized possession is an autographed programme from their 1952 tour of Britain. I went along to the Liverpool Empire to see them and, as I was too shy to approach them myself, I sent my brother to get them to sign our programme. I've kicked myself ever since! That was the only chance I had to meet them and I threw it away."

✱ Derek Malcolm, film critic in *The Guardian*, was personally entertained as a small boy by Laurel and Hardy in their dressing room after a London theatre matinee. He recalled, "I just asked to see them and miraculously got in." At the time Oliver ordered tea and buns for his awed guest, deliberately sat on one of the buns and then passed the flattened object to Stan, who started to cry.

✱ Albert Smyth wrote in the anthology *Carry On Writing*, "I cherish one memory that sums up the real Stan Laurel. In one of his letters he stated that he now appealed to a much younger audience. Some of the neighbourhood kids would knock on his door. When he appeared they would ask, 'Make a funny face for us, Mister Laurel.' Stan would oblige in his inimitable way and off they would go, laughing."

✱ Patsy Kelly said of her work in Hal Roach two-reelers, "We all had such a good time that I didn't feel right taking the money."

✱ Reg Harrison, now retired and living in Australia, operated spotlights in a Manchester theatre. He and his fellow workers took it in turns to go backstage to meet artistes. He said of Laurel and Hardy, "What amazed me most was the transformation of the two. One minute before going on stage you would have thought they were ordinary people and next Laurel and Hardy as their fans knew them. They treated all the stage staff with respect and they were never overpowering or snobbish, just two wonderful gents, never to be forgotten. It was one long laugh for the twelve nights they performed. While they were in Manchester they never went out together and never in their bowler hats. On the streets they were just two ordinary gentlemen."

✳ The late historian William K Everson expressed admiration for Robert Youngson, whose film compilations did much to revive interest in Laurel and Hardy:

> I was with him when he was looking at most of the films in negative form. I saw *The Battle of the Century* with him when he first looked at it. I remember him being so delighted at the pie fight scene. But even then the first reel was in terrible shape. He salvaged what he could, but a lot of that film was gone even when he got it and this is going back to the 1950s. As soon as he ran the negative and knew what he wanted, he right away would make fine grain masters. If those silents hadn't been brought out into the open and used when they were, we might have lost most of them.

✳ Geoff Lovell reminisced, "My pal and I went to the show [at the Bradford Alhambra] and afterwards to the stage door for autographs. It was a filthy night and we couldn't get near the famous duo so we legged it across town to the Midland. We beat the taxi, but the doorman would not let us into the foyer. Ollie, however, insisted we be allowed in and sat us down and chatted to us for fully ten minutes. They then both signed our programmes and escorted us outside and thanked us most graciously, to cap an evening to remember."

✳ T Marvin Hatley, composer of the Laurel and Hardy theme tune and much of the Laurel and Hardy music, said, "Stan Laurel had a wonderful, sweet personality. He was very humble and he was always ready for a laugh. And Hardy was more reticent. That is, he didn't mix in as much as Stan Laurel did." The Hatleys would have Laurel and Hardy over for spaghetti dinner. "You'd be surprised how they eat. Fat Hardy just nibbled at a little plate of spaghetti while Stan ate three or four big plates of it. Most astounding thing I've ever seen. And then he (Stan) went out and jumped in the swimming pool and almost cracked his head open."

✳ The picture most people have of Oliver Hardy is the sweet, lovable "Ollie" of the Laurel and Hardy films. But, according to Leo Brooks, "Nothing could be further from the truth. Oliver Norvell Hardy was a very complex, often angry and driven individual. Not even his third wife, Lucille, realised until the final months of her life just how complex the man she thought she knew so well was. I have spent over fifteen years on research in getting to know the real Oliver Hardy. I met him in person in 1953 in London and shall treasure that meeting as long as I live. I love and admire his film work, but do not think I would have cared to have had him as a friend."

Complicated?

Drawing by Steve Mullin

CHAPTER 11: STAR QUOTES

✳ Barry Norman: "Together they were funnier than any other screen comedians the cinema has yet produced. The contrast between them was perfect, the naïve, well-meaning but terminally dimwitted Stan being the perfect foil to Ollie who, though equally dimwitted, was never aware of it and nurtured intellectual and social ambitions way above his station."

✳ Bob Monkhouse: "I fell in love with Laurel and Hardy because of the sweetness of their nature and that fantastic combination that reaches across the years."

✳ Dick Van Dyke: "I suppose there are people who think of Laurel and Hardy as relics of yesterday, shadows on grainy film. They're hardly that. Their comedy is being used today in every medium – begged, borrowed or stolen. Stan Laurel was not just an actor, not just a comic; he was the truly complete performer. He created his own comedy situations, developed and polished them and worked out the action, step by step."

✳ Brent Spiner, who plays the Android Data in *Star Trek: The Next Generation*: "I don't really trust someone who doesn't think Laurel and Hardy are funny."

✳ Richard Briers on Christmas 1994 viewing: "I'm praying for my favourites to be on TV: Harold Lloyd, Laurel and Hardy, Tommy Cooper and Morecambe and Wise."

✳ Eric Morecambe's son Gary, when asked who his father's influences were: "Laurel and Hardy. He thought they were the best ever."

✳ When he visited America, Tony Hancock went to see Stan Laurel and observed: "He doesn't get a penny for any of the [television] repeats. There he is, the poor bugger; another genius who got screwed."

✳ Paul McCartney: "I love them and I love all their films. I don't have an out-and-out favourite, but I particularly like *The Music Box*. I prefer their short films and I love to see Stan cry."

A Stan trademark – the crying game

✳ Robson Green: "I've always had so much respect and admiration for Stan Laurel. If I ever did a one-man show, I'd love to play Stanley. His story has got the lot – pathos, humour, the works. It'll come along one day . . . with a bit of luck!"

✳ John Cleese: "I think Oliver Hardy is one of the greatest comedy actors I've ever seen – I just think he's sensational."

✳ Ronnie Barker: "Oliver Hardy is charm itself when he's setting out to woo a lady – this big, fat man flitting about so lightly. Behaving in such a pansy way, so fastidious when he flicks a drop of rain off his hat, a bit of fluff off his sleeve."

Logic for Dinah

✳ Michael Bentine: "Stan Laurel and Oliver Hardy complimented me on my original approach to comedy and told me that their own approach was always instinctive first and that they would develop the situation along logical lines later. I was fascinated as they explained to me how they would develop a gag from a vague flash of inspiration – like trying to get a donkey into a hayloft – and then the painstaking process that followed, as they slowly and logically built up the whole sequence."

✳ George Stevens, the one-time Roach cameraman: "Until I met Laurel and Hardy, I didn't know that comedy could be graceful and human."

✳ Cannon and Ball, doing a slapstick routine, decked out in overalls and bowler hats: "It's not as easy as it looks. Your timing and movements have to be exactly right. Laurel and Hardy were the masters of this."

✳ Paul Eddington: "For years I've felt terribly guilty about not liking Chaplin films. Bernard Shaw did him a great disservice when he called him a genius. For my money, Laurel and Hardy are head and shoulders above Chaplin."

✳ Barry Humphries: "When I see a bowler hat it is not Chaplin I think of, but the more lovable and humanly engaging personalities of Laurel and Hardy."

✳ Richard Wilson: "The funniest act ever has to be Laurel and Hardy. They were always my favourites from childhood. I have seen all their films[15] and they still make me laugh my head off and I don't laugh very easily. They were brilliant and had wonderful timing."

---

[15] All their films? *Hats Off* and *The Rogue Song* are lost.

CHAPTER 12:
SIGHTINGS AND CITINGS IN PRINT

✳ *The Picturegoer* in 1929 had an account of a live appearance of Laurel and Hardy:

"Good evening, ladies and gentlemen. We wish that you could be here with us tonight." These were the words of brilliant wit, uttered by Oliver Hardy. [Later Stan explained . . .] "We are like everybody else, with a regular business. Comedy is our business. We can't go around all the time, doing comedy falls and hitting each other." Oliver added, "Then, if we did try to be funny, and didn't succeed, people would say, 'Oh, they're not half so good as we thought they were,' so we refuse all requests to appear in public, and keep what funniness we have for the screen."

✳ Henrietta Grayne wrote in *Film Weekly* in 1930:

Oliver Hardy's chief characteristic is pomposity. We never fail to see humour in those who assume a dignity out of keeping with their appearance and the fact that Hardy's pomposity is generally assumed deliberately to impress those whom he intends to gull only adds to its savour. Stan Laurel is meek. We are told that the meek shall inherit the earth; our general experience of life is that they receive their inheritance in instalments – by having it thrown at them in clods. Laurel is no exception and the patient resignation with which he accepts each new buffet of fate, and the pale, wan smile with which he returns the rare smiles of fortune, endear him to us all. Thus far the twain are divided; now for the irresistible combination. Underlying all their give-and-take adventures, in which the big man gives and the little man humbly takes, is a sense of comradeship which only awaits a moment of common danger to bring it to the surface.

The Picturegoer's Guide to Pictures 8 page Art Souvenir Inside

Picture Show 2D

Laurel and Hardy
Just a Couple of Clowns

Two unlikely pilgrims were front page news in 1932

✳ Margaret Chute wrote in *Royal Pictorial Magazine* in the early 1930s:

The reproduction of the sound made by smacking a man's head, or "socking him one" on the jaw (frequent occurrences in comedy films), is a tricky business. The action itself does not record through the microphone as it ought to sound, so some other noise has to be substituted. In silent picture days someone in the orchestra would have gone "bump" on the drum, when Mr Hardy hit Mr Laurel on the head. But when the actual thump was recorded, it sounded flat and quite unreal. So the noise was made by a man hitting the brake drum of a car with a wooden mallet and the loud "clank" that resulted caused a roar of laughter. When Oliver Hardy has to fall down – "blump" – a large empty barrel is dropped on the floor. When Stan Laurel falls a very little barrel is dropped. That makes the right-sized crash for both of them.

59

✳ In 1933 E R Moak reported in *Photoplay*:
Even today, secure as they are in the cinema's arena of plenty, tears well in Stan's sad eyes as he recalls the times when, penniless in strange lands, he felt his frail body couldn't cling to life against continued hunger, while a lump rises in Oliver's silvery throat as he speaks of how he, alone and "broke", lay fever-ridden in a cheap lodging house, awaiting the end he believed inevitable.

✳ Stan Laurel said in *Film Weekly* in 1935:
Laurel and Hardy must always remain in character. I could think of thousands of funny things we could do to get laughs, if we didn't have to study this character problem. But Laurel and Hardy must never be "wise guys". They may only keep on thinking they are and act accordingly. They must never be "fresh" or resourceful; they must be just plain dumb. Their exploits must end right way up, not through their ingenuity, but in spite of their blundering. Coincidence can be exaggerated, but must still loiter somewhere within the realm of possibility.

Laurel and Hardy have been used in countless advertisements over the years, including this cigarette advertisement in 1934

✳ Basil Wright wrote in *World Film News* in 1937:
Maybe you don't find them funny? Then you are my enemy, and I hope you will many times be forced to sit through a Laurel and Hardy feature film, tortured by the unceasing laughter of an audience of ordinary people who realise, if only subconsciously, that they are looking at a film which sums up more simply than any philosophical treatise the need for laughter.

✳ In her autobiography *On the Other Hand*, Fay Wray (*King Kong*'s leading lady) claimed that she had a six month contract at the Hal Roach studios during which time she had what she terms, "an ingenue lead with Stan Laurel". Unfortunately she quoted no title.

✳ *Gas-tly Mistakes* is a safety booklet first produced by Air Products in the 1970s, with artwork by Laurie Richards.

✳ One of the most bizarre references to Laurel and Hardy has to be a review of the poems of Theodore Roethke in *The Times* in 1985:
Laurel and Hardy in a single poet. His rhythms fall naturally into dance-time, waltzing with what they mean, stamping sometimes up and down, achieving once in a while a strange dignity, a kind of whirling, accidental, dervish grace, like a fat man who, by sheer inspiration and close attention to the pattern of the music he hears, has managed to release the thin man inside him so that the thin man spins off dancing like a ghost.

✳ The smallest Laurel and Hardy book in the world comes from Germany and measures 80 x 60mm. It has 128 pages and is entitled *Dick + Doof*.

This advertisement was in a South African newspaper, The Star Tonight, *in 1987. It wasn't a joke!*

✸ Roger Kettle and Andrew Christine, whose adventures of Beau Peep (below) appear in the *Daily Star*, wrote:
> They call it the Legion of the Lost, or the Legion of the Damned. Now, for the first time in strip cartoon form, the other side of the story is told, the story of Beau Peep, the Legionnaire who has taken over where Laurel and Hardy left off.

✸ The *Daily Express* in 1989 asked:
> How do top models wind themselves up in the morning and wind down at night? "With some great music first thing," they report. "And watching classic funny videos like Laurel and Hardy at night."

✸ David Ort had the following to say in *Classic Images* in 1990:
> My own personal choice for the most intriguing film-that-might-have-been has to be the project Billy Wilder dreamed up to follow *Sunset Boulevard*. According to Maurice Zolotow, "Wilder was now toying with the notion of a screwball comedy with . . . Laurel and Hardy!" He envisioned a film opening, "with a longshot of that famous 'Hollywood' sign and zoom in for a close-up, very

tight, and we'd see Stan sleeping in an 'O' and Ollie sleeping in another 'O'. They are movie extras. Oh, yes, the story was about Hollywood during the Mack Sennett custard pie comedy era. They lived in a cemetery. A rich widow, coming to pay her respects to her late husband, falls in love with Ollie – but hates Laurel." Wilder approached Oscar winning screen writer Norman Krasna, who found the idea irresistible, but who also found Wilder difficult to work with. Edwin Blum became Wilder's collaborator and the film might have been made had not Oliver Hardy fallen ill. Think for a moment of what might have been. Billy Wilder writing and directing a film specifically tailored to the talents of Laurel and Hardy at a time in their careers when they certainly could have used another great movie.

✸ The *Times* in 1992 reported a waiter being jailed for six years for threatening to poison tubes of toothpaste. He and an accomplice had written a series of blackmail letters, signed "Laurel and Hardy".

✸ The *Bradford Telegraph* (1993) reported that two men trying to pass counterfeit banknotes were caught because they looked like Laurel and Hardy. A toy shop assistant described the men as "a Laurel and Hardy pair" and police had no difficulty finding them in Bradford city centre.

✸ The *Sunday Mail* in 1993 said:
> A country's upper crust are being plagued by a custard-pie thrower! Dedicated to deflating egos, he's pounced on politicians and film stars in France. Police laugh off the attacks, and say he's paying homage to Laurel and Hardy.

✸ There are more relatives of Stan Laurel living in the Dewsbury area in Yorkshire than anywhere else in the world, according to a Dewsbury newspaper in 1993.

✸ Two leaflets surfaced in 1994, advertising the Banque Populaire. Stan's face was on one and Ollie's on the other.

✸ Even a Mensa publication had Laurel and Hardy on the cover in 1994!

✳ The *Highland News* had details of a visit to Inverness in 1994 by a mass choir from Finland. The headline in the newspaper was, "Another Finn Mass".

✳ The *Independent on Sunday* in 1994 had a feature on fat men. John Goodman wrote:

Look at early photographs of Hardy and you don't see a fat man at all. The frowning weather-beaten face of 1925, with its full, assertive moustache not yet foreshortened into that clipped badge of absurdity, might be that of the young Ernest Hemingway. Between, say, *The Music Box* (1932) and *Way Out West* (1937), Hardy swells from stoutness to obesity, the face losing all definition, inflated into a medicine ball, the eyes like narrow slits for laces. Perhaps, by then, the thanklessness of his comic persona had dawned on him. Well might he have sought solace in food and drink, as his self-image dwindled and he was left playing a fat fool – clumsy, stupid, hot-tempered, and hypocritical (tetchily dismissive of Stan, but unctuously polite to outsiders: "Why, thank you, Ma'am"). He was allowed to wallow unhappily in his image of himself as fat and useless. He was, after all, funny not because he was fat, but because he was a comic genius: a master of timing, of dummying the audience into relaxation, before taking a hit; and the creator of a character whose real humour lay as much in its exaggerated courtesy and inarticulate exasperation as its humiliations.

✳ The magazine *100 Years of Moving Pictures*, issued in 1995, stated:

Pathos was at the root of the most successful comedy team in the history of the moving pictures, Laurel and Hardy. Their portrayal of two pathetic characters, the feather-brained Laurel and the short-fused Hardy, is a study in frustrated dignity. Laurel and Hardy's success bridged the way for the great comedy teams, from Bing Crosby and Bob Hope's Road pictures of the 1940s and 1950s to Cheech and Chong's *Up In Smoke* (1976) and the immortal Monty Python group.

"Offbeat" is the word for Maurice Sendak's In the Night Kitchen *(1970), written for very young children. It had three Ollies!*

✳ *Another Fine Dress* by Jonathan Sanders (1995) found little favour with some aficionados, being a provocative and unorthodox look at the films of Laurel and Hardy. The author's exposition of role-play was considered obsessive and even distasteful to some, while others recognised a new and perceptive perspective.

✳ In *Films in Review* in 1995 was the story that Gerald Potterton, the director of Buster Keaton's movie *The Railroader*, went to see Keaton in Los Angeles and said:

He had promised to introduce me to Stan Laurel. Buster had told Stan that I had named my youngest son after both Stan and Ollie – Oliver Stanley Potterton. Stan howled with laughter. That was a great moment for me.

✳ In the 1990s the Abbey National had a four-paged brochure with the slogan, "Get into one of life's fine messes and we'll help get you out." Photos of Stan and Ollie were splattered throughout and there were many quotes including, "Say, Ollie, every year there are three million accidents around the house." "If I had that many accidents, I'd move house."

✳ A Tesco Club booklet in 1996 had a photo (from *Busy Bodies*) of Stan directing a hose pipe into Ollie's mouth in an item called *How to Handle a Hangover*.

✳ If there are errors in this book, the *Laurel & Hardy Quote Unquote* book offers comfort – it quoted a film title as *The Laurence and Hardy Murder Mystery*.[16] Three mistakes in five words!

---

[16] The correct title is *The Laurel-Hardy Murder Case*, by the way.

CHAPTER 13: MUSIC

＊ The song *The Trail of the Lonesome Pine* from *Way Out West* does not date from the thirties. As early as 1913 it had been recorded on an Edison cylinder! Most of the songs heard in Laurel and Hardy films were decades old when the Boys sang them, but *The Old Spinning Wheel* is an exception – the song Ollie hums and Stan "pom-poms" to in *Them Thar Hills* was a popular hit during the summer of 1933, the actual time of filming.

＊ Oliver Hardy's singing sessions include *Somebody's Coming to my House* (in *Chickens Come Home*), *Lazy Moon* (in *Pardon Us*) and *Shine on Harvest Moon* (in *The Flying Deuces*). Stan's melodious moments include accompanying his partner singing *Let Me Call You Sweetheart* (on a tuba in *Swiss Miss*) and *The World is Waiting for the Sunrise* (played on his bed-springs in *The Flying Deuces*).

＊ Stan's wild tromboning in *Saps at Sea* almost drove Ollie crazy, while his clarinetting (in *You're Darn Tootin'*) caused Mr Hardy to destroy the instrument! They lost their double bass and organ in *Below Zero* and the same film afforded us *In the Good Old Summertime*, before a couple of well-aimed snowballs ended all.

＊ We have been treated to shorter musical pieces too: Stan's fish horn in *Towed in a Hole*, the swallowed harmonica in *Pick a Star*, a bubble-blowing organ in *Swiss Miss* and Ollie's inaudible guitar picking in *Them Thar Hills*.

＊ There were some instruments we didn't hear, like the cello Stan left behind on a train in *Berth Marks*, a set of bagpipes in *Bonnie Scotland* and that steamrollered French horn in *You're Darn Tootin'*.

"That's nothing, lady . . . just wait till we yodel!"

"I hate and detest pianos"

✳ Pianos have been played (*Another Fine Mess*, *Chickens Come Home* and *Beau Hunks*) and destroyed: Billy Gilbert axed one in *The Music Box*, as did Stan in *Big Business* and Ollie ruined one in *Beau Hunks*. In *Swiss Miss* the Boys deposited a piano in a gorge and in *Way Out West* they went in one end of a piano and out of the other! Ollie's head was jammed between a piano and a piano leg in *Wrong Again* and who can forget the one that rolled into the street to be crushed in *Call of the Cuckoos*?

✳ Who were the musicians heard on the original Laurel and Hardy film soundtracks? When and where were they recorded? In spite of years of research, nobody has yet found the answer. Not a single musician active around that time recalls playing at these sessions, or even hearing about them – which is odd, considering that musicians generally make it their business to know about these things.[17]

✳ Laurel and Hardy's theme tune, *The Dance of the Cuckoos*, was originally a jingle on a local Los Angeles radio station.

✳ T Marvin Hatley, the music maestro of the Hal Roach studios, composed *The Dance of the Cuckoos*. Hatley was seen on screen on more than one occasion. He played the piano during the *Honolulu Baby* number in *Sons of the Desert* and he was the

17 Source: Piet Schreuders's booklet issued with the Beau Hunks Orchestra recording in 1992.

accordionist in the barrack room sequence of *Bonnie Scotland*. Hatley was nominated for an Oscar for Best Score in *Way Out West*.

✳ Between April 24th and 27th, 1929 about a dozen 78 rpm records were recorded in the Hal Roach studios in Culver City; accompanied by Le Roy Shield at the piano, Thelma Todd recorded three songs – *Let Me Call You Sweetheart*, *If I Had You* and *Honey*. Thelma sang the latter with Eddie Dunn, who was the taxi driver in *Me and My Pal* and had other roles in Laurel and Hardy films. This record was never released.

✳ In 1930 Le Roy Shield and the Victor Hollywood Orchestra made a record in Hollywood with the titles *Sing-Song Girl* and *Song of the Big Trail*. The vocalist on the second title was Bud Jamison, who appeared in hundreds of two-reelers and was one of the highway robbers in *On the Wrong Trek*.

Laurel and Hardy made only one 78rpm record, recorded and released during their UK tour in 1932

✳ Director Leo McCarey wrote more than a thousand songs, only one of which was moderately successful: *Why Don't You Sit on Your Patio?*

✳ Most existing prints of *Berth Marks* (1929) derive from a 1936 reissue print that features *The Dance of the Cuckoos* over the opening scenes. An interesting anachronism since the song wasn't written until 1932!

✳ The Beau Hunks Orchestra (Netherlands), The Nighthawks (USA) and Ronnie Hazlehurst and his Orchestra (UK) have released modern, but faithful, reconstructions of Laurel and Hardy music on tapes and discs.

✳ An unusual version of *The Dance of the Cuckoos* was produced in 1994 by the Midlands based Dance Music Federation, headed by Ravi Gill and Mark Telfer. Ravi explained, "The whole idea came to me when I was eleven. The first record my mum ever bought me was *The Trail of the Lonesome Pine*. We had two Hi-Fi systems at home and I used to mix this with Adam and the Ants." Ravi then procured a copy of the 1932 recording of *The Dance of the Cuckoos* and it just stuck in his brain.

✳ The ever-popular *At the Ball That's All* from *Way Out West* was one of the selections made by Billy Connolly when he was on *Desert Island Discs*. When asked to nominate just one of his eight choices, this was the one he picked. Virginia Bottomley chose *The Trail of the Lonesome Pine* as one of her records on the programme.

✳ Little and Large, dressed as Laurel and Hardy, sang the Bowie and Jagger hit *Dancing in the Street* on television in 1986.

✳ As part of the 1987 British Record Industry Awards, Boy George presented the Pet Shop Boys with a trophy for the best record of the year. Astute viewers noticed an Oliver Hardy badge on George's hat.

✳ On Abba's album *Waterloo* the ladies sported badges of Stan Laurel – Agnetha had one and Anni-Fried had two.

✳ In a live concert of Big Country in 1991, and during the instrumental break of *Field of Fire*, self-confessed Stan Laurel fan Stuart Adamson broke into *The Dance of the Cuckoos* on his guitar.

✳ When Ken Bruce played a record by Meatloaf and Larry Adler on Radio 2 in 1995, he referred to them as being musical equivalents of Laurel and Hardy!

✳ Many pop songs contained references to the Boys. Examples are *The Old School Tie* by the Western Brothers ("famous school fellows like Laurel and Hardy") and *Pamela Pamela* by Wayne Fontana ("when Laurel and Hardy were shown at the flicks"). Squeeze's *Christmas Day* included the lyrics, "So what would Christmas be without Mary or Joseph, Morecambe and Wise, Laurel and Hardy?" Also a group called Laurel and Hardy took a song called *Clunk-Click* to number 65 in the pop music charts.

✳ All four Beatles were Laurel and Hardy fans long before Paul McCartney mentioned Ollie in the lyrics of *Junior's Farm*. At Paul's request both Stan and Ollie were included on the front cover of the Beatles' *Sergeant Pepper* album. McCartney also wore a bowler hat on the cover of his single *My Brave Face*.

✳ On a John Lennon and Yoko Ono album track called *Nobody Sees Me Like You Do*, Yoko Ono likens herself and John to Laurel and Hardy.

✳ Even Laurel and Hardy film titles pop up in the most unlikely musical contexts. The Rolling Stones had an album called *Dirty Work*. A band called Babes in Toyland toured America in the mid 1990s and a group called Atoll K played in Britain. There was a group called Laughing Gravy and a group called Way Out West had a hit called *The Gift* in the charts, as did Blue Boy[18]. There is also a group called Sons of the Desert.

✳ Jan and Dean had a single called *Laurel and Hardy* and Eric Burdon and War had a song titled *Laurel and Hardy* on their album *Black-Man's Burdon*.

✳ The Kinks had Stan and Ollie on the cover of their album *Everybody's in Show Business*.

---

[18] We know Blue Boy better as a horse and a painting in *Wrong Again*.

Though frequently posing with musical instruments, Stan's forte was wrecking pianos

*Ollie's
downfall
was a
horn*

CHAPTER 14: PLAYS AND MUSICALS

✳ John McCabe, a specialist in Shakespeare, recalled:

> I told Stan a number of years ago that there is a similarity between Laurel and Hardy and Andrew Aguecheek and Toby Belch in *Twelfth Night*, a play he had not read and so he timidly asked me if I would read him a scene or two, which I did with great gusto. I mimicked him when I read Aguecheek and he was delighted. The fact is that Laurel and Hardy are traditional comics going back to five hundred years before Christ.

✳ Samuel Beckett's play *Waiting for Godot* (1957) was influenced by Laurel and Hardy. The two main characters wear bowler hats and there is much "business" with hats. When Estragon attempts to remove his boots, the struggling Ollie in *Be Big!* immediately comes to mind. Vladimir, like Ollie, often puts incorrectly pronounced emphasis on certain words and has Ollie's quirk of making his partner feel obligated to him, saying, "But for me . . . where would you be?" Estragon says, "There are times when I wonder if it wouldn't be better for us to part."

✳ Tom McGrath first staged his play *Laurel and Hardy* in 1975 at the Traverse Theatre in Edinburgh. Kenny Ireland played Ollie and John Shedden was Stan. The play toured Scotland and played the Citizens' Theatre in Glasgow in 1976 – its first appearance in a large theatre – and the place was packed! It went to the Mayfair Theatre in London and the same critics who raved about it in Edinburgh turned against it in London, but the play survived.

✳ When McGrath's play was staged in Miami in 1991, George Capewell reviewed it in *The Miami Herald*:

> The touring British production is an extremely likable, nimbly written work that places the duo in purgatory, awaiting their entry to heaven. The respite gives them a chance to evaluate their emergence as stars, their romantic entanglements and, most of all, their lifelong friendship. More than anything else, the play captures the love shared by these two men – a love so deep that Stanley continued to write gags for his partner eight years after Oliver's death. Maybe it's that affection that has made their humor so endurable.

✳ When, however, the play came to Radio 4 in 1996, John Sessions was not at all convincing as Stan and Robbie Coltrane was not much better as Ollie. The play simply did not adapt well to radio.

✳ *Stan and Ollie* was a musical for which Ron Day wrote the words and Nicky Paule wrote the music. With songs such as *Call Me Babe*, *We Live for Laughter* and *Twenty-Five Years* the show had its world premier at the International Convention of the Sons of the Desert in Ulverston in 1984.

✳ Eight months later *Stan and Ollie* had a five-day run at the Tameside Theatre in Ashton-under-Lyne. Roy Brandon and Dennis Garner captured Stan and Ollie's mannerisms accurately. Many scenes were interrupted by Stan finding fault with a prop or theatre technique, much to Ollie's disapproval, he preferring to proceed with the show. "The audience loved it which is judgment enough," said a reporter.

✳ A musical *Block-Heads*, based on the lives of Laurel and Hardy, opened in 1984 at the Mermaid Theatre, London, but was withdrawn after only two weeks.

✳ The Merseyside Festival of Comedy in 1990 included *The Little Feller*, a short play written and performed by Roy Brandon and Barbara Andrews. Billed as "the life and laughter of Stan Laurel", it consisted of impressionistic vignettes, projecting Stan's screen persona side by side with the real Stan in conflict with the women in his life. Stan aged from the days of Fred Karno to his death bed. One routine had him trying to put his coat on a coat-stand. It kept falling off. He took a pen from his pocket and drew a butcher's hook on the door, hung his coat on it and walked away, with the coat hanging perfectly. The play reappears from time to time.

✳ Graeme Wells's one-man show *Stan* featuring Roy Castle as Stan Laurel had its premiere at the Theatre in the Forest, Grizedale, Cumbria in August, 1991.

✳ *The Laurel and Hardy 70th Anniversary Show* toured in 1997. Stan and Ollie were played by Pete Lindup and Steve King.

✳ *Anything for Laughs* was in Edinburgh in 1997. A press review said, "The Fun Factory's production explores the hitherto unknown path which Stan and Charlie Chaplin shared together on the English music hall circuit." The play suggested that Laurel invented Chaplin's distinctive walk.

CHAPTER 15: FOUR GIANTS

DAN LENO (1860-1904)

✳ In his youth Stan studied many comedians, but his idol was the popular Victorian music hall comedian, Dan Leno.

✳ Dan Leno was born in 1860 and died when Stan was fourteen years old. There was a strong physical resemblance. Both men had squeaky voices at times, no doubt further exercised to enhance their comedy routines, and both comedians had cheeky laughs. Their humour concentrated on real life situations with which audiences could identify.

✳ When Stan sailed to America with the Karno company, one of the troupe was Whimsical Walker, who had known Dan Leno.

✳ Dan was Champion Clog Dancer of the World in the early 1880s; Stan took part in a clog dancing competition in Sunderland in the first decade of this century. He did not win, but then neither did another entrant, Charlie Chaplin!

✳ Leno was one of a group of comedians who founded the Grand Order of the Water Rats; years later Stan and Babe were both proud members of that organisation.

✳ Both Stan and Dan presented convincingly attractive females when dressed in skirts, a trait of the music halls and pantomime. They were also both able to portray working girls sympathetically – Stan in *Another Fine Mess* and *Duck Soup* and Dan in *Mrs Kelly* and *I'm Waiting for Him Tonight*.

✳ The most notable similarity between Leno and Laurel humour is perhaps the "word mix-ups". Stan's opening speech in *Towed in a Hole*, when he suggests that he and Ollie catch their own fish, reflects *The Poppies*, in which Dan sings of walking "alone, side by side". In *The Robin* he is describing his Christmas dinner and, instead of saying, "You all eat the pudding," he says, "and you all sit on the pudding and eat the robin."

✳ Also in *The Robin* Dan invites us to hear the robin sing. He introduces the bird. Silence. He says, "I forgot to tell you, you can't hear the robin singing as he sings out of sight." This is reflected in *Pack Up Your Troubles*, when Stan says he didn't think he would be heard in the cupboard as it was so dark.

✳ Dan sings in *The Huntsman*, "I've just come back from where I've been," which reminds us of Stan's reply to Ollie in *Helpmates* – "I was here with me."

✳ A "Kinora" reel of Dan Leno still exists, lasting only thirty seconds and consisting of many small but clear paper prints. It shows Leno and his wife in a burlesque attempt to open a bottle of champagne.

HAL ROACH (1892-1992)

✽ Hal Eugene Roach was born in Elmira, New York, on 14 January, 1892.

✽ His first job in movies was in 1912, when he was one of seventeen picked from three hundred as film extras. His early careers included gold prospecting and mule skinning.

✽ Unlike Mack Sennett, Roach never worked before the camera as a comedian, though he did appear in westerns for Universal Studios.

✽ As a raconteur his style and timing were impeccable. At his Guardian lecture at the National Film Theatre at the age of ninety-five he showed he could bring the house down with a pause.

✽ Roach maintained that Laurel and Hardy were adults who behaved like children and that this was the principal reason for their success. Roach thought that comedy couples, "Usually consist of one funny man and one straight man. Laurel and Hardy were each funny and straight; one's comedy complimented the other. They would tease and fight each other, but if anyone else started a fight with one of them, the other would go to his rescue and the audience liked this reassurance."

The Boys on the set with the Boss

✽ Roach gave his employees more opportunity to be creative than other studios. The lot was non-union and Hal paid lower wages, generally paying by the week or per film. So he laughed all the way to the bank when his workforce put in twelve to fourteen hour days and worked at weekends.

✽ Roach won two Academy Awards for best short subjects for Laurel and Hardy's *The Music Box* (1932) and Our Gang's *Bored of Education* (1936). In 1984 he was awarded an honorary Academy Award for his "unparalleled record of distinguished contributions to the motion picture art form."

✽ Hal Roach is quoted as saying, "Comedy does not belong in feature pictures because you just can't laugh that long."

✽ When the Hal Roach studio provided lunch of a sandwich and fruit for its extras, Hal Roach ordered that the fruit was to be a banana as the skin had an obvious reuse.

✽ Roach was a pioneer of television, establishing the Hal Roach Television Corporation in 1948. He began turning out "quickie" half-hour drama and comedy shows for television. Hal, more than any other producer, anticipated the quick dominance of television. He leased sound stages to other television producers and he sold nearly all of the hundreds of comedies in his stockpile. Hardy's widow Lucille and Stan Laurel received not a penny.

✽ Thirty years later he said, "If a Laurel and Hardy picture were on the television, I wouldn't watch – I have seen them so many damn times."

✽ He sold his studio to his son, Hal Jnr, in 1955.

✽ In 1987 at the launch in London of video tapes of Laurel and Hardy's films Hal said, "Video is something of a fad . . . I don't think it will be a big, lasting business. For me tape is as disposable as magazines. Personally I have no interest in them whatsoever. I don't own any part of the material."

✳ In reply to a question about the process of colouring some of his films he commented, "The process is inferior. It doesn't make the film any funnier."

✳ In 1985 Hal Roach was asked, "How much of Laurel and Hardy's material did they write or improvise themselves?" His answer revealed, "Babe Hardy was a very good actor and the little mannerisms were his and the way he played his part was his. But as far as story construction, it was up to me to decide the kind of picture they made and it was up to the writers to write it. There would always be one or two gag men on the set who would help, with Laurel and the director, to make a scene funny if it wasn't funny as written. In my experience, fifty per cent of a story wouldn't play as it was written. Maybe just a little adjustment, and it would be funny . . . and that was where Laurel was invaluable. If something didn't work, he could go back over his experiences in vaudeville and pantomime in England and all these thousands of gags that were done over the years. He could always come up with something that either he or someone else had done."

✳ At the age of ninety-five, Roach was surprisingly disparaging of Stan Laurel: "Laurel tried to be like Chaplin and do everything. Sure, he was great when working on individual gags, but his construction of pictures was absolutely childish. His ambition was to be able to carry the whole film himself, but he wasn't capable of doing that. I always had to tell him what to do, only the bigger he became, the more he resented my involvement."

Long-lasting Hal Roach

✳ At the age of one hundred, he still supervised his business interests.

✳ When Hal Roach died on 2nd November, 1992, the *Daily Telegraph* described him as, "The last surviving giant of the silent film industry." He outlived two wives and two of his five children.

✳ A question once asked of Roach was, "How do you think that Laurel and Hardy's popularity has stood the test of time and lasted so long?" His answer was, "Never mind that. I don't know how I've lasted so long!"

✳ When confronted with a fancifully worded menu at a top London hotel, Hal reportedly said, "Gimme chicken."

LEO McCAREY
(1889-1969)

✳ A graduate of the University of Southern California Law School, Leo McCarey had just begun practising when he entered films in 1918, as assistant director to Tod Browning on the film *The Virgin of Stramboul*.

✳ He started out at Roach as a gag writer and director of the Charley Chase comedy shorts and became Vice-President at the Hal Roach studio.

✳ It was no coincidence that, shortly after McCarey became Supervisor of Comedy at Roach, Babe Hardy was signed by the studio. Leo had long been an admirer of Hardy's work.

✳ Much of the Boys' best work was done during the Leo McCarey era. He is credited as having created the team of Laurel and Hardy and was a supervisor and/or story writer for thirty-one Laurel and Hardy films. He often worked on the story line.

✳ McCarey won Academy Awards for Best Director, for *The Awful Truth* (1937) and *Going My Way* (1944), and a third for writing *Going My Way*.

✳ According to *Katz's Film Encyclopedia* Jean Renoir said, "Leo McCarey is one of the few directors in Hollywood who understand human beings."

CHARLIE CHAPLIN
(1889-1977)

✳ In the book *Charlie Chaplin, A Centenary Celebration* by Peter Heining is a 1929 interview with Stan Laurel in which Laurel says, "Charlie was the ringleader in everything. Even then we all felt there was something in him which was different from other men. We didn't know what it was; we couldn't put our fingers on it; but it was there. He was always trying to do queer and unusual things." Elsewhere he adds, "He was always terribly impatient and nervously active. Nothing annoyed him so much as delay of any kind."

✳ In *Six Men* Alister Cooke referred to Chaplin and Laurel sharing seedy rooms during their early vaudeville days and added, "I don't think he saw much of Laurel in Hollywood, certainly not in my time, but he spoke affectionately of him and told me why. There was a time during a provincial tour when Chaplin was often absent from his lodgings, till one Saturday night he came back petrified with fright that his girl in the show was pregnant. Laurel evidently confronted this life crisis as mildly as he contemplated the crasser ordeals of Oliver Hardy. He went off to his trunk and fumbled around in it for a while and came back with a handful of pound notes. They were such savings as he could have scratched up from a fifteen-shilling-a-week salary. Chaplin never said whether the offer had to be taken up, but the memory of it made him more indulgent to the antics of Laurel and Hardy than to any other of the Hollywood comedians, of whom he was uniformly contemptuous."

✳ In his extensive autobiography, Chaplin didn't once mention Laurel.

✳ John McCabe included Stan's recollections in his biography of Chaplin.

✳ Richard Attenborough included Stan in his film *Chaplin* but the role was fleeting.

✳ In *The Legend of Charlie Chaplin*, by Peter Hainey, Stan Laurel said of Charlie, "I remember that he drank only once in a while and then it was always port. He read books incessantly. One time he was trying to study Greek, but he gave it up after a few days and started to study yoga."

✳ Stan Laurel's valet, Jimmy Murphy, told the story that, "At one famous restaurant, Charlie Chaplin used to make a show of preparing his own salads in front of all the customers. Stan couldn't stand pretentiousness. He was not on speaking terms with Chaplin at the time. He entered the restaurant grandly, clapped his hands and called, "James – my salad!" I was dolled up as a waiter and dragged in a big tin bath full of cabbages, beetroots and other vegetables, which Stan started chopping up with a hatchet. Then I had to pour a gallon of vinegar over them and trample them with my bare feet. Stan ate some of his salad and the customers laughed their heads off. Chaplin was sitting at a corner table fuming."

✳ In a 1993 issue of *Filmfax* magazine, an interviewer asked Lita Grey Chaplin, Charlie's second wife and mother of two of his children, "You once said that your sons preferred the films of Laurel and Hardy to their father's films. Was Chaplin aware of this, and was he angry or hurt?" Lita laughed and replied, "No, in fact he thought it kind of amusing. Here he was, their father, considered the greatest comedian in the world, and his sons say they prefer the films of two other comedians. It's funny, children loved Charlie, they laughed at the way he walked and moved, but they didn't really understand him. Laurel and Hardy's comedy was so obvious they understood them and they could associate with them."

✳ In Sheridan Morley's *Tales from the Hollywood Raj* Morley quotes Stan as saying about Fred Karno, "He didn't teach Charlie and me all we know about comedy, but he taught us most of it. I was Charlie's room-mate on tour. He was very moody and often very shabby in appearance. Then suddenly he would astonish us all by getting dressed to kill. It seemed that every once in a while he would get an urge to look very smart.

CHAPTER 16: MOVIE MELTING POT

✳ Laurel and Hardy appeared together in thirty-five silent films, all two-reelers (approximately twenty-five minutes), spanning the years 1921 till 1929.[19]

✳ They appeared together in forty-three sound shorts, spanning the years 1929 till 1935. These are generally regarded as representing their best work. Thirty-five were two-reelers (approximately twenty minutes) and eight were three-reelers.

✳ They also appeared together in a sound one-reeler in 1943, their only coloured short.

✳ Laurel and Hardy appeared together in nineteen feature films (one actually a featurette) between the years 1931 and 1940. One was in colour.

✳ After leaving Hal Roach they appeared together in nine feature films between the years 1941 and 1951. Views on these are varied and emotive.

✳ Hal Roach played the cowardly lion in the 1912 version of *The Wizard of Oz* and Oliver Hardy played the Tin Man in the 1925 version.

✳ Hardy used the name "Babe" in his silent screen career right through till some of his films with Laurel. At the end of *Habeas Corpus*, Stan is carrying a sack containing a "body". Puzzled, he stops and calls Ollie, but what he actually shouts is "Babe!" And in *Big Business*, when Stan mistakenly thinks that Fin is going to order a Christmas tree, he again attracts his partner's attention by calling, "Babe!"

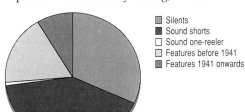

- ▨ Silents
- ▰ Sound shorts
- ☐ Sound one-reeler
- ☐ Features before 1941
- ▨ Features 1941 onwards

✳ The staircase in *Early to Bed* is the same as that used in *The Second Hundred Years*. The intricate scroll work on the bannister provides the clue.

✳ When Ollie first sees a huge crowd of people flocking round Stan in *Putting Pants on Philip*, a small dog appears for a second and yaps at his feet. Ollie seems to be taken by surprise and this, coupled with the fact that the dog is seen in only this one scene, suggests that the incident was fortuitous, but was left in because it was so funny.

✳ How is it that a successful farce like *Hats Off*, of which hundreds of copies were distributed, disappeared almost without trace, though a script survives as do stills and publicity merchandise? It is much more remarkable that only a few of the hundreds of Hal Roach productions are missing. As far as Laurel and Hardy are concerned these are, besides *Hats Off*, the first half of *Now I'll Tell One* and *Battle of the Century*, extant prints of which are less than half of the film, sequences being missing from the middle and end.

Whatever happened to Hats Off?

---

[19] The list is by no means definitive, as discussed in Chapter 26.

* Also missing is *The Rogue Song*, an MGM production.

* *Why Girls Love Sailors* was thought lost until discovered by Leo Brooks in 1986. What was to be expected? Director Fred Guiol's notes bore no resemblance to the film and Stan's outline, though substantially correct, needed to be modified because the "rough sea captain" was played not by Hardy but by Malcolm Waite. Hardy's role was the ship's mate. Stan was a fisherman. Hardy claimed to have first used the tie twiddle in *Why Girls Love Sailors* but there is no sign of it here, nor of the water throwing which, he said, inspired it. Peter Mikkelsen also discovered the film; see page 166.

* Laurel and Hardy's silent films of 1927-29 were shot a little faster than was standard. The speed of around 22 fps (frames per second) compared to the normal 16 fps made them smoother than other silent films. The sound films were all shot at the standard 24 fps. When shown on television they are speeded up to 25fps, for technical convenience.

* The Our Gang films offer something special for Laurel and Hardy enthusiasts, with familiar locations, sets and music as well as faces from the Roach "Stock Company" among the supporting cast. Some of the gags and situations are familiar – a result of the cross-fertilisation of ideas that took place on the Roach lot. The Gang appeared in *The Stolen Jools*, though not on the screen at the same time as Laurel and Hardy; and Stan and Ollie guested as kids in the Our Gang short *Wild Poses*.

* A still from the Buster Keaton film *Sherlock Junior* (1924) shows a cinema queue near a poster advertising Stan Laurel's *Mud and Sand*, released in 1922. This scene was not in the released film, so it must have been either a publicity shot or a sequence filmed and then deleted. It would be good to think that the choice of poster was intentional homage to Stan.

* Buster Keaton appeared with Stan and Ollie in *Hollywood Revue of 1929* and *The Stolen Jools* (though not in the same scene) and wrote gags for *Nothing But Trouble*. David Macleod's book *The Sound of Buster Keaton* documents the numerous Laurel and Hardy players to be seen in Keaton's films.

* Laurel and Hardy won an Academy Award for *The Music Box* in 1932 – their only Academy Award, we are repeatedly told. But Robert Youngson's *The Golden Age of Comedy*, which centred firmly on Laurel and Hardy's shorts, won not one but two Academy Awards in 1958.

* Many compilation films brought Laurel and Hardy to new audiences in the 1960s and most were well concocted, but *The Crazy World of Laurel and Hardy* had extracts which were generally too short and the wonderful Hatley music was removed and replaced by insipid tunes.

* The compilation film *Laurel and Hardy's Laughing Twenties* broke a thirty-year record by producing two hundred and fifty-three laughs during one showing.

* The US Library of Congress in 1989 declared a list of the twenty-five greatest films, which is now considered sacred. Included on the list were Chaplin's *Modern Times* and Keaton's *The General*, but there was no mention of Laurel and Hardy.

* One authority on Laurel and Hardy says that Stan was never happy about their making features, preferring to make twenty minute shorts. Hardy on the other hand really enjoyed making features, according to Lucille Hardy Price.

✳ Ten freak endings: Laurel and Hardy have their legs broken off and tied around their necks in *Going Bye-Bye!* Stan is miniaturised and pops out of an egg in *A-Haunting We Will Go.* Ollie turns into a monkey in *Dirty Work.* The Boys end up looking and sounding like each other in *Thicker Than Water.* Ollie "comes back" as a horse in *The Flying Deuces.* Stan and Ollie have their heads twisted around in *The Live Ghost.* Stan is sucked down the bath's plug-hole in *Come Clean.* Our heroes are turned into a dwarf and a spindly giant in *The Bohemian Girl.* They are actually killed in *The Midnight Patrol.* Stan balloons out of shape after drinking some water in *Below Zero.*

Fra Diavolo *had its British television premier on May 4th, 1981, forty-eight years after its initial cinema release!*

✳ "Because Stan Laurel added two inches to his waistline and ten pounds to his weight while Oliver Hardy's belt had to be drawn up several inches owing to a loss of forty pounds in but a few months, producer Hal Roach insisted that his famous comedians consult a dietitian and rigidly follow his orders until they had resumed their normal measurements." As the date of the edition of *Seeing Stars* which carried this item was 1935, could it be that the reported weight problem was the inspiration for the role reversal gag at the end of *Thicker Than Water*? The comment, "El Flaco and El Gordo are getting *vice versa*" reinforces such an idea.

✳ The title *Midnight Patrol* had already been used for a low-budget Monogram picture of 1932.

✳ Laurel and Hardy's *Way Out West* was not the first film to bear that title. It was used for a silent two-reeler which featured comedian Hank Mann in 1920 and for an early MGM talkie in the 1930s, in the cast of which was Charles Middleton (the Foreign Legion commandant in *Beau Hunks* and *The Flying Deuces*).

✳ *The Trail of the Lonesome Pine* is not only a song, but a film made by Paramount in 1936. Film buffs know it as the first Technicolor feature to be shot on location, but it is of interest to us for certain names among the supporting players: Charles Middleton, Spanky McFarland (the reluctant photographic subject in *Wild Poses*), Richard Carle (the mad professor in *Habeas Corpus*), Otto Fries (the dentist in *Leave 'Em Laughing*) and Henry Brandon (Silas Barnaby in *Babes in Toyland*).

✳ Hal Roach was out of town when *Them Thar Hills* was being filmed. Stan was able to take advantage of the situation by inviting back Billy Gilbert, whose contract had not been renewed by Roach.

✳ In *Way Out West*, when the Boys first arrive in Brushwood Gulch and are taken up to see Lola (whom they think is Mary Roberts) by the unscrupulous Mickey Finn, the latter trips, falls upstairs and is helped to his feet by Ollie. This action seems so natural that it would seem that Finlayson really did trip accidentally and the incident wasn't scripted.

✳ In *The Music Box*, in an obviously unplanned moment when Stan begins to open the crate with a hammer, a giant splinter of wood hits him in the face.

✳ Earlier in *The Music Box*, when the maid laughs and says, "Of all the dumb things . . ." Stan kicks her. She punches Stan's nose and his hat falls off. Ollie laughs. She removes Ollie's hat and hits him over the head with a bottle. As she replaces Ollie's hat, Stan replaces his own in perfect unison!

✳ The sequence in *Perfect Day* in which Stan and Ollie repeatedly bid their neighbours, "Goodbye, goodbye," originated in a music hall sketch of Harry Tate's.

✳ In his book *The World of Laurel and Hardy* Thomas Leeflang accused James Finlayson of swearing in *Way Out West*. In the final scenes, when Ollie ties Finn to the light fitting, it was claimed that Finlayson shouts, "You son of a . . . !" Not so. He actually shouts, "You'll suffer for this!" Finlayson's Scots accent was a little too strong for some ears.

✳ Leeflang suggested that there are bodies of women who are so unintelligent as to disregard completely Laurel and Hardy films as "anti-women". Not all Laurel and Hardy wives are spiteful or bullies. Two notable examples are Stan's wife in *Our Relations* ("Don't rush me, lover") and *Sons of the Desert* – she initially gave him permission to go to the convention and finally gave Stan the chance to confess, rewarding him with cigarettes, chocolates and a kiss.

✳ Randy Skretvedt ponders the matter of Laurel and Hardy aging. "It is an unusual thing about Laurel and Hardy that their characters seem to become more infantile as Stan and Babe grow older. Could you imagine a film such as *Chickens Come Home*, wherein Ollie is happily married and in a position of authority, being made in 1939 or '40? Sweeping the streets is a more typical level of occupation for Mr H in their later pictures."

✳ Stan and Ollie have to prepare a meal in *Saps at Sea*. As there are no proper ingredients, they substitute string for spaghetti, sponge for meatballs, soap for cheese and paint for sauce. Fifty-six years later (in 1996) Harry Hoppe had eighty recipes based on Laurel and Hardy films in his German book *Das Lustige Laurel & Hardy Kochbuch*.[20]

---

[20] The book's title translates as *The Merry Laurel & Hardy Cookery Book*.

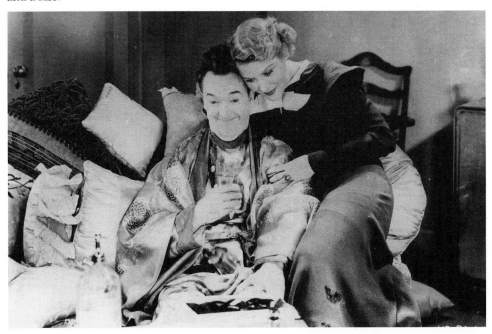

Affection for Stan in Sons of the Desert

* The preview of *The Bohemian Girl* went very well on December 11th, 1935. Five days later Thelma Todd was found dead, slumped behind the steering wheel of her car. Hal Roach resolved to prevent any scandal from encompassing the film, so most of Todd's scenes were removed and Mae Busch took over the leading role. So what we see today is far from being the original version.

* On its original release, *The Bohemian Girl* was banned by the Nazis in Germany because of a dislike for gypsies.

* Rather dubiously it is often stated that *Tit for Tat* is the only sequel Laurel and Hardy made – a sequel to *Them Thar Hills*. When Stan and Ollie visit the grocery store of Mr and Mrs Hall, the Boys recall a dispute they had in *Them Thar Hills*. There was no need to have this reference in *Tit for Tat* as it was no more pertinent to the action than many of their other quarrels.

* Bob Watters and Juggie Read have pointed out that we should consider *Bonnie Scotland* a sequel to *Pardon Us*. In *Bonnie Scotland*, when Stan is asked to produce evidence to verify his identity, he produces his prison record card and it is the same record card that was used in *Pardon Us*, with Stan having the same identification number (44634). The dialogue further confirms the association when it is revealed that Stan and Ollie have been in prison for around three years – the gap between *Pardon Us* and *Bonnie Scotland*. The Boys explain that in order to arrive in Scotland in time for the reading of the will, they had to escape from prison, "with only one week of a three year sentence left to serve." *Pardon Us* was indeed made three or four years previously. All this prompts the assumption that for Stan's indiscretion at the end of *Pardon Us*, whereby he tried to secure an advance order for a keg of beer from the prison governor, the Boys were given a further three years' custodial sentence.

* There is another "sequel". In *Babes in Toyland*, Ollie tells Stan that anything Stan can do, Ollie can do too. Stan disagrees and reminds him of the kneesie-earsie-nosie routine, which Stan had used in *Fra Diavolo* the year before.

Babes in Toyland can be considered to be Fra Diavolo 2

* It may also be relevant to note three other "ties". . . . . The sign outside Stan and Ollie's shop in *Tit for Tat* reads, "Open for Big Business". In *The Big Noise* a gag is reworked from *Habeas Corpus* and then the words "Habeas Corpus" are spoken. In *Way Out West* Stan calls his adversary a "Toad (Towed) in a Hole."

* For *Babes in Toyland* Hal Roach originally intended including all his big stars – Charley Chase, Patsy Kelly, Our Gang etc.

* How many readers have seen the film *Toyland*? Not *Babes in Toyland*, just *Toyland*. It was the 1934 film *Babes in Toyland*, on re-release in the cinemas in sepiatone in 1969.

* In *Our Relations* Stan asks to use Ollie's spectacles to see a photograph more clearly, although he knows very well there is no glass in them (an instance of Stan's special sense of humour). Later, when Alf and Bert walk over to join Alice and Lily in Denker's Beer Garden, Alf takes his own chair over to replace one already there.

Beer garden conviviality with Alice and Lily

✳ Observe that the mountain of washing the Boys have to work through in *The Flying Deuces* matches in shape the real mountain behind it!

✳ If the actors who appeared with Stan and Ollie managed to find regular work in the Leon Errol and Edgar Kennedy short comedies, how could it be that in 1939, when the Boys made *The Flying Deuces* for the same company (RKO), they weren't asked to do a series of two-reelers? Perhaps they were asked and turned down the offer.

✳ Eugene Stratton (1861-1918) was an American black faced singer and dancer who was very popular with British music hall audiences as well as with his peers. Contemporary reports described his dancing as "thistledown," "too beautiful for words," and said, "He moves like a spirit of the air." Stan possibly witnessed Stratton's act and could have been sufficiently impressed to imitate it in his own dance to *Lazy Moon* in *Pardon Us*.

✳ *Pardon Us* is a close parody of MGM's *The Big House*. Leo Willis appeared in both! Discussion once centred on whether Hal Roach used MGM's sets from *The Big House* for *Pardon Us* or built his own. The latter proved to be the case. There are similar prison surroundings and atmosphere and a close adherence to the broad framework of the MGM feature as well as many individual scenes being close replicas.

✳ In *Babes in Toyland*, when Santa and the toy maker discover that Stan has made a mistake with Santa's order and has produced one hundred soldiers each six feet high, instead of six hundred soldiers each one foot high, Ollie's response is his most famous catch-phrase, "Here's another nice mess you've gotten us into." Right? Wrong! Strangely he omits the word "nice".

✱ According to a pressbook, Frank Clark, Hollywood's veteran stunt pilot of twenty-two years at the time of making *The Flying Deuces*, was the first man to change planes in midair without a ladder, though not in Stan and Ollie's film. He was also the first to hang by the tail and then climb back to his seat, a feat he did not try a second time.

✱ The magazine *Variety* predicted that *Sons of the Desert* would, "have to be satisfied with sub-normal receipts". It proved, however, to be one of the top ten grossing feature films of the time.

✱ June Lang and William Janney starred with Laurel and Hardy in *Bonnie Scotland*. June's hobby was collecting china dogs and William's was tennis, according to publicity for the film at the time of its release. It was also stated that Stan's collection of rare plants and beautiful flowers won first prize in a home garden contest in Los Angeles.

✱ In a pressbook for *Saps at Sea*, Stan Laurel is quoted as being convinced that it's harder for an actor to get a laugh than a tear. "And a comic's failure is a lot more embarrassing than the inability of a tragedian to get over," he said. "If the latter doesn't quite put across the dramatic content of a scene, the audience merely feels let down and disappointed. But when a comedian flops, he makes a silly ass of himself and the audience squirms in embarrassment."

✱ The name "Ruth" is to be seen clearly on the side of the old boat the Boys attempt to renovate in *Towed in a Hole*. This is quite a coincidence as the film was made in November 1932 and Stan did not meet Ruth Rogers, his future wife, until the spring of 1933.

✱ There is a sequence in *Towed in Hole* where Stan is incarcerated inside the boat and amuses himself by drawing a picture of Ollie on the wall, poking it in the eye and playing naughts-and-crosses with himself. Leo Brooks says, "Knowing Hardy like I do, I would venture to say that he could not have been amused by Stan's solo venture. When Hardy was not happy about something he went straight to Hal Roach. He would not have vented his anger on Stan, but on George Marshall, who directed the sequence."

Babes in Toyland was one of Laurel's favourite films. It has also been claimed that it was one of Hardy's favourites, but Lucille said that she could remember only one occasion when Babe even mentioned the film and that was not favourably.

✳ Felix Knight, who played Tom-Tom in *Babes in Toyland*, was once interviewed by Leo Brooks, who stated in his thought-provoking magazine *Shifting Sands*:

> Felix pulls no punches. He describes Babe as cold, unfriendly and a volcano, ready to explode, when on the set. Babe came to the set ready to act and if a fellow actor (except Stan) started blowing his lines and caused retakes, Babe would blow his top. There have been hints of this for years. In the spring of 1987, I interviewed Babe's two nieces, who worked in the Boys' films in the early 1930s and they confirm Felix's story. They said that their uncle was a very unhappy man during this period.

✳ In *Come Clean* the sold-out ice cream flavours were listed in the script as orange, walnut and chocolate. Someone changed this during shooting, prompting one of the great Charlie Hall lines, "We're out of orange, *gooseberry* and chocolate!" It's hard for anyone to sound menacing when saying "walnut", but when Charlie hisses "gooseberry" through those gritted teeth, you know he means trouble.

✳ In *Saps at Sea* escaped convict Nick bullies Stan and Ollie at gunpoint. However, he pays a coin for his newspaper, so he's not all bad!

✳ In 1926 *Variety* announced, "Hal Roach, producer, is negotiating for a downtown theatre to be devoted exclusively to short product. He will also endeavor to line up a similar house in San Francisco. Only one and two reel subjects are to be screened."

✳ Many films of Laurel and Hardy are richer for the blatant celebration of insanity. Seven cuckoo stars deserve mention here . . . Charley Chase, one of the lunatics in *Call of the Cuckoos*; James Finlayson, inmate of the same cuckoos' nest, who, in *Thicker Than Water*, proclaimed, "You're all nuts!"; Richard Carle, the nutty Professor Padilla in *Habeas Corpus* who offered the theory that, "the human brain has a level surface"; Lucien Littlefield, the mad Professor Noodle in *Dirty Work*; everyone's favourite eccentric, piano-hating professor, Billy Gilbert (as Theodore von Schwarzenhoffen, MD, AD, DDS, FLD, FFF&F) in *The Music Box*; Mae Busch whose moments of brandishing a knife in *Oliver the Eighth* have cut a place deep in our hearts, along with Jitters, the butler (Jack Barty), who excelled at serving imaginary food with make-believe cutlery.

CHAPTER 17: THE ROGUE SONG

❋ Among many hundreds of lost films is the 1930 two-strip Technicolor movie *The Rogue Song*. Even if the can were to be found in a studio vault, the film itself may well have disintegrated, as has much early celluloid. Old Technicolor film stock was less stable than black and white nitrate film, which itself was notoriously unstable.

❋ The gala premiere took place on Friday 17th January, 1930 at Grauman's Chinese Theater on Hollywood Boulevard, Los Angeles. Tickets were priced $5, $3 and $2. The New York premiere followed on January 28th, 1931 at the Astor Theater where the film ran for five months.

❋ Over one thousand prints were released by MGM in 1930 through their various distributors. After multiple screenings, worn prints were destroyed.

❋ The film was not revived in the way that the true Laurel and Hardy comedies were revived. It was never shown on television.

❋ As *The Rogue Song* was released at a time when cinemas were converting to sound, prints were offered with the sound on either film or disc.

❋ Lawrence Tibbett (1896-1960), born in Bakersfield, California, played the part of a singing bandit. In real life his father, sheriff of Kern County, was killed arresting a bandit.

❋ The *Los Angeles Times* (20.1.30.) reported: The singer was signed yesterday to a six-year contract to appear in at least one film yearly.
Only two years later, after three more films (*New Moon*, *The Prodigal* and *Cuban Love Song*), MGM cancelled his contract. Their newest star returned to the world of opera, concert and radio.

❋ The *Morning Oregonian* (13.4.30.) stated: The introduction of Laurel and Hardy was little less than a stroke of genius. Their antics form the best kind of comedy relief and turn the film into excellent entertainment for all classes and types of moviegoers. The film was directed by Lionel Barrymore, which in itself should be something of a recommendation.

❋ The story was based on *Gypsy Love* (*Zigeunerliebe*), an opera by Franz Lehar. It had additional music and songs by Herbert Stothart and Clifford Grey.

❋ So that you know what to expect if *The Rogue Song* is found, note this publicity material from MGM at the time of the film's release:
The picture that will change motion picture history! A powerful, tremendous, amazing panorama of love and life dominated by a dramatic personality – the greatest dramatic and romantic star that has emblazoned the screen in this generation. Drama flaming with passion – sparkling spectacular scenes – scintillating with glorious music – sparkling with riotous comedy!

✳ A contemporary musical from Universal, *The King of Jazz*, was also filmed in the original two-strip Technicolor process and has survived, providing a pointer to the colour quality we can expect in *The Rogue Song* if found.

✳ Hal Roach personally directed the Laurel and Hardy sequences, of which there were eight.

✳ A writer encountered the Boys in the studio café and described their outfits: "Hardy in a long rose-pink smock, Laurel in a purple satin doublet with red flannel underwear showing at neck and sleeves."

Sheet music from the film survives

✳ The search for *The Rogue Song* has produced rumours and false trails. One report was of a print dubbed into Russian for the troops in the former East Germany.

✳ In most adverts Laurel and Hardy are just a footnote though, as the opera star himself was later to recognise, they assisted the film's promotion in small town America.

✳ Can we prosecute MGM under the Trade Descriptions Act? In their publicity they said, "It will live forever!" It didn't!

✳ Parts of *The Rogue Song* do exist. A clip with Laurel and Hardy seeking shelter in a cave and being chased by a bear was found in Boston in the collection of an American projectionist. A ten minute silent compilation of scenes with Lawrence Tibbett, but without Laurel and Hardy, has been preserved by the Czech Film Archive in Prague.

✳ A trailer for the film was found in an MGM film vault and very recently a twelve-inch soundtrack disc for the trailer has been found.

✳ The entire soundtrack of *The Rogue Song* has survived, complete on discs.

✳ Summaries of the Laurel and Hardy scenes with dialogue can be found in the book *Big Quizness*.

✳ Possible sources for the discovery of a complete print: mislabelled film in the Roach archives, a print in a private collection, among rubbish in someone's loft, in an old cinema, or a foreign film archive with a print bearing a foreign title.

CHAPTER 18:
DELETIONS AND VARIATIONS

✳ Fascinating revelations emerge from the analysis of existing scripts and comparison with the finished films: three chimps instead of one in *Dirty Work* and three babies instead of one in *Their First Mistake*, for example! Promising scenes, in scripts but not filmed, include a bicycle ride in *Sons of the Desert* and a dance in *Block-Heads*. It is even more galling to learn of treasures which were actually filmed but lost on the cutting room floor, an example being the first reel of *Any Old Port*.

✳ Another casualty to the cutting room floor is a finale to *Pardon Us* with Laurel and Hardy in their old age sitting beside a river, Stan fishing and Ollie in a wheelchair.

✳ Randy Skretvedt explains the ice cream gag deleted from *Come Clean*:

> Mae Busch has bid the world adieu. Preparing to save her, Ollie takes off his coat. Stan also does this, then begins to remove his trousers. Ollie stops him with, "That won't be necessary." Stan goes to find a rope. He returns just as Ollie is making a running jump over the dockside wall. Ollie trips over the rope and lands in seventy-five cents' worth of chocolate ice cream.

So now we know why the Boys arrive back empty-handed with Ollie having to make up an excuse about the ice cream.

Tiny Sandford, Fin and the ostrich – all deleted from Any Old Port

✻ As originally scripted, when the Hardys and the Laurels dine together in *Come Clean*, Stan takes a second helping of everything. Ollie turns to Mrs Laurel to comment on Stan's appetite. A cut back to Stan shows him already wiping his plate clean with a piece of bread.[21]

✻ The still below, from *From Soup to Nuts*, seems to be from deleted footage of the Boys' arrival at Mrs Culpepper's house. One can only wonder how the parrot got into the scenario and what is said to cause such embarrassment to all in earshot.

✻ The *Old Boys' Cinema Annual of 1933* reviewed *Any Old Port* in story form, with original dialogue from the film. Many written phrases were completely different from what was actually said. According to this cinema book and William K Everson's book *The Films of Laurel and Hardy*, the ending is very different from the one we know. After Stan had won the fight (which, the annual says, he entered to raise money for the girl whom they had rescued), the girl's boyfriend turns up and the next scene shows Stan and Ollie at her wedding. The two-reeler was at one time intended to be a three-reeler, but the parts reportedly cut show not a hint of the above story.

✻ A publicity sheet for *The Midnight Patrol* includes some ideas that were changed in the released version:

While on patrol in a suburban section, a call from headquarters informs them that a couple of thieves are stealing their tyres. Ollie sends Stan back to look over the situation. The thieves escape and Stan

returns to the car. "Who were they?" queries Officer Hardy. "I dunno," shrugs Officer Laurel. "I never met them before!" Another call instructs them to hurry to a private home. A prowler is said to be at the premises, but the Boys fail to get the address. Officer Laurel goes to a drug store being robbed by a burglar and asks permission to use the phone. He wants to call up headquarters to find out about the prowler. The burglar gives him the address, explaining that it came over the radio in the store.

✻ Two highlights actually filmed for *Bonnie Scotland* were then rejected. Stan was to play a native pipe, thereby causing a snake to rise up over Ollie's shoulder. In *The Lives of a Bengal Lancer*, Gary Cooper makes an Indian prisoner talk by threatening to put him in a pigskin: this is echoed in *Bonnie Scotland* by a similar interrogation scene involving Ollie. Some existing stills are now the only consolation for these deleted episodes. The same thing applies to the opening sequence at the blacksmith's with the deletion of a comedy routine in which Ollie encounters a red-hot horse shoe and a tub of water. In an interview given to *Film Weekly* (28.6.35.) on the set, Stan's outline of the film included a scene where some veterans of the regiment pursue the mirage hoax after the music played on the accordion by Marvin Hatley out of sight of the two gullible recruits: "They take us to the horse races. We can see no horses, but all the boys go rooting and cheering their fancies. Another mirage."

✻ Some shots in the trailer for *The Bohemian Girl* were not seen in the feature as released. Among these is dialogue in which Mae says to Ollie, "How can you be so cruel and hard-hearted?" In response, Ollie turns to the camera and declares dramatically, "It's the gypsy in me."

✻ An early scene in the script of *Way Out West* has the Boys tramping along in the middle of nowhere, trying to find Brushwood Gulch. A signpost points the way, but it keeps shifting direction with the wind. The gag developed but was used only in early releases of the film and no prints of the sequence are now known to exist.

---

[21] Telescoping of time *does* occur in *Way Out West*, *Helpmates* etc. See page 103.

* When Laurel and Hardy's silent films were being made, two cameras were often run simultaneously, one negative being reserved for overseas markets.

* Starting with *Night Owls* (1930), Laurel and Hardy made some of their sound films in French, German, Spanish and Italian (listed in Appendix 2). After a film had been previewed in English, each scene would be reshot in three or four foreign languages, with interpreters as they could not actually speak the languages.

* Margaret Chute, writing in *Royal Pictorial Magazine* in the early 1930s, explained:
    They go over the dialogue sentence by sentence, so that they are perfectly familiar with all the business and timing. The words are written on a large blackboard, just out of sight of the camera; and, having tried to memorise the sentences, the comedians cast a sideways glance at the blackboard if they come to grief.

* Spanish versions of Laurel and Hardy films contain many surprises. All are longer and contain scenes either intended for the American prints but deleted or designed solely for foreign audiences. Different dialogue, musical scores, camera angles and supporting cast provide a treasure house.

* There were plans to make Laurel and Hardy films in Mexico. Prior to the deal with Twentieth Century Fox in 1940, Stan was set to produce an independently financed Laurel and Hardy version of *Don Quixote*. There was also almost a deal for a series of Spanish language comedies (for Latin American distribution only) which would begin production at Mexico's Azteca Studios in the summer of 1941.

* *Berth Marks* was not specifically refilmed in other languages but out-takes and actual footage from it were dubbed and added into foreign releases of *The Laurel-Hardy Murder Case*.

* Not only is the existing English language *Blotto* a reduced reissue of its former self, with a replaced music track, but even on first release it lacked Laurel and Hardy footage to be found in the foreign language versions. After seeing these, the familiar *Blotto* can never be the same again.

* Dubbed versions of Laurel and Hardy films were also successful, often with strange titles. In Germany *Sons of the Desert* was released as *Adventures in Honolulu, Help – We Are Drowned* and even *Fat and Stupid in Africa*.

Stan manicures his nails, but the editor's cut is the deepest for this scene which was deleted from Two Tars

A fire-fighting sequence with June Marlowe was originally in only the Spanish version of Pardon Us

＊ *Pardon Us* is the only Laurel and Hardy feature to have been shot in foreign languages (the German version of *Hollywood Revue of 1929* omitted the Laurel and Hardy scenes). *Pardon Us* has been the subject of several "rediscoveries" – in 1985, a longer, earlier cut of the English-language film was released on laser disc in the USA and more recently the Spanish version, *De Bote En Bote* has been found and shown on the AMC cable network. And in 1995 a longer version of *Pardon Us* for UK video release used sequences that originally existed only in the Spanish version. Now, if we can only find *Sous Les Verrous*, the French version, *Hinter Schloss und Riegel*, the German version, and *Muraglie*, the Italian edition . . . Stills exist from these which indicate that there are several scenes (for example where a bomb is delivered to the prison governor as a present) still not included in English versions.

＊ What are Laurel and Hardy called in other countries? Here's a list, compiled from different sources, but the correct spelling is not guaranteed:

Finland:	Min & Fin
Egypt:	El Tikhin & Ouel Roufain
Portugal:	O Bucha e O Estica
Greece:	Xonapoe & Azsnoe
Palestine:	Hashamen ve Haraze
Norway/Sweden:	
	Helan & Halvan
Turkey:	Sisman ve Zaif
Italy:	Crik e Crok
Germany:	Dick und Doof
Spain/South America:	
	El Flaco y El Gordo
Netherlands:	De Dikke en de Dunne
Denmark:	Gog og Gokke
Poland:	Flip i Flap
Hungary:	Stan es Pan
Rumania:	Stan & Bran

Spanish posters for Our Relations *and* Swiss Miss

CHAPTER 19: SLIPS

✳ Continuity errors and other slips exist in a huge percentage of films, even the biggest blockbusters. Try looking for wristwatches in biblical epics, "dead" bodies moving, TV aerials in Victorian melodramas or pneumatic tyre tracks in westerns. They all exist! Discontinuity in Laurel and Hardy films can sometimes be explained by "out of sequence" filming. The examples that follow are noted as a result of loving study by Laurel and Hardy scholars and it is hoped that readers will accept them in that spirit. In fact, even in the early days of cinema, spectators were watching the screen with a critical eye, so a well-established tradition is being continued.

✳ *Love 'Em and Weep* (1927)
From inside the hall the view outside is in darkness, yet Laurel and Hardy emerge in broad daylight. In silent days, as now, night shots were often shot in daylight, and the film then tinted blue. This was perhaps the case with original prints of this film.

✳ *With Love and Hisses* (1927)
We see Fin on a travelling train, breathing fresh air through an open window. In the adjoining carriage Stan is seen throwing a pie out of his window. If you look closely in the next shot you can see a hand throwing the pie into Fin's face!

✳ *Do Detectives Think?* (1927)
Ollie loses his hat in the graveyard and Stan looks at him, wearing his own hat. The camera looks into the graveyard and we see both Stan and Ollie's hats in there, though only Ollie's blew in. This scene is included again later when both their hats have blown in and was obviously included by mistake in the earlier shot.

✳ *Putting Pants on Philip* (1927)
Why do crowds gather to gaze at Philip yet the other, similarly dressed, Scot whom Ollie encounters provokes no such reaction?

✳ *The Battle of the Century* (1927)
The dentist and the pie salesman behind the counter are played by the same person (George K French).

As the Boys leave the pie fight, they move out of the picture area (right of frame), both holding a pie. As they enter the next shot (left of frame), Ollie's pie is missing. Although the existing footage of the pie fight sequence has been edited, these two shots do seem to fit together despite the sudden disappearance of one pie!

A man about to have his photo taken receives a pie in the face. To the top right of the frame can be glimpsed the blurred hand or arm of the props man who threw the pie.

✳ *You're Darn Tootin'* (1928)
On the first street corner the same woman walks by twice from the same place.

✳ *Should Married Men Go Home?* (1928)
When Stan knocks vigorously with his golf club on the door of the Hardy household, the marks on the door at the point of impact are already clearly there – presumably caused during a rehearsal or a previous take.

✳ *Two Tars* (1928)
The cable that was used to tow the Boys' squashed car out of the railway tunnel in the final shot can actually be seen in the bottom right corner of the frame.

✳ *Wrong Again* (1929)
If you look carefully at the sequence where the horse drinks from the fish tank, in the first shot it is drained to about one quarter full. Shortly afterwards the horse turns away and chases Stan and the tank is full again, illustrating the problems the crew had – it's difficult to make a horse do what is required in sequence!

✳ *Berth Marks* (1929)
At the beginning of the Spanish version, after one of the Boys loses his hat in front of their berth, a hand in the lower left corner parts the curtain and hands back the hat.

On location in Hollenbeck Park

Stan poses with Gloria and Anne

*A fruit machine solves the Boys'
financial embarrassment*

✻ *Men o' War* (1929)
Pay attention to Stan's sailor scarf ties hanging over his chest. They change in length from scene to scene, especially during the soda parlour scene when the ties lengthen and shorten with almost every shot of Stan.

Just before Ollie passes the flirtatious brunette over to Stan ("meet the general"), there is an inserted close-up of him reacting to the girl's observation ("I just love soldiers"), but the position of his arms does not match the previous mid-shot where he has taken hold of the girl's arm.

✻ *The Hoose-Gow* (1929)
The film ends with a car backing into a truck. Two barrels of whitewash tip over just before the impact!

✻ *Night Owls* (1930)
When Finlayson rolls down the staircase, he shatters a large vase at the bottom. Several scenes later, the vase is intact!

✻ *Brats* (1930)
Ollie resets the draughts board having been soundly beaten by Stan. In the next shot we see, without any apparent lapse of time, Ollie has been reduced to having only a couple of draughts pieces left.

The draughts board is the wrong way round. This is perhaps intentional!

When the Boys play pool, the balls change their positions on the table between shots. Also the chalk on the side of the table disappears as Ollie tears the cloth, then reappears.

Later the bath appears to be filled with remarkable speed because the cutaway material is too short. Moreover, Ollie emerges from the bath water yet his soaked pyjamas seem forgotten in the following shots (a boxing match and pretending to be asleep in bed).

✻ *Below Zero* (1930)
Where did Frank Holliday go on holiday? While waiting for the meal to be served, Ollie asks, "Where are you going to spend your vacation this summer?" We never hear the police officer's reply.

Stan removes the unwanted pigeon's egg from his mug and places the mug on the organ with his right hand, the handle being on the left. In an instant the handle changes position to the right.

✳ *Hog Wild* (1930)
When the Boys are on the roof for the first time and Stan is to go to one end and erect a pole, the garage doors in the background are closed, yet when Ollie has fallen off the roof and returns, the doors are ajar.[22]

Despite his immersion in an ornamental pond, Ollie (with no apparent time lapse) appears on the roof in subsequent shots with dry clothes.

No explanation is provided as to how Mrs Hardy gets so quickly from her home to the location in town where the street car crashes into Stan's car.

✳ *Another Fine Mess* (1930)
Lord Leopold Plumtree is wearing a handkerchief in his top pocket. This appears throughout the film, randomly ranging from being barely visible to hanging halfway down his jacket.

✳ *Chickens Come Home* (1931)
At the end of the film, Ollie escorts Mae Busch on Stan's back. Stan's coat reaches down to his garters. In the following shot it doesn't and in the next again shot it does.

✳ *Laughing Gravy* (1931)
The Boys are struggling on the roof with their dog, Laughing Gravy, who walks off the screen to the left. In the next shot the dog is back. True, there is a cut-away shot of Charlie Hall, but the music and tempo suggest no adequate time lapse.

Watch the plant pots on Charlie Hall's window ledge. After one has been knocked off, it reappears and disappears again.

Charlie Hall's suicide is impressive. He manages to shoot himself twice!

✳ *Our Wife* (1931)
On Stan's arrival at the household of the Justice of the Peace (Ben Turpin), so that Dulcy Darling and Dimple Dumpling (Ollie) can wed, Blanche Payson shouts, "Pa" to make Turpin come and perform the ceremony. Later, after Turpin has become horribly confused and marries Stan to Ollie, as well as kissing Ollie for Dulcy, Blanche shouts, "William!" and hustles him from the room.

Best not to tangle with the Tiger

✳ *Pardon Us* (1931)
In the schoolroom sequence, Fin announces that he will call the roll, but in fact proceeds with a general knowledge test.

During the test a prison warden slowly walks past in the background. As we change to a close-up of Fin the warden has vanished.

While Stan and Ollie are listening to the singing prisoners, Ollie's jacket goes from closed to open and back again during the chorus.

Stan has a dental problem – his tooth buzzes! He silences the tooth by putting his finger on it. On release from solitary confinement, Stan speaks without having his finger on his tooth, but no buzzing sound is heard.

Stan and Ollie escape from prison with Walter Long. A shot shows the Chief Warden in his office as the alarm sounds. The next clip, albeit brief, shows mayhem as officers try to gain control. The prison gates are shut and Stan and Ollie can be seen among the prisoners who have not escaped!

Stan and Ollie, having escaped, are disguised as black cotton pickers. Ollie beckons two dogs. While bending down to pat the dogs, Ollie speaks, but his lips don't move!

---

[22] The doors seem to be the same ones as in *The Chimp*.

❋ *Come Clean* (1931)

In the ice cream parlour, the cash register behind Charlie Hall is showing 5 cents. As he goes to ring in the 75 cents change for the Boys' chocolate ice cream, the amount on the till has changed to 10 cents.

❋ *Beau Hunks* (1931)

Stan notices a bald man crying over his picture of Jeanie Weenie. He is wearing a white shirt. We next see him wearing just a vest. Not enough time has elapsed for him to have taken off his shirt, as he is still crying, broken-heartedly, "You didn't oughta have done it, baby."

Stan smells Jeanie Weenie's scented letter and his hat flies off. When his hat comes back down a cross of sticky paper is seen inside it – probably used in pulling off his hat.

When the two legionnaires topple over the summit of the sand dune, Stan drops his rifle. When they reach the bottom and collide with Captain Schultz, Stan has his rifle to hand again.

❋ *Any Old Port* (1932)

The pool balls move around between shots, exhibiting the same capacity as in *Brats*.

The Boys flee the Mariner's Rest, leaving all their money in their room. They meet their old friend who can "throw fifty bucks" their way. Given the fifty bucks, they sit down to eat, so they *must* spend some of the money, yet near the end, when Ollie is paying out the lost bet to the drunk at the boxing, he pays him fifty bucks!

❋ *The Music Box* (1932)

The crate has a sloping side and, during one of the many times it returns to the bottom of the steps, it starts off with the sloping side one way then, when it rides over Ollie, the slope is on the opposite side, then the piano reaches the street with its original orientation.

Various wet items dry miraculously!

The shadow of a tripod, camera and the crew can be seen on the piano as it passes down the steps.

❋ *The Chimp* (1932)

After Stan has dropped the cannon ball on his foot, Ollie (wearing his circus hat) bends to lift it. In the next shot he appears without his hat and has to retrieve it from the ground – it would appear to have fallen off while he was picking up the cannon ball, but we are not shown this piece of action.

When Stan and Ollie try to put Ethel the Chimp into a crate, Ollie says, "Maybe she likes you better than she likes me." Then he says, "Get some rope and we'll tie *him* up," and, "Get *him* in there."

Billy Gilbert's wife doesn't match the photograph we were shown of her. The photograph is of Dorothy Granger, but the actress who appears as Mrs Gilbert is Martha Sleeper.

❋ *County Hospital* (1932)

Stan lifts up from the floor a weight, which is attached to a rope and pulley, which in turn is keeping Ollie's plastered leg in the air. In this shot a chair is seen beside Stan. After a brief cut to the visiting doctor, the next shot sees the doctor approach Stan to put the weight back where it belongs. The chair, though, has mysteriously vanished from Stan's side.

❋ *Scram!* (1932)

The almost instant inebriation of the judge's wife strikes a false note: a simple time-lapse device would have created a smoother effect.

Hasty mirth from Mrs Beaumont

Watch that tie

* ***Pack Up Your Troubles*** (1932)
  In the jail scene in which the Boys render cook George Marshall unconscious, his prostate position on the floor doesn't quite look consistent. As if to correct a continuity lapse the unconscious cook can actually be seen moving a leg!

* ***Towed in a Hole*** (1932)
  Ollie has some continuity problems with his tie. In the first few minutes sometimes it's inside his bib and sometimes outside. When Stan slams him into the mast, Ollie's tie barely touches it, but after a cut there is paint all over his tie!

  When the anchor chain rolls down to join the anchor in crashing through the bottom of the boat, we first see the chain moving from left to right, then the next shot shows it moving from right to left.

  When we see Ollie painting the mast, the sawing sound is slower than the shots of Stan in the cabin.

* ***Twice Two*** (1933)
  When Mrs Hardy has chastised Ollie by telling him that he's forgotten more than Stan will ever know (in his little finger!) she walks from the living room to the kitchen. When leaving the living room she is wearing on her forearms two ridiculous furs which spontaneously disappear upon her arrival in the kitchen.

  At the end of the film the wives have a disagreement and Mrs Hardy prepares to leave. While waiting for her cape, Mrs Hardy sings in order to annoy Mrs Laurel. At this point the camera moves to Mrs Laurel for her facial expression and you see that her dress has been torn. It is not until a few moments later that Stan actually rips the sleeve in an attempt to restrain his wife.

* ***Fra Diavolo (The Devil's Brother)*** (1933)
  When Stan and Ollie are laughing, because Stan is spiffed, they both laugh loudly. Zerlina comes in and Stan sings the song she sang the night before. Ollie realises this could mean big trouble and he stops laughing and tries to silence Stan, without success. Cut to Zerlina, talking to Lorenzo, and in the background we can still hear Stan and Ollie laughing.

Drawing by Alessandro Rossini

✳ *The Midnight Patrol* (1933)

During the conversation with the burglar, Stan and Ollie argue among themselves about their time off duty and Ollie says, "We were off last Monday." At the end of the film, when confronted with the Chief in the police station, Ollie pleads, "Pardon us, Chief. We only started this morning."

When Ollie hands the burglar his summons, there's a sudden edit before the burglar reveals he can't appear next Tuesday. The burglar's gun suddenly appears to be deeper down in his pocket and his cravat seems to be more prominent, as does the handkerchief in his breast pocket.

When Stan and Ollie crash through the stairs with their "battering ram", the Police Chief is already on the stairs with his gun, yet he still comes down the stairs and falls through the freshly made hole and looks surprised at doing so.

There are some "wet and dry" discrepancies.

Even though it is obviously not uniform, Stan hangs on to his character by still wearing his bow tie.

✳ *Sons of the Desert* (1933)

There is a slight *faux pas* by Ollie while the Boys are singing, "We are the Sons of the Desert." When the line, "Far from our sweethearts and wives" arrives, Babe appears to forget the words and then picks up again at the end of the line.

It is really only noticeable on a very big screen that in various fezzes there are dents which appear and disappear by magic.

At the convention Charley Chase says, on the telephone, "It's your *little* brother Charley." Ollie says to Mae Busch, "So this is Charley's sweet *little* sister."

When the Boys return from the convention, they are each wearing two garlands (or leis) around their necks – a light-coloured one and a medium-coloured one. When they are seen in the attic shortly afterwards, Stan has only one around his neck (he may have removed the other) but Ollie still has two, one light-coloured and the other is now dark-coloured. The garlands also change colour while the Boys are in the living room.

At the end of the film, when Ollie is being bombarded with crockery, the editor cuts backwards and forwards to shots of reactions from Stan. In the commotion, a picture on the wall behind Stan falls to the floor, as does a stuffed bird. The picture and the bird reappear on the wall in subsequent shots.

✳ *Oliver the Eighth* (1934)

Stan unbuttons his waistcoat after eating the fictitious soup and is immediately summoned away to be told that it is not the butler who is "nuts" but the lady host. Lo and behold, Stan's waistcoat is fully rebuttoned!

✳ *Them Thar Hills* (1934)

When Ollie climbs onto Stan's back, his jacket is open, but by the time he hits the water in the bath a few seconds later, it is closed! If it were the other way around it would not be remarkable. A closed jacket could easily pop open in the struggle, but not *vice versa*.

Charlie Hall drives up to the well, stops and exits his car. The camera angle changes to a side view of the car, where a large boulder can be seen up against the front wheel. As Charlie continues to walk, the camera shot changes back to the front view of Charlie's car and the boulder is missing.

Ollie's tie seems to shorten when he puts on an apron to make a meal. When Charlie Hall returns and evicts Mae Busch in preparation for the tit-for-tat sequence, keep an eye on that apron. From being fully on, it suddenly changes. The bib part appears to have been slipped off and left to sit in Ollie's lap, revealing the tie in all its glory again.

During the altercation in the trailer a plate of beans flies off just *before* Mr Hardy's fist comes down.

* *Babes in Toyland* (1934)

When the soldiers advance on the Bogeymen, Barnaby confronts them, holding Bo Peep in his arms. Cut to a cannon firing. Cut back to Barnaby knocked to the ground – but Bo Peep has vanished! A subsequent shot shows her hiding with Tom-Tom.

The addition of colour provided a new variation to the "spot the continuity error" game. The police have green tunics – except in the height of the grand finale, in the middle of the rout of the Bogeymen, when two of the clockwork soldiers suddenly appear with green tunics. This may not be so much a colour error as a continuity error. The two "soldiers" in green tunics are, in fact, dressed as the town's policemen (and therefore correctly coloured), but the actors appear to have the red-cheeked make-up of the toy soldiers and are acting and moving as toy soldiers in time with the marching music.

* *The Live Ghost* (1934)

When the captain clonks Stan on the head, Ollie, who is supposedly unconscious on the floor behind them, looks up with interest at them both.

* *The Fixer-Uppers* (1935)

There is a life-sized painting of Mae Busch on the wall of her apartment, presumably painted by her artist husband, Pierre. It is seen clearly in the sequence when the Boys are questioning Mae about her troubles. Later in the film, when Ollie is having the duel with Pierre, it is seen again, but this time it appears to have been severely ripped. Could there be a deleted sequence in which the jealous Pierre slashes the painting to shreds with his knife?

* *Thicker Than Water* (1935)

Daphne Pollard dons her hat and coat and gives a final squirt of perfume, which blows her hat off. Next minute she walks into the living room minus coat and talks to Fin ("she gave it to you and he gave it to him"). Then we see her in the bank sporting both hat and coat!

During the auction, the woman makes a bid and then she bids again.

* *Bonnie Scotland* (1935)

The Scottish band in India features a euphonium. British military bands did not use this instrument – only American bands. And the clock on the mantelpiece in the lawyer's office is an American-made clock – unlikely to be available in Scotland at that time.

Towards the end, after Stan has failed in his order to shoot himself, watch the gun magically change from being held in his left hand to his right.

* *The Bohemian Girl* (1936)

In the released version, Count Arnheim's medallion changes hands without explanation. The count gives it to his child, Arline, but later Mae Busch is seen wearing it (1) when she introduces Arline to Ollie as his daughter and (2) when she persuades Stan to take Ollie's savings. Mae departs (presumably wearing the medallion) with her lover. After a lapse of twelve years, the adult Arline is seen wearing the medallion during the breakfast scene in the caravan. For once, a continuity lapse can be explained by reference to the script which underwent considerable revision during production: (1) after the abduction, Mae takes the medallion from Arline and wears it herself (2) Stan, whose dexterity as a pickpocket has been well established, "removes" the medallion from Mae while she is coaxing him to agree to her plan (3) during breakfast there is a conversation about Arline's birthday and Stan gives her the medallion as a present. Continuity restored!

The wine-bottling sequence has many cutaways to the barrel containing the diminishing fermenting wine. The emptying rate is completely out of step with the much slower rate at which Stan in filling the bottles.

✱ *On the Wrong Trek* (1936)
The speed of Charley Chase's car does not match that of the tracking shot (from the car's viewpoint) revealing Stan and Ollie as hitchhikers.

✱ *Way Out West* (1937)
The white terrier that discovers the piece of meat in Stan's shoe (because it is as tough as leather!) can be seen amongst the group of dogs squabbling over the meat in the next shot. We cut back to Stan and the terrier is still at his feet. Never work with children and animals!

✱ *Swiss Miss* (1938)
The Boys take Della Lind to her husband's room. The husband places a "do not disturb" sign on the door. The chef finds Stan and Ollie and chases them down the stairs. Shortly afterwards the chef is successfully locked in the kitchen cupboard. The Boys return to the bedroom and the "do not disturb" sign has gone.

✱ *Block-Heads* (1938)
Several people run down the stairs prior to Hardy's street fight with Finlayson. One man disappears!

Hostile Finlayson meets an "overstuffed pollywog" – there's going to be a fight!

✱ *A Chump at Oxford* (1940)
Stan and Ollie, as street cleaners, turn a street corner pushing their cart. Before they turn, the pointed stick is pointing towards Stan. However, in an inserted medium shot it points towards Ollie, before reverting to its original slant in the long shots.

Lord Paddington (Stan) throws one of the students out of the window and he lands in the pool. The next student he ejects crashes into not one but several students climbing out of the pool.

✱ *Saps at Sea* (1940)
When Ollie is overcome by the noise in the factory, he complains of "horns to the left of me" but at the same time gesticulates wildly to his right. Because from our viewpoint the direction is towards left of frame, the discrepancy is not immediately apparent. This audio-visual mismatch may have been intentional, however, due to confusion brought on by hornophobia verging on hornomania.

When Dr Finlayson examines poor Ollie, in one shot the mirror on his head is central. In the following shot, in mid-conversation, it has moved distinctly to his left. It returns to its original position in the next shot. Watch the handkerchief in the doctor's breast pocket too.

✱ *The Dancing Masters* (1943)
Stan sits down on the left of scaffolding, saying he'll wait there for Ollie. But he has moved when Ollie falls through – some pretty nifty footwork!

✱ *The Big Noise* (1944)
Stan's pipe and magnifying glass shoot off the table when he accidentally overturns the table. In the next shot they can be seen in their original position – and then they are gone again.

✳ *Three solos*

Finally, three lapses from the Boys' "solo" work. . . .

In *Kill Or Cure* (1923), after Stan's lack of success at house number 1313, his bag miraculously appears just as he's about to knock on 1311's door.

In *Somewhere in Wrong* (1925) Stan is wearing a ring on the third finger of his right hand. It can be clearly seen as he looks in a mirror at the reflection of a safe and when he is stuffing doughnuts into his jacket. Not only is this decoration at odds with his role as a penniless tramp, but it is also highly unusual to see Stan so adorned.

In *Zenobia* (1939) we are reminded that elephants never forget. We cannot say the same about film makers. A newspaper headline spells the central character's name as "Dr Tibbitt". A letter addressed to him likewise spells his name. In the credits at the end of the movie, we see his name written as "Tibbett".

The good doctor with his wife (Billie Burke) and daughter (Jean Parker)

CHAPTER 20:
THE LATER FILMS IN PERSPECTIVE

* The American magazine *Filmfax* said very succinctly:

   While the duo's forties comedies are definitely among their weakest, the resulting films are not entirely without interest – or laughs. The fact that these pictures turned a profit is often (and conveniently) overlooked.

* Stan had been the principal creative force behind the vintage films at the Hal Roach studios, his influence being felt at all stages of production. His live theatre background persuaded him that the Laurel and Hardy comedy style could best be served by shooting in continuity, a method long since discarded by other film makers. The script was merely an outline of the routine that was to be worked out on the set.

* The world of MGM and Twentieth Century Fox was one of detailed scripts, writers unappreciative of Laurel and Hardy's style, tight wartime production schedules and shooting out of sequence. More importantly, the studios did not rate their new performers so highly that they were prepared to grant them unlimited time and money to do things in their own way.

* By way of contradiction, a pressbook for *Great Guns* said:

   In the past, the Laurel and Hardy comedies have never had a story – instead they worked from day to day and when filming commenced no-one could tell how the story would end up. Under their new contract, they have a clause which permits them to OK the script before they work on the picture. According to preview critics, this system has worked out much better for all concerned. There was plenty of room for the comics to improvise – and they did insert several spontaneous gags which hit them on the spot – and brought belly laughs at the preview. But the important point is that *Great Guns*, unlike most of the Laurel and Hardy comedies that have gone before, has a definite beginning, middle and ending.

* Laurel and Hardy never talked directly to the Fox executives, but let their lawyer, Ben Shipman, deal with their affairs. Shipman convinced them that everything would be all right.

* In the early days of their teaming Hardy was involved in the planning of their films and in shaping their characters. Once they became established, Hardy wisely stepped back and exerted his influence from a distance. This all changed during the period the Boys were at MGM and Twentieth Century Fox. Stan's private life was a shambles and, once he learned that he would have little control over their films, he seems to have lost interest completely. As a result, Hardy quickly took control of their film careers, as much as the studios permitted him. According to Lou Breslow (a Fox writer) and Dante (their co-star in *A-Haunting We Will Go*), among others, Stan seemed to have his mind on things other than their films and was rather quiet on the set. Hardy was more of a driving force.

* Under Babe's guidance the Ollie roles became bigger and broader, while the Stanley character regressed from simple to unbelievably dimwitted at times. Later Stan would tell a different story, but Babe confided to friends during that period that he was enjoying himself. After they retired from films, Babe, out of loyalty to Stan, would agree with him "in public" on Stan's complaints about this era.

* The fact that Stan and Ollie looked no longer in their prime is not a persuasive shortcoming of their later careers. Contemporary audiences would have accepted their aging as natural and did not allow it to diminish their enjoyment, as seen in the reception from the live audiences during the British tours of 1947, 1952 and 1953-54 when Laurel and Hardy were up to eleven years older than when they made their last American film.

❋ Two feature films were scripted for filming in 1942, but never shot. The story of *Me and My Shadow* concerned two Nazi agents, some important microfilm, a wax museum, a baby, gangsters, spies and a dummy of Napoleon! It was so bad that Sal Wurtzel, the Fox "B" movie producer, refused to produce it. *Untitled Laurel and Hardy* was to have had foreign agents, a St Bernard dog called Bernardine and an overweight cook named Olga, who was madly in love with Stan. The Boys were to have been the proprietors of Alpshaven, a sanitarium located in a very remote corner of the Swiss Alps.

❋ In *Great Guns* (1941), "We haven't eaten for three whole days – yesterday, today and tomorrow" is reworked from *One Good Turn* but is wasted. Not much better is the plank-carrying routine, repeated from *The Finishing Touch*. Several of the Boys' established characteristics are evident – Stan, as always, tries to go through the door first and is still able to change from uncontrollable laughter to a straight face in an instant. *Great Guns* contains the "asking the time/spilling the drink" gag beloved by Laurel and Hardy impersonators. The submerged car gag at the end of *Leave 'Em Laughing* and *Perfect Day* is transferred to an army jeep in a river.

Sgt Hippo with three of his new recruits in Great Guns

❋ *A-Haunting We Will Go* (1942) has one of those "inability to pay for the meal" situations and a series of special effects gags: climbing a rope, striking a gong, magic booths plus a freak ending.

❋ In *Air Raid Wardens* (1943) are reworkings of the sale of fertiliser (*Chickens Come Home*), scattering of jigsaw puzzle (*Me and My Pal*), Ollie buried under a load of sand (*Block-Heads*), faulty steering wheel (*The Flying Deuces*) and altercation with Edgar Kennedy (*Unaccustomed As We Are, Leave 'Em Laughing* and *Angora Love*). Highlights include scenes of chaos caused by a dog at a Civil Defence meeting, some slapstick with posters and Stan and Ollie's dismissal as air raid wardens – an almost symbolic humiliation.

Colonel Watterson Bixby and his valet Potts

❋ In *Jitterbugs* (1943) Ollie, masquerading as a Southern gentleman, engages in romantic exchanges with Lee Patrick, who is pretending to be a Southern belle. Stan gives his most sophisticated female impersonation. There are three pleasant musical numbers and some frenetic jitterbugging from the Boys.

✳ *The Dancing Masters* (1943) has reworkings which include an auction/grandfather clock sequence (*Thicker Than Water*), a passing-round-objects gag (*Our Relations*), Ollie in a hospital bed with his foot in a plaster cast (*County Hospital*), a banana peel destined to cause Stan's accident (*Battle of the Century*) and falling bricks (*Dirty Work*). Highlights are Stan and Ollie as dance instructors and a runaway bus.

✳ *The Big Noise* (1944) contains a slight reworking of *Oliver the Eighth*, the scenes with a "sympathetic meal" being very funny. This film was most unfairly included in the book *The Fifty Worst Films of all Time*. Admittedly the reuse of the dressing-for-bed-in-the-top-bunk routine from *Berth Marks* would have been improved by situating it afresh in an aeroplane as Laurel wanted. Yet in some ways the second version is preferable to the obviously ad-libbed and too long original, particularly when we are surprised by the introduction of a drunk into the scene. Our favourite "drunk" actor, Arthur Housman, had died the previous year – the scene could have become another classic with him!

✳ *Nothing But Trouble* (1945), their last American film, has Stan and Ollie as butler and chef in what was really an extended reworking of *From Soup To Nuts*. The warmth of the relationship between Stan and Ollie and the boy king has an old-fashioned charm. A football supporters' song provides a musical *leitmotif*. Highlights are refereeing a football match and serving a steak *à la* Oliver.

✳ Reworkings in *The Bullfighters* (1945) are signing a hotel register (*Double Whoopee* and *Any Old Port*), acting as witnesses at a trial (*Going Bye-Bye*), an egg smashing routine (*Hollywood Party*) and a swooning gag (*The Fixer-Uppers*).

✳ After *The Bullfighters* Laurel and Hardy decided to call it quits – not the studios or the movie-going public. But Laurel and Hardy tried once more in 1950 with a French/Italian film called *Atoll K*. Most connoisseurs consider it Laurel and Hardy's poorest film. Ill-health, production problems and a poor script made this a disaster movie and a painful end to their film careers. There are a few funny moments, though.

✳ Even after *Atoll K*, Laurel and Hardy were considered for supporting roles in a Technicolor musical comedy called *Two Tickets to Broadway*, to be produced by Howard Hughes at RKO. A Japanese studio made the team a tentative offer, as did an Italian stage company. In May 1952, the Scalera Film Company captured Stan and Babe's interest in making a musical comedy version of *Carmen*, to be produced in Rome. Alas, none of these projects materialised.

Laurel and Hardy's film career sank along with the atoll

Wartime publicity.
Above: Stan gives the military a hand.
Opposite: Is this plane now airworthy?

CHAPTER 21: MIXED REVIEWS

Contemporary reviews of Laurel and Hardy films were sometimes kind but often hostile. We select here some issues of the trade magazine *Variety*, noted for its racy language; it is important to remember that the reviews were written for the benefit of exhibitors, not the film-going public. After the *Variety* examples come a few press reviews aimed at the public.

VARIETY

Fra Diavolo (The Devil's Brother)
This 11-reeler has sufficient Laurel and Hardy and connecting story to cut down to six spools and get an entertaining Laurel and Hardy feature, thus eliminating the slow and old-fashioned opera that has been recorded probably in the manner of its initial presentation in 1830. The comic team dish up some hearty sequences, notably a sleeping powder gag, wine cellar scene and laughing gag. Henry Armetta foils well for them, as does Dennis King, who sings and plays the title part with dash and ability. Thelma Todd looks her most seductive opposite him. James Finlayson is Miss Todd's nearsighted husband and good, too. Le Roy Shield has arranged and conducted the music, a tough job capably done. Only interpolation is the Laurel and Hardy *Coo Coo* trademark. Photography is under-lighted in many spots and otherwise handicapped by the 10-20-30 exterior sets. Picture is underway 15 minutes before Laurel and Hardy make their initial appearance.

24 March, 1933

Bonnie Scotland
The pressbooks read "sixty minutes of fun". It's fair fun, but it doesn't total up to sixty minutes, and if the press sheet meant that's the running time, it also errs. Preview was ninety minutes on the coast and, by best eastern daylight saving time, it clocks seventy.[23] Carved to Laurel and Hardy specifications, release measures up for fair family trade returns, but no more.

28 August, 1935

The Bohemian Girl
A comedy with little or no comedy. Laurel and Hardy are not going to be able to gain forgiveness save among the most undiscriminating for the sheer silliness of the comedy sequences while the more serious implications of the plot, dealing in a heavy-handed way with kidnapping, infidelity, torture and thievery, are downright unwholesome. Laurel and Hardy are snatch-purses with an 18th century band of roving gypsies. In retaliation for the flogging of a fellow member (Antonio Moreno), caught red-handed in an attempted burglary, the gypsies steal the child of a nobleman and bring her up as one of their own. In the end the customary tell-tale medallion saves the peeress and restores her to her daddy. Chained to such a scenario the picture has the additional liability of inept direction. Camera angles are dreadful, revealing many of the singers as self-consciously aware of the lens or catching the femmes in undainty waddling, rear view. Mae Busch is especially abused by the photography and the late Thelma Todd, who goes through the motions of singing (a mere bit) with the voice poorly synchronised to her lips, seems strangely unlike herself. (A good deal of her footage, fortunately for her rep, was cut out just prior to release.) There is not a good performance in the production.

19 February, 1936

---

[23] Even the trailer advertised this 80 minute feature as "60 minutes of joy."

Darla Hood from Our Gang poses with her surrogate father and "Uncle Stan"

✳ Swiss Miss

Just a filler-in and not a very good one. Some chuckles from Laurel and Hardy, but story, production, acting and direction suggest a revival of early sound filmusicals presented with stage technique. Of little box office value, except for the children on Friday nights and Saturday mats. Comedy team turns up at a Swiss mountain resort with mouse-traps for sale, on the theory that cheese makers must be bothered by rodents. Other characters are an operetta composer, who is in hiding, his prima donna wife, who masquerades as a hotel chambermaid and sings in the village fiesta, an irate chef, a hotel keeper with a Yorkshire dialect, and a stuttering valet. There also are peasants who sing and dance hesitantly. Most pleasing views on the screen are some stock shots of snow-decked Alpine peaks used for atmospheric purposes. *Swiss Miss* misses by a mile and a furlong.

10 May, 1938

✳ A Chump at Oxford

With *A Yank at Oxford* whipping up interest in the old English school and its traditions, Stan Laurel and Oliver Hardy's farce is mildly comical without offending. *Chump* is not successful as outright comedy until more than half completed. Time-worn gags clutter up the earlier footage and only when Laurel and Hardy, as new initiates into Oxford, actually move into the dean's home does the action speed up. Early episodes have Laurel as a maid and Hardy as a butler in a rich man's home. It looks as though it had been tacked on in order to make up footage.[24] James Finlayson is the wealthy host in this episode but not given any cast credit. The dinner party brings in all the familiar dress-tearing, pastry-flinging, cork-popping and shot-gun gags. But once the comedians land in England they fare better. Outside of the lost-in-the-woods stunt and ghost-at-midnight routine, the gagging and all-round material brightens up. Picture is all Laurel and Hardy. They have more witty dialog than usual and it seems to help overcome the necessity of so much old-fashioned hoke panto.

February, 1940

✳ The Big Noise

Practically every gag the fat boy and his partner use in this melange has been used on the screen before, either done by themselves or others. Mal St Clair is a much better director than his job in this one would have you believe. But even they were hampered by an obviously poor screenplay.

Autumn, 1944

---

[24] This is exactly what had happened!

WORLD FILM NEWS

✳ Way Out West

Everything in *Way Out West* is built up on simple but beautiful gags, most of them probably by Laurel, who is the producer and is now reported to be supervising Wild Westerns as well (what vistas of future joy!). Gags of incident, gags of dialogue, gags of sound, gags of Keystone vintage and gags brand new from the inexhaustible bowler; the flaming finger, the ritual eating of Hardy's hat, the vast dent in mother earth where Hardy fell from the roof, the vamp tickling Laurel into hysteria, the mule sneering from the bedroom window, the poignant cry of, "Oh, my apple" as the golden chain tightens round Hardy's neck, Laurel's apocalyptic changes of voice as he sings the poignant ballad of the *Lonesome Pine* – all these, and many more, are the life blood of the picture. There is even a continuity gag: Hardy, divested of all but decent covering in search for a locket, departs into an inner room and gets dressed in the twinkling of an eye. Laurel, unguarded innocent, inquires, "How did you get dressed so quickly?" "Never you mind," replies Hardy, sublimely summing up the history of the *avant garde* movement in three pregnant words. It is a film I would choose to see on my deathbed.

Basil Wright (January, 1938)

✳ Block-Heads

So, *Block-Heads* is their last film[25]; and it is fitting that it should be, in every sense, the Laurel and Hardy to end all Laurel and Hardys, a lunatic swansong, plotless, reasonless but yet the final distillation of all they have done. From the purist point of view we shall be compelled to rate it below the shapely and consistent *Way Out West*; but as fans, and may the curse of the Ritz Brothers[26] light on all who are not, we may blast away all critical reasoning on the wings of a giant guffaw. The opening gag is irresistible. While shells burst and the troops go over the top in 1918, Laurel is left behind to guard the empty trench. A serious farewell to Hardy – a date change to 1938 – and behold the faithful soul is still guarding the trench, now well overgrown with weeds and shaded by a monstrous pile of empty Bully-Beef [27] tins. It is only when he shoots down a passing private plane that he learns that there is no longer a war. So the scene is set for his reunion with Hardy at a home for aged soldiers.

Basil Wright (1938)

---

[25] It was widely expected to be their last film, but fate decreed otherwise.

[26] An inferior comedy team of the thirties.

[27] Actually beans.

LOS ANGELES TIMES

❋ *The Rogue Song*

This picture is efficacious entertainment, and its comedy moments, which are thrust into the story at times with scant regard for their suitability, succeed in delighting the audience. It is amazing what a chorus of laughs accrued to that terribly hokumish scene of the bee buzzing in Stan Laurel's pyloris, wherein even the sound itself is not adequately realistic. However, the justification of the presence of Laurel and Hardy is that they cause no end of hilarity and, after all, boobery such as they portray can perhaps exist in the make-believe anywhere, even in the Russian Romany.

20 January, 1930

A couple of weeks later the same newspaper had changed its tune somewhat . . .

All the reviews are favorable, though tempered by caution, the highlights focusing on the star rather than the picture. The latter is only moderately interesting, tastefully produced, but brilliant never, and always quite incredible save in one scene, that of a bandit's murder of the prince. Staged with imagination, distinction and fine tragic feeling, this episode more than any other identifies Lionel Barrymore as the director. His hand seemed conspicuously missing from the comic relief,[28] supplied at intervals as regular as the filling between layers of cake, by Laurel and Hardy. A joy in their own place, they bored as intruders in this.

2 February, 1930

---

[28] Hal Roach directed the Boys.

Cheers! – from Fra Diavolo

CHAPTER 22: PRESSBOOKS

✳ Pressbooks were aimed at telling the press of the day what the press should say. In the selection which follows, original spelling and grammar have been retained! Statements are to be taken with a few grains of salt!

✳ *Perfect Day* (1929)
A huge mudhole was excavated and filled with water in one of the Hal Roach studio streets. As two family men who start out for a Sunday picnic, Laurel and Hardy end their perfect day with a final plunge beneath the muddy waters. Only their famous derbies are left floating on the water as Laurel and Hardy, their wives, Uncle Edgar and their car all sink beneath the surface. The mudhole, eight feet deep, twenty feet long and twelve feet wide, was fitted with pulleys so that the automobile could be lowered to the bottom without accident.

Fifty windows were smashed in one hilarious scene. The celebrated clowns started a throwing match which involved an entire neighborhood, its windows and its windshields.[29]

Catchlines:
Filmdom's Favorite Funsters.
A smash hit – as Stan and Ollie break every window in the neighborhood.
Gloom takes a holiday – as Stan and Ollie set out for a picnic!
Today is fun-day . . . They thought they were having a picnic – until their flivver sank in a mudhole!

---

[29] A typical pressbook exaggeration.

✳ *Blotto* (1930)
The smartest cocktail of the season has nothing on the drinks that Mrs Laurel mixes. Laurel and Hardy think it is the real stuff, and imagine they get drunk from the results of it. Only when Mrs Laurel tells them it is nothing but cold tea do they sober up.

Catchline:
The Boys were whooping it up – until their iced tea let them down!

✳ *Come Clean* (1931)
All Laurel and Hardy comedies are laugh successes because these boys seem to have the capacity to extract fun from the most everyday things in life. Laughter is spontaneous throughout one of their comedies because of their famed Laurel and Hardy manner. To bump one's nose is maddening, but to bump one's nose in the Laurel and Hardy way is quite laughable.

The script is very short, but with the comedians shooting from the cuff – adding more action with each scene shot – the desired amount of film was ready at the completion of the comedy. Laurel and Hardy know their own comedy capacity and act accordingly. Of course, they have many times used a script complete in every detail which they have followed scene by scene, but whether they have this finished story or not, all of their comedies so far have been pronounced laugh successes.

✳ *Beau Hunks* (1931)

When is a movie director not a director? When he's an actor! Such was the position in which James Horne found himself during filming. Not only did he essay the role of an actor, he also took orders from actors. It all came about while filming night scenes for the picture. A small but important part was open in which some ambitious actor might score individual honors as a chieftain of Arabian Riffs. Three different players were rehearsed for the part but none of them came up to the expectations of director Horne. It was too late at night to get another actor to the studio for the part so with grim determination Horne donned a Riff chieftain's attire, plastered some hirsute adornment over his face and took his position before the camera. Action of the scene forced Horne to take orders from Laurel and Hardy, who, as legionnaires, held him captive.

It's not always fun being funny. Laurel and Hardy testified to this. For several days these two comedians drilled and tramped under a sizzling California sun with the temperature tickling 100 degrees, dressed in heavy woollen uniforms of the Foreign Legion and packing full military packs on their backs. On top of this they spent two days in a movie produced sand storm.

Catchlines:
Four reels of furious fun!
One long loud laugh!
They took to the desert to forget the gal who deserted them!
Sit down in the desert. . . . When the Boys put tacks under their bare feet the Riffs couldn't stand it!

✳ *County Hospital* (1932)

That old wheeze, "Did you ever hear about my operation?" served as inspiration to Laurel and Hardy for the writing of *County Hospital*. During a session of cards someone at the table, in an effort to break the tenseness of the game, pulled the old bromide about their operation. It got a laugh and also started to work the imaginative minds of the two comedians.

The business of making movie audiences laugh is no laughing matter to Laurel and Hardy. Oliver Hardy hung suspended by one leg with his head down for approximately one hour. Of course, he did not hang the full hour at one time as the scene was photographed several times before the desired effect was obtained. In this particular scene Hardy was drawn up by a leg encased in a huge plaster cast, supposedly a broken leg. The comedian was lying in a hospital bed and his partner Stan Laurel accidentally dropped the weight out of the window causing Hardy's sudden ascension. Considering the comedian's weight the gag in itself was a big undertaking. The greatest difficulty was experienced in getting the proper lighting on the star's face while he was suspended in the air as the blood would rush to his head and he would photograph very dark. After several experiments he used a very light make-up which photographed natural.

Catchlines:
Oliver's broken leg gave Stan a pain in the neck!
Making laffs no fun for comedians.

✱ *Twice Two* (1933)

Hardy portrays a doctor, specialising in brains, while Laurel is seen as an associate adviser, specializing in the delicate task of handling the telephone switchboard.

A special talking trailer measuring 50 feet[30] has been prepared on this comedy – and similar trailers will be available on each release of this series. These trailers combine the most effective use of selling titles and scene footage from the picture itself.

The six foot lobby cutout which has just been made available should be in every theatre playing the series. The cost per release comes to but one dollar for the black and white and one dollar and a quarter for the color cutout.

Have you a motion picture projection machine in your home? It is unnecessary to answer the question, because Laurel and Hardy furnish all the answers on how not to run it in *Twice Two*.[31]

✱ *Thicker Than Water* (1935)

Nearly everyone has a pet aversion. Stan Laurel's is wiping dishes, for as a child he was called upon to perform this rite nightly for years. So when a scene in *Thicker Than Water* made it necessary for him to dry dishes as Ollie Hardy washed them, Stan did not relish the duty but reluctantly complied with the director's orders for art's sake. His only satisfaction was in seeing the crockery destroyed before the scene was completed.

Probably the most interested spectator on the set was an aged English gentleman, Arthur Jefferson. For hours at a time he would sit in rapt attention watching the filming of the picture, occasionally offering a comment in subdued tones to his wife, who accompanied him. It was quite apparent that the spectator, who was in his middle seventies, had more than a casual interest in the proceedings. Mr Jefferson,

father of Stan Laurel, was enjoying his first visit to America and his initial experience in an American motion picture studio. He came over from London especially to spend a few months with his "boy" of whom he is extremely proud.

Everyone on the set got a great "kick" out of the enthusiasm the old gentleman displayed. He was interested in the cameras and the other mechanical paraphernalia common to all studios as well as the work of the actors. Nothing escaped his eyes.

So much did the interior sets used as background in their new fun short appeal to a California college professor who visited the Hal Roach studios while the picture was being filmed, that he asked permission to copy the plans for a new home he was about to build.

Promotional suggestion:
Three or four days prior to opening, have blotches of paint daubed on the streets, sidewalks and plate glass windows of vacant stores. The color should be a vivid red or scarlet to resemble blood but should be easily removable to avoid complications with the authorities. The opening day of the picture, letter in white over the red blotches, "See Laurel and Hardy in *Thicker Than Water* at the . . . Theatre."

Catchline:
Merrily they roll along gathering no moss but leaving a trail of giggles and guffaws!

---

[30] The playing time was around thirty seconds.

[31] Such a sequence was scripted but not used in the film. It provides an example of how press material was prepared well ahead of a film's completion and release.

❋ *Pack Up Your Troubles* (1932)

Hardy said, "First of all, comedy is harder to stage than drama. In creating film comedy a momentum must be started. When once this has been put into effect, laughable situations invariably follow one another in quick succession. Drama is much easier than comedy. The dramatic story can and does permit occasional lapses in interest. The momentum is strong, powerful and thus makes allowances for the breaks. On the other hand, it can be readily seen that comedy demands creation of laughter and it does not permit long lapses in the interest."

[Laurel] is shy and retiring, but is an excellent conversationalist when the barrier of reticence is broken. He is a convulsing mimic, his favourite imitation being that of Queen Victoria.

Throughout the film colony little Jacquie Lyn is known as "the wonder child". Jacquie is just three years of age and can imitate the mannerisms and characteristics of the most famous film celebrities. And that isn't all. She has an uncanny facility for remembering dialogue, and often prompts grown players when they forget or stumble over their lines. . . . Never having seen the child act before, the comedians had one question before engaging Jacquie. Could she imitate the mannerisms of Messrs Laurel and Hardy? She could, and proceeded to convey the bashful expression on Hardy's face when he twirls his tie, and the dumb stare of Laurel when he scratches his head.

Catchline:
Pack Up Your Troubles is three times as long and 100 times as funny!

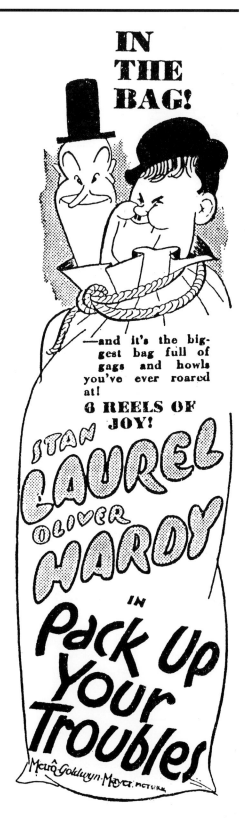

IN THE BAG!

—and it's the biggest bag full of gags and howls you've ever roared at!

6 REELS OF JOY!

STAN LAUREL

OLIVER HARDY

IN

Pack Up Your Troubles

Metro-Goldwyn-Mayer PICTURE

they're back in their new full-length feature picture!

HAL ROACH *presents*

Stan **LAUREL** *Oliver* **HARDY** in **SONS OF THE DESERT** with **CHARLEY CHASE**

An M-G-M Picture

✳ *Sons of the Desert* (1933)

Members of Hollywood's famous American Legion Post, numbering more than one hundred, appear in atmospheric roles. Included in the group are a drum and bugle corps, chanters and a drill team. The Santa Monica, California, Lodge of Elks is also represented in the picture in parade scenes which were photographed during a state convention of the antlered herd in the bay city a few months ago. During the actual filming more than one thousand extra people were given employment as members of the supporting cast.

For the first time in his career since he attained stardom, Charley Chase, popular Hal Roach comedian, is appearing in the cast of a picture other than his own. Reading the script of *Sons of the Desert*, Chase was intrigued by a "good time Charlie" part in the story and he immediately sought out director William Seiter and suggested that he be given the role. When Seiter recovered from the shock of a star offering to appear in support of others, he immediately secured Charley's signature and then asked the actor to explain himself. "Why, there's no catch to it," explained Chase. "I'm delighted at the opportunity to work with Stan and Oliver and the part, as I see it, is made to order for me." He and Laurel and Hardy have been warm friends since they first met on the Roach lot and each is an admirer of the other's peculiar comedy talents. There has never been any professional jealousy among the three funsters and on many occasions they have exchanged ideas for their respective comedy offerings.

* *Swiss Miss* (1938)

Gags spring up like mushrooms and thrive like sunflowers on the Laurel and Hardy set. Practical jokers enjoy an open season and there's no limit on the ingenuity of any prankster. One may find dry-ice in one's pocket when reaching for cigarettes or may sit in a pool of water on a chair that was as dry as the Sahara the moment before. "Hot-foot" is in order at all hours and the substitution of props keeps the entire company on the alert for mischief-makers. Usually the routine is accomplished in "dead-pan" silence. To show indignation is to invite further disaster. In fact, to show any emotion is a violation of the rules of the game. While *Swiss Miss* was in production, Stan Laurel was the victim of a gag that not only surprised him but gave him the laugh of a lifetime. Instead of wearing the colorful Tyrolean garb worn by all members of the cast, Ham Kinsey, Laurel's stand-in, appeared one morning dressed as Abraham Lincoln. With the aid of the costume and make-up departments Kinsey was arrayed in the sombre black suit of the '60s, with shiny top hat, beard and even the distinguishing mole on the face of the martyred President. In retaliation for the gag Laurel made Kinsey learn the entire Gettysburg address and recite it with appropriate gestures to Oliver Hardy, Della Lind, Walter Woolf King and other members of the cast.

Imagine the consternation of the property department at the Hal Roach studios when in the dish-washing scene the plates, cups and saucers, roughly manhandled by the comedians, failed to break. One of the crew was sent up thirty feet into the flies with a cup. He dropped it to the kitchen floor. It bounced two feet and came to rest without even a nick. Investigation disclosed that the floor had been so well insulated by the sound department that it was almost cushioned.

✳ *The Flying Deuces* (1939)
To James Finlayson, veteran comic of the Sennett days, Stan Laurel and Oliver Hardy virtually owe their teaming. [In 1927] Hardy and Finlayson were teamed in a series of pictures in which Hardy appeared as the heavy. When Finlayson went with another company, a partner was sought for Hardy. Laurel was employed with the same company at the time as a gag writer and the two were brought together.

Harry Langdon, star of silent comedies, made his debut as a caricaturist in *The Flying Deuces*. The former comedian, credited as one of the writers of the Boris Morros Production for RKO Radio, is an able charcoal artist and clay modeller. When a sketch of Laurel and Hardy was needed for an opening sequence, Langdon provided the drawing. The scene depicts a French sidewalk café artist sketching the two comedians. The camera shows Langdon's work, however.

"Hundreds of stories have been submitted to us that we've been compelled to turn down," explained Hardy. "Not that they haven't sufficient elements of comedy, but because they don't fit the characters that we have established as fundamentally ours." Both comedians insist that the moment they departed from their proven screen formula, their star-tenure would be at an end. Consequently, each is a factotum of

every picture. Not only do they act, but they write, help produce and aid in direction. They "eat and sleep" the picture with writers, directors and producers. They approve their supporting cast.

Audiences who have a sharp eye are liable to discover many an old timer of vaudeville in *The Flying Deuces*. More than twenty actors appearing with Laurel and Hardy in this picture owe their jobs to Stan. Most of them appeared on vaudeville bills with him at one time or another years ago. Anxious for work in Hollywood, they somehow reach the comedian and offer a plea for work. Laurel is always receptive. At the actor's ranch in San Fernando Valley are employed four old timers, who have come to California in need of a job. Two are former acrobats, one having been injured in a fall. Laurel has never turned a deaf ear to an actor's plea for work of some sort.

✳ *Saps at Sea* (1940)
Both members of the famous comedy team give forth with several gag ideas a day during the shooting of a picture. They have different mental techniques, however. Babe Hardy, the corpulent one, uses the isolationist method for cerebrating. He really sits down and thinks. He says to himself: "Now for some solid, uninterrupted, mental functioning. I'll devote 15 minutes to getting ideas for gags. I want to be alone, too."

Stan doesn't consciously strive for his gems. "I never got any results by reminding myself that I ought to take time out for evolving new business. I've tried, often in bed before going to sleep. Gag ideas, whether funny or not, come to me in strange places and at unusual times. Often on the set where, of course, conditions put you in a mental state conducive to creating funny situations. But occasionally I get ideas in such places as the dentist's chair or in the shower. They seem spontaneous, but, of course, they aren't. Mental processes directed to one end – the thinking up of gags – are unconsciously operating. It's fairly mechanical."

Both Hardy and Laurel agree that a slight fever or a blow on the pate are also helpful in the origin of comedy situations.

✳ *Great Guns* (1941)

Monty Banks [director of *Great Guns*] in the industry's earliest days was a member of Mack Sennett's Keystone comedy troupe, the cradle of so many top actors and directors. From acting, Banks went to producing and directing, and while directing a Gracie Fields picture in England he met and married the great British comedienne. Back in the 20s Banks vied with Charlie Chaplin for the world's laughter. He starred in some 160 comedies himself. All of which equipped him to handle the director's chores for Laurel and Hardy, themselves among the handful of great visual or "sight" comics of show business.

Stan Laurel and Oliver Hardy, unlike many other teams of comics, are not jealous of each other and try to present the laughs in a picture effectively without regard to the part played by either in obtaining the laugh. The script called for Stan to deliver the punch line. As they prepared to go into the scene, Stan said, "You know, Ollie, I think this would go better if you gave it the clincher." He then went on to explain why. Ollie, however, wasn't sure, and they discussed the matter, each more or less urging the other to take the major part.

✳ *Nothing But Trouble* (1945)

Imagine Stan and Ollie, mingling in high society, as chef and butler, nearly poisoning a prince, ruining a royal reception and generally creating hilarity in the comical story of the servant problem and intrigue in the rarefied atmosphere of a foreign government in exile.

Oliver Hardy once remarked, "The stories that we picturise are nearly always based on actual incidents – most of them serious – many of them garnered from newspaper files. Although our humorous sequences in *Nothing But Trouble* are without basis of fact, we have drama threaded throughout the entire production to set off the comedy scenes." He continued, "Those who have seen some of our feature pictures will remember that much of the comedy was, in reality, inverted drama. For the same reason that people will laugh at the embarrassment of a dignified old chap who slips on a banana skin and at the misfortune and simplicity of others, they will sometimes roar at our screen predicaments although they are at times rather tragic."

The comedy antics of Stan Laurel and Oliver Hardy always refused to be confined to a story or a screen play, no matter how near perfection either might have been. Following the practice laid out by the pioneers of funmaking, they persisted in doing a lot of their work "off the cuff". Almost any incident happening on the set suggested comedy developments. In addition to the observations of Stan Laurel and Oliver Hardy, there were nearly always on the set the shrewd and comedy-appraising eyes of members of the writing staff, alert to better even the best situation with new dialogue or new bits of business.

CHAPTER 23:
LAUREL AND HARDY IN COLOUR

✳ It could be only a convention that we have come to regard the world of Laurel and Hardy as black and white. Our viewpoint might have been differently coloured if *The Rogue Song* had survived. But coloured Laurel and Hardy films do exist. . . .

✳ A Kodachrome silent home movie survives, shot during a 1942 performance in Philadelphia as part of the Hollywood Victory Caravan. For one and a half minutes Laurel and Hardy appear on stage during the introduction of their *Driver's Licence Sketch*.

✳ The five minute wartime short *Tree in a Test Tube* shot on Kodachrome in 1943 remains unknown to the general public and now has only curiosity value as a colour record of Laurel and Hardy in close-up shots, marred by a patronising commentary.

✳ In 1956 a young fan named Andy Wade persuaded Stan Laurel to let him shoot a home movie of Laurel and Hardy, on the condition that Andy keep the film only for his personal use. Andy loaned the film to a friend and on his way home to Florida from California he was killed in a car crash. When Andy's dad tried to retrieve the film from the friend, he was told that he had lent the film to someone else and had committed suicide. Soon afterwards copies of the film were made available to the public, upsetting Stan terribly. Lasting three minutes and in colour, it was released as both *Stan Visits Ollie* and *Laurel and Hardy at Home*. It is an intrusion into a family gathering with Stan ill at ease and Babe virtually unrecognisable due to loss of weight. Stan has a very pronounced limp, the result of his recent stroke. Babe isn't wearing a tie so he twiddles Stan's! Babe also does a perfect double take when Andy shows up and both Boys nod their heads in perfect unison at one point.

✳ In the BBC *Omnibus* programme *Cuckoo* in 1974 were thirty seconds of colour footage showing Stan in his Santa Monica apartment. This sequence too has a "home movie" atmosphere with silent, informal shots of Stan smiling at the camera and happily manipulating two bowler-hatted marionettes.

✳ A short colour film exists which shows Stan's 1964 birthday party.

✳ At the dawn of the computer colouring age, the first planned transfer of black and white Laurel and Hardy film was *The Dance of the Cuckoos*. Reservations were expressed not so much on the use of colour, but on the proposed rearrangement of vintage material to create a revised storyline. The project made slow progress and was never completed, due to technical difficulties.

✳ The opportunity to assess the impact of a colorized two-reeler came in 1984 with the showing of *Helpmates* at the National Film Theatre, with large screen video projection. The colour, unobtrusive shading with a limited tonal range, was pleasing enough not to detract from the comedy element in the film but was substandard.

✳ By the time a colorized version of *Way Out West* appeared on video tape in 1985, considerable improvements in technique had been effected and the film revealed a much wider range of colours.

✳ Lois Laurel approved the colorization of her father's "personal favourite", *Way Out West*, and expressed the opinion, "My father would surely have raised his derby."

It is said that Stan had reservations about the use of colour in comedy but wanted to use it in Babes in Toyland

✳ Hal Roach stated that *Babes in Toyland* was to have been shot in Technicolor. Henry Brandon, who starred in the film, testified that screen tests and the first week of filming were in Technicolor, but financial considerations forced Roach to complete the film in black and white.

✳ According to historian Richard Bann, Hal Roach "experimented with colour for some of his early Laurel and Hardy musicals, but rejected it for stylistic and budgetary considerations."

✳ The texture of the images in *Swiss Miss* supports the view that this feature was filmed in colour. Della Lind, one of the film's stars, certainly thought that it was and recalled being impressed at the premiere by the colourful flag waving sequence. Stan Laurel recalled that there was experimental use of colour in the film.

✳ Laurel and Hardy aficionados have had lengthy debates on the acceptability of colorization of Laurel and Hardy films and many prefer the original black and white. Others argue that admiration of Laurel and Hardy is even more justified, not only because the classic comedy they have given the world is standing the test of time in colorized versions, but also because their work is thriving on modern technology. Certainly they attract the younger generation, for whom colour is the norm.

✳ When one group of Sons of the Desert were asked if they approved of computer colouring of Laurel and Hardy films, 44 said "Yes", 29 said "no", 12 said "don't know" and 4 gave no answer. An often expressed proviso was that the black and white versions should be retained for viewing.

✳ Colour films were technically possible very early in the cinema's history, but were uncommon for reasons of taste, aesthetics etc. It prompts the thought that, if films made in the 1920s and 1930s were made in black and white through choice, what right do technocrats have to colorize them now?

A shot not in the film so we don't know if Stan is about to shout or give a colourful yodel

CHAPTER 24: CARTOON FILMS

* Many cartoons shown in the cinemas in the '30s and '40s had Stan and Ollie caricature appearances. In our selection here all the cartoons are of approximately seven minutes' duration.

* *Battling Bosko*
    (1932, Warner Brothers, b/w)
    An ostrich delivers *Dance of the Cuckoos* in this early *Looney Tune*.

* *Bosko's Knight-Mare*
    (1933, Warner Brothers, b/w)
    The Boys play Knights of the Round Table in another *Looney Tune*.

* *The Organ Grinder*
    (1933, Warner Brothers, b/w)
    This *Merry Melody* has a dancing monkey and impressions of Laurel and Hardy.

* *Mickey's Gala Premiere*
    (1933, Walt Disney, b/w)
    This cartoon (aka *Movie Star Mickey*) was the last item to be broadcast on BBC Television before the station shut down because of World War II. The broadcast was terminated midway through the film. When the station recommenced broadcasting at the end of the war, their first programme was – *Mickey's Gala Premiere*. The large array of film stars includes Stan and Ollie.

* *Soda Squirt*
    (1933, Ub Iwerks, b/w)
    Stan and Ollie are among the Hollywood stars invited to Flip the Frog's gala opening of a soda fountain where "Jekyll and Hyde" cocktails are a speciality. The images move at a brisk pace helped along by occasional dialogue and a jazzy tune.

* *Buddy's Adventures*
    (1935, Warner Brothers, b/w)
    The Boys are seen imprisoned in stocks in Sour Town, where music and laughter are banned. From the *Looney Tunes* series.

* *Mickey's Polo Team*
    (1936, Walt Disney, colour)
    A frenetic sporting event features a host of caricatured film stars determined to win the polo match against Mickey's equally enthusiastic team. The Boys have difficulty mounting a horse and feature in a freak ending worthy of the Laurel and Hardy films themselves. The bright hues and rapid animation are breathtaking.

Hollywood's best comics appeared in one of Disney's best cartoons, Mickey's Polo Team, *directed by David Hand*

* *The Novelty Shop*
    (1936, Columbia, colour)
    This has a charming fairy tale quality using subdued colours and delightful music yet with equally imaginative animation. When the novelty shop owner departs, the whole store comes to life as star caricatures cavort with the animated novelties. Laurel and Hardy join in the fun, getting into a nice mess – with toothpaste – and Stan engages in some monkey business at the fade-out.

* *Coo-Coo Nut Grove*
    (1936, Warner Brothers, colour)
    This marvellous cartoon is built around a vast collection or movie star characters at a night club and our pals are included.

* *The Case of the Stuttering Pig*
    (1937, Warner Brothers, b/w)
    Another in the *Looney Tunes* series, this has a caricature of Ollie only.

* *Hollywood Picnic*
  (1937, Columbia, colour)
  Stan and Ollie can be seen on a see-saw in this success from the *Color Rhapsodies* series.

* *Porky's Five and Ten*
  (1938, Warner Brothers, b/w)
  Stan and Ollie appear as fish in this *Looney Tune*.

* *Mother Goose Goes Hollywood*
  (1938, Walt Disney, colour)
  In this delightful *Silly Symphony*, nursery rhymes are brought to life, the linking theme being Bo Peep's search for her sheep. Stan and Ollie play Simple Simon and the Pie Man (who whistles *The Dance of the Cuckoos*). Ollie has a stack of pies which Stan decides to raid. Stan takes one pie from the middle of the pile, but by some luck they do not fall over. Ollie tries to repeat this feat and in so doing becomes covered in pies. All the mannerisms are there with tie twiddles, head scratches etc. At the end of the film all the cartoon film stars reappear for a musical finale with Ollie on trombone and Stan on clarinet.

* *You Ought to be in Pictures*
  (1940, Warner Brothers, b/w)
  A superb *Looney Tunes* cartoon using mixed live action and animation. Oliver Hardy is played by Porky the Pig!

* *Putting on the Act*
  (1940, Paramount, b/w)
  Olive Oyl runs into the sitting room and disturbs a resting Popeye with a newspaper proclaiming that vaudeville is back. They dart upstairs and, with Sweet Pea, they go through their old act together. In his act Popeye moulds his pliable face into that of Stan Laurel and he does a very neat, but all too brief, imitation.

* *Timid Toreador*
  (1940, Warner Brothers, b/w)
  In this *Looney Tune* Porky Pig is a vendor of hot tamales at a bullfight. He beats a bull that no other matador can. In the final scene everyone throws hats at him and a bowler lands on his head. Porky does a superb Oliver Hardy impression.

* *Hollywood Steps Out*
  (1941, Warner Brothers, colour)
  This was an Academy Award nominee in the *Merry Melodies* series.

* *Hop, Skip and a Chump*
  (1942, Warner Brothers, colour)
  The main characters are two birds who resemble Stan and Ollie. The plot revolves around the birds trying to catch a grasshopper for dinner. Director Friz Freleng tried to give this *Merrie Melody* the flavour of a Laurel and Hardy short, but didn't quite pull it off.

* *Holiday For Shoestrings*
  (1946, Warner Brothers, colour)
  In this *Merrie Melody*, based on *The Elves and the Shoemaker*, Stan and Ollie appear as elves in one sequence.

* *Hollywood Canine Canteen*
  (1946, Warner Brothers, colour)
  Hollywood celebrities appear as dogs and the Boys wag their way across the screen in a *Merrie Melodies* showcase.

* *The Big Snooze*
  (1946, Warner Brothers, colour)
  Looney Tune with Bugs Bunny and Elmer Fudd.

ALSO WORTH SEEING:

Walt Disney
1933 *The Pet Store* (b/w)

Ub Iwerks
1931 *Movie Mad* (Flip the Frog, b/w)
1934 *The Brave Tin Soldier* (colour)
1935 *Balloonland* (aka *Pincushion Man*, colour)

Warner Brothers
1933 *Bosko's Picture Show* (b/w)
1933 *Bosko's Garage* (b/w)

Columbia
1933 *Scrappy's Party* (b/w)
1933 *Movie Struck* (Scrappy, b/w)
1936 *Doctor Bluebird* (colour)
1936 *Merry Mutineers* (colour)
1936 *Two Lazy Crows* (colour)

Walter Lantz
1934 *Toyland Premiere* (colour)

TOONS LORE

✳ Frank Tashlin worked as a gag writer for Hal Roach on two-reelers featuring Laurel and Hardy and others and in 1945 he returned to live action films as a writer and director, but in the interim he became one of Cartoonland's most respected names, working for the Van Beuren Studios, Ub Iwerks and Walt Disney. By 1941 he was production manager at Screen Gems and by 1943 he was directing Bugs Bunny, Porky Pig and Daffy Duck at Warner Brothers. He included caricatures of stars such as Bing Crosby and Frank Sinatra in his cartoons and had "Ollie" in *The Case of the Stuttering Pig* (see above). We know of no instance of his having used "Stan" but there is undoubtedly more than a trace of Laurel and Hardy in many of his cartoons.

✳ According to Joe Adamson's book *The Walter Lantz Story*, Lantz (whom we all know through his Woody Woodpecker character and others) went to work for Leo McCarey at the Hal Roach studios for no payment. He just wanted experience of two-reel comedies. He was there when *Hats Off* was filmed and is credited as having drawn the animated herd of elephants in *Flying Elephants*.

✳ A 1936 Warner Brothers *Merrie Melodies* cartoon from Tex Avery, called *I Love to Singa* (sic), has a radio station called Radio Gong. Jack Bunny conducts auditions for his amateur hour. Various birds queue to play or sing. The first act is a bird playing the same tune that Laurel and Hardy play in *Pick a Star*.

✳ What-A-Mess is a very scruffy dog. Frank Muir wrote the stories and provided the commentary on these cartoons, which were made for Central Television and which have appeared on satellite television. In one of the cartoons, *What-A-Mess at the Seaside*, two flies feature and their resemblance to Laurel and Hardy is unmistakable – bowler hats, distinctive moustache, silly grin. . . .

✳ The Pingu cartoon titled *The Circus* has a piece of Laurel and Hardy's signature tune when Pingu is trying to lift a heavy set of weights, sets it down and his little sister Pinga walks into frame, picks up the so-called heavy weights very easily and exits to *The Dance of the Cuckoos*.

✳ Last, and some would say least, Larry Harmon's Laurel and Hardy cartoons, made by Hanna-Barbera for television in the sixties, are frowned on by most buffs, but children love them!

Before video, collectors in Britain often had to be content with cut-downs,
as was the case with a two-reel version of the three-reeler The Music Box

CHAPTER 25: FILM COLLECTING

✳ In the UK video release of Laurel and Hardy's films has seen ongoing exploitation of collectors. First the films were released in black and white with poor reproduction, then as colorized versions, also with poor reproduction, and then in 1995 came a batch of releases this time in black and white with much improved reproduction and, in nearly all cases, additional footage absent from earlier releases. In 1997 came yet another issue of Laurel and Hardy films, in colour and in black and white, claiming to be even further "updated", but in reality often identical with the 1995 issues.

✳ The 1995 issue of *Pack Up Your Troubles*, for example, had all the opening titles and censored scenes reinstated. The *pièce de résistance* though was *Pardon Us*, the most fragmented and frustrating Laurel and Hardy feature. With scenes restored there was the semblance of a complete film but not quite. Still missing was a bomb sequence as well as a final riverbank scene. Nor can we see the French, German and Italian language versions *Sous les Verrous*, *Hinter Schloss und Riegel* and *Muraglie* for they have joined the legion of lost films.

Posed shot for restored prison fire sequence in Pardon Us

✳ UK video releases have been mainly from Virgin and Vision Video Ltd (originating from the Kirch Group).

✳ David Oyston from Bradford created excitement in 1984. Through a senior citizen friend who had been a lifelong film collector, a very rare 35mm film of Oliver Hardy was discovered. *Something In Her Eye* dates from 1915 and seemingly predated any other known extant film of Hardy. Parts of the film were in the early stages of decay, but other parts were perfect. To preserve it for all time, a copy was made on safety stock and copies are available on video for collectors. Earlier Hardy films have now been found, but *Something In Her Eye* remains a landmark.

✳ An amateur silent film has survived which shows part of Laurel and Hardy's 1932 visit to Edinburgh. Thanks are due to Alan J Harper who recorded some memorable highlights, which are available to collectors on video and super 8.[32] Quite remarkable even by Beatlemania standards are the scenes of the crowd besieging the car bringing Laurel and Hardy to the Playhouse Cinema. Although their appearance on stage suffers from lack of sound, the subsequent shots of impromptu clowning convey the highly-charged atmosphere. Also recorded is Laurel and Hardy's visit to the North-East of England in the same year.

✳ Babe was interviewed for a television programme called *Ship's Reporter* just before he sailed for Paris on the RMS Caronia on 10th June, 1950, to make *Atoll K*. The film is in the super 8 and video collections of many aficionados.

---

[32] Super 8 (preceded by standard 8 aka regular 8) is the gauge, 8mm wide, most popular among "film" collectors, as opposed to video collectors. 16mm is also popular, generally with better definition, but is more expensive.

✳ Before the appearance of the Laurel and Hardy filmographies in the sixties, listing all the original American titles, the film collector had a headache caused by the UK distributors' practice of releasing prints under fanciful titles of their own making and sometimes the synopses were ambiguous. Some titles were predictable: *Aerial Antics* was *Hog Wild*, *Stone Age Romance* was *Flying Elephants*, *Double Trouble* was a compilation of *Them Thar Hills* and *Tit For Tat* and *The Bodyguard* was *Do Detectives Think?* But *Caught With Their Pants Down* turned out not to be *Liberty* but *You're Darn Tootin'*.

✳ In 1977 the Romney, Hythe and Dymchurch Railway in Kent celebrated its fiftieth anniversary and released a short film which became available to home movie collectors. One highlight was a visit (in March 1947) from Laurel and Hardy, who reopened the line after its wartime disruption. The snippet (mute apart from "canned" laughter) lasted only one minute and twenty-five seconds, during which the comedians clowned with a gigantic key.

✳ Walton Films were perhaps the best friends Laurel and Hardy super 8 film collectors ever had in Britain. There were complaints though about Walton's insistence upon editing shorts and features to standard lengths. Collectors complained too about the variable quality, the selection of subjects available and the price. They even found fault with the packages in which the films were marketed. In 1983 Walton Films went into liquidation and overnight became lamented champions. Today a large percentage of Laurel and Hardy films shown on super 8 are Walton prints and when second-hand Walton prints become available they fetch more than corresponding brand new prints of other subjects.

✱ In the USA Blackhawk Films were the champions for Laurel and Hardy home movie collectors on 8mm and 16mm. Print quality was usually outstanding and it was policy to release versions which were as complete as possible. Blackhawk films now exist mainly as rare, used prints, with high market value.

✱ While 16mm collectors are fewer than video and 8mm collectors, their collections often tend to be of rarer material and more durable, making 16mm the "more serious" collectors' gauge. Private collections exist on the pioneering 9.5mm gauge, which is now almost extinct, and even on 35mm, the gauge most common in cinemas.

✱ Super 8 film collectors were able to buy a real curio in the early 1980s. *Perfect Day* had a dubbed German soundtrack and one could not help but wonder at the reception it must have received when it originally went the rounds of German cinemas. Stan and Ollie repeatedly mouthing "Goodbye" to the incompatible sound of "Auf Wiedersehen" is most strange.

✱ A series of Italian videos had Stanlio e Ollio in various titles. One turned out to be five sound shorts strung together to form a feature; the voices were dubbed and Stan's voice was so high that it might have belonged to a woman.

✱ A lucky collector paid £20 (in 1986) for a used 16mm projector. Along with it came two spools of film which turned out to be a complete print of *Our Relations*, in pristine condition. Another chap bought an 8mm copy of *A Chump at Oxford* and discovered it had a very rare trailer for *The Flying Deuces* attached to it!

✱ In 1994 excerpts from Pathé newsreels covering the 1947 and 1953 tours were made available on super 8 as an eight minute disjointed compilation without any linkage or additional explanation. Shortly afterwards the material was also released on video.

"How many?"

CHAPTER 26: FILM 107 AND BEYOND

✳ For years it was accepted that Laurel and Hardy appeared in 105 films together, though not always on the screen at the same time. In 1989 careful study of *Now I'll Tell One* (1927) established that Laurel and Hardy both appeared in this Charley Chase Pathé two-reeler, Stan as a lawyer and Babe as a policemen – and history was rewritten as the magic number was raised to 106.

✳ The definition of a "Laurel and Hardy film" is vague and the new total of 106 films is somewhat arbitrary. It does not include newsreel material or *This Is Your Life*, but does include cameo appearances and the novelty item *The Tree in A Test Tube*. Researchers are on the lookout for film 107. . . .

✳ *Memories of Famous Hollywood Comedians*: This film is a 14 minute short released in 1951 as part of Columbia's *Screen Snapshots* series. Running for an incredible thirty-eight years (1921-58), each *Screen Snapshot* cobbled together into a themed short often unrelated clips of the stars at play or at home. By the early 1950s the need for such shorts was dwindling, as were budgets. In an effort to economise, "new" *Screen Snapshots* were put together from old footage. Laurel and Hardy perform a gag alighting a train. They aren't in costume, so the film must have been shot during a promotional trip. Probably the clip was filmed in the 1930s, possibly during the 1932 tour. Stan, in a smart suit, stands beside a train, fanning himself with his straw boater. Ollie, also in suit and boater, is about to alight the train but looks dubiously at the step. Stan obligingly wipes it with a handkerchief. A satisfied Ollie nimbly steps down and exits the frame. Stan looks after him, then very quickly steps onto and then off the small platform before following Ollie. This amounts to about twelve intriguing seconds.

Announcing Film 107 coming soon

✳ Is *The Rent Collector* (1921) a contender for film 107? In 1994 it was certainly considered a possibility as the following item shows:

Two facts are not in dispute. Firstly, this Vitagraph comedy was a Larry Semon two-reeler with Babe as the supporting heavy. Secondly, Stan included this title in his personal listing of films. Now for two claims. Camillo Moscati, Italian film author, included this title in the Laurel and Hardy filmography in his book *Stanlio e Ollio* because he believes he clearly recognised Laurel with Hardy in the scene where Semon steals a pumpkin. He claims that Stan also appears in other scenes in different costumes in this film. In the second edition of *The Magic Behind the Movies*, Randy Skretvedt writes, "Noted film historian David Shepard has seen a print in Italy, and is quite certain that Laurel and Hardy are both in the film, but have no scenes together." The pumpkin scene has Babe helping himself to the produce on a vegetable stall while the stall holder vigorously protests. Unknown to both of them, Larry (the replacement rent collector) abets two children at a window above to spear a pumpkin and lift it from the stall. The gag ends when the pumpkin slips and splits open on Babe's head. Is the stall holder with a large moustache Stan? How can we account for the title being included in Stan's list? Because it is third on the list, chronologically long before 1921, could it refer to a different film? Why would Larry Semon, after dispensing with Stan as a scene stealer following their three films together in 1918 (*Huns and Hyphens*, *Bears and Bad Men* and *Frauds and Frenzies*) want to reemploy him three years later for *The Rent Collector*?

Whatever the answers to these questions, others who have now seen the film (including three "solo film" researchers) are not prepared to wager their rent money that Stan is in the film.

✳ In the Pathé short *Roughest Africa* (1923), which features Stan as an intrepid explorer, some viewers were sure that they saw Babe playing the part of one of the natives. The lavish make-up prevented a clear look at his features and the date needed to be reconciled with his work at Vitagraph. Research on the solos established this claim as a case of wishful thinking.

✳ The suggestion that *Get 'Em Young* (1926) had some footage of Babe as the butler (which was actually shot before Stan assumed the role) left in the film always sounded unlikely and was not substantiated when the film finally resurfaced.

✳ A handful of Laurel and Hardy film archivists have been hoping to unearth a short piece of film, commonly referred to as the *Lollipop* film. It was taken, it was believed, during the Boys' stay in Northampton in 1953, for use on a film promoting road safety. The only evidence of its supposed existence was a photograph of Hardy standing on a zebra crossing and Laurel about to cross with a party of schoolchildren. After exhaustive research, A J Marriot revealed that, far from being lost, this Laurel and Hardy film never existed. Marriot interviewed the police constable who instigated the photo-call and one of the schoolchildren. Both stated authoritatively that a photograph is all that was shot.

✳ Nor need we concern ourselves any further with *The Voice of Hollywood* series; the rumour that Laurel and Hardy appeared in one episode is now explained in one word – lookalikes!

✳ A film was made during a visit of Laurel and Hardy to the Carlsberg Brewery in Copenhagen.

✳ *The Autobiography of a Jeep* is a one-reel propaganda film with a strange reputation. Laurel and Hardy's appearance in it is relished by buffs, but lasts only seconds. It has appeared on Channel 4 television.

Keep searching

CHAPTER 27: SUPPORTING PLAYERS

✳ A spin-off from the study of our favourite duo has been the interest aroused in the supporting players who so richly enhance the films of Laurel and Hardy. In no other series of films has the supporting cast achieved such fame and glory.

On the occasion of Oliver Hardy's centenary, artist Johan Amssoms of Antwerp revived some of the supporting players. Beneath the Boys are (clockwise from top left) Anita Garvin, Arthur Housman, Walter Long, James Finlayson, Charlie Hall, Mae Busch, Edgar Kennedy, Charles Middleton, Billy Gilbert, Charley Chase and Tiny Sandford

JAMES FINLAYSON

✳ James Finlayson was born on 27th August, 1887 in the Scottish village of Larbert. One of nine children, it looks as though Jimmy was about the third eldest in the family. James Finlayson was his christened name and he resisted advice in later years to change it.

✳ He attended Larbert High School, but left at an early age to become an apprentice with Jones and Campbell, Larbert's first foundry. Although his chosen trade was that of a sheet metal worker, it is doubtful whether he had any real choice in the matter; employment was not easily found.

✳ From childhood he had entertainment aspirations and some reports have him singing in church choirs. So it came as no surprise when Jimmy joined the amateur Larbert Opera Company. His parents were very angry when he joined a touring company founded by the actor/manager John Clyde, father of Andy Clyde, who also became a film comedian in Hollywood.

✳ In 1910 Clyde's company, with Jimmy in the cast, appeared in the melodrama *Rob Roy* at the Metropole Theatre, Stockwell Street, Glasgow, where Stan Laurel's father, Arthur Jefferson, was the lessee. So it's quite possible that Finlayson and Laurel met in Scotland before they both emigrated.

✳ As was the trend for entertainers in the early 1900s, Jimmy couldn't resist the call of America, which coincidentally claimed young Arthur Stanley Jefferson. Stan emigrated in 1910, Jimmy in 1911.

✳ Laurel recalled that Finlayson toured with Alec Lauder, brother of the famous Sir Harry, in vaudeville throughout America in a very successful sketch, *The Concealed Bed*.

✳ Several years on the stage in the United States led to Jimmy's eventual appearance in the movies. First came Jack Blackstone's L-KO comedies, then Mack Sennett comedies. He had some freelance work with First National, Paramount and RKO, but it was the promising Hal Roach organisation which was to become his most successful base.

✳ In 1924 he was made the star of a series of Roach comedies and it was on this project that Stan Laurel earned one of his earliest accomplishments as a director. The film was *Yes, Yes, Nanette*.

✳ In 1927 Finlayson appeared in his first film with Laurel and Hardy. The title was *Love 'Em and Weep* and in this he played the central character. It was later reworked with Oliver Hardy in the main role as *Chickens Come Home*.

Sugar Daddies: *Hardy and Finlayson*

✳ James Finlayson's role in Laurel and Hardy films can be equated to that of Margaret Dumont in the Marx Brothers' movies. Although several stars appeared in more Laurel and Hardy films than Finlayson did, somehow the public always identifies James Finlayson as being Stan and Ollie's number one supporting star.

Sugar Daddies: *Laurel and Finlayson.*
Jimmy's trademark squint and stance are virtually identical in this and the previous photo

✳ Whether Fin[33] is obstructing the Boys in their well-meaning endeavours in *Way Out West*, being quarrelsome in *Block-Heads*, or taking advantage of their naïveté in *Our Relations*, we can scarcely find a redeeming aspect to endear him. Yet we love him.

✳ James Finlayson appeared on the screen with Marlene Dietrich and Judy Garland. His directors included Ernst Lubitsch and Alfred Hitchcock.

✳ He appeared in three films with the title *Big Business*; in addition to the classic conflict with Stan and Ollie in 1929, the film title appeared again in 1931 and 1934.

---

[33] On the lot technicians and actors referred to Finlayson as "Jim" or "Jimmy". Scripts always called him "Jim" and never "Fin". The latter sobriquet seems to have been inspired by his character's name in *Our Relations* and *Way Out West*, though it was spelt "Finn" there.

✳ In May, 1933 *Fra Diavolo* was released in England. Hal Roach, James Finlayson, Dennis King and Thelma Todd made personal appearances at the Empire Theatre in London, to promote the film. Instead of returning to the States with the others, Finlayson decided to spend some time in his beloved Scotland, visiting friends and relatives.

✳ His film career in Hollywood was floundering. Over the years he had been reduced from starring roles to playing bit parts in Roach comedies. Even that work had begun to dry up and he had to freelance all over Hollywood to find work. That work was mostly bit parts in two-reelers for RKO. In England he appeared in a number of feature films for Gaumont-British and also toured England in a number of stage plays. In March, 1935 Hal Roach talked him into returning to Hollywood to appear in *Bonnie Scotland*. He had been missed by the Boys during his two years' absence from Roach.

✳ In later years Larbert welcomed home the Hollywood star for his annual holidays. Jimmy used to stay at the Station Hotel for a month or six weeks and visited his family. He played golf at Falkirk Tryst.

✳ He also returned to the foundry in which he had worked as a lad and, in order to demonstrate perhaps to himself as much as to others that he still possessed his old prized skills, he produced ash-pans for domestic coal fires. They rapidly became valued souvenirs. One of his greatest delights was also to frequent an old favourite haunt: the fish and chip shop close to Dobie Hall, nearby his childhood home.

✳ He was a member of the Santa Monica Race Club, Masquers, Screen Actors Guild and Lambs Club. He was also a life member of the Masonic Lodge in Scotland.

✳ Co-star Dorothy Granger said that one of Finlayson's big toes was missing, but another account alleges he had six toes on each foot!

✳ In 1939 the *Los Angeles Times* reported, "It will be a trek to the altar for Jimmy Finlayson, the comic, and Stefani Insull, English stage star now living in Hollywood." He never married!

✳ He made a total of thirty-three films with the Boys, his last being *Saps at Sea* in 1940. He made his last screen appearance in the 1951 Paramount feature *Here Comes the Groom*.

✳ He was found dead in bed on 9th October 1953, apparently of a heart attack.

✳ As part of the Cinema 100 celebrations, the Scottish Film Council in 1996 presented a plaque for James Finlayson to Falkirk District Council. The plaque was in fact the second one – the first recorded that Finlayson was born in Falkirk (a common misconception).

The bushy moustache he wore in the Laurel and Hardy films was artificial

MAE BUSCH

✴ Mae Busch was born Annie May Busch in Australia on 18th June, 1891.

✴ The search in Australia for information on Mae, and for her birth certificate in particular, encountered many red herrings but perseverance was rewarded in 1993 when her birth certificate was finally found.

✴ "May" was a popular girl's name of the period with its variant "Mae" common in America. Just when "Annie May" became "Mae" is not known, but she was certainly known by her latter name during her Keystone days.

✴ It is thought that her father was a musician and her mother a professional vocalist. She had British nationality but from the age of thirteen she lived in America.

✴ Despite being brought up in a convent, she started her career on stage in musical comedy and vaudeville. In Hollywood she made her debut with the Flying A Film Studios in 1912 and went on to work with Mack Sennett at Keystone.

✴ The first Laurel and Hardy film in which Mae appeared was *Love 'Em and Weep*.

✴ The only scene in which Mae Busch plays a happy part with the Boys is in *Them Thar Hills*. She sits in a caravan with Stan and Ollie, drinking, singing and giggling. In *Tit For Tat* and *The Fixer-Uppers* she is also a sympathetic character, but her forte was the portrayal of shrewish wives or beguiling, wayward women.

✴ The discovery of her death certificate revealed her date of death as April 20th 1946, the location as the Motion Picture Country Home, her residence as 1219 N Beachwood Drive, Los Angeles and the cause of her death as cancer. Her cremated remains were left in a shoe-box. Thanks to the work of the Sons of the Desert, Mae now has a plaque and an urn at the Chapel of the Pines in Los Angeles.

✴ Most surprising are the inaccuracies provided on the death certificate by the informant (Thomas C Tate, her third husband). Her length of stay in the USA was given as only thirty-seven years, her occupation as an "actress" in "silent motion pictures" and her date of birth as June 19th, 1901!

✴ "Elusive" is the word for Mae. Gaps in her life story persist and questions remain unanswered. After fifty years the "ever-popular" Mae is still keeping us guessing.

Beguiling Mae with Stan in Chickens Come Home *phones Ollie on* GRANITE *3648*

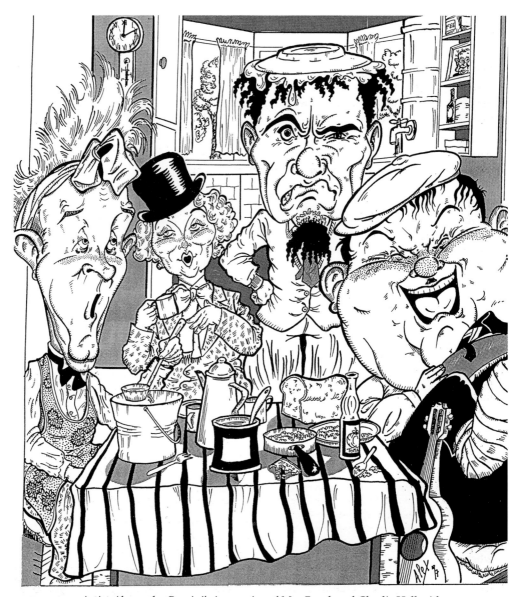

Artist Alessandro Rossini's impression of Mae Busch and Charlie Hall with
Stan and Ollie in Them Thar Hills

CHARLIE HALL

✳ Charles Hall was born on 19th August, 1899 into a working class environment in Birmingham, England. He was the second in a family of eight.

✳ After he left school at the age of fourteen he did some acting on the amateur stage while making a living as a carpenter.

✳ Eventually he found himself in Los Angeles, where he occasionally played very small parts in films and did odd jobs as a carpenter.

✳ In 1926 the small, scrawny Hall appeared for the first time in a Hal Roach comedy. The first time he appeared in a film with Laurel and Hardy was in *Love 'Em and Weep* in which Charlie was the butler of the rich business man Titus Tillsbury, played by James Finlayson.

✳ In most Laurel and Hardy films Hall was the adversary of the two friends and the victim of escalating violence.

✳ In *The Battle of the Century* his brief presence is perhaps symbolic. He is the man who starts the pie fight by slipping on a banana peel.

✳ The difference between Hall and Finlayson was that the Scotsman had a much more comical expression. From Charlie Hall there radiated a more realistic threat.

✳ One of Charlie Hall's most memorable appearances is as a cab driver in *Double Whoopee*, with Laurel and Hardy as hotel attendants. Charlie is really belligerent when he steps out of his taxi, pulls Ollie's whistle from its cord, crushes it under his heel and tears the peak of Ollie's cap. Stan immediately pulls the peak of Charlie's cap over his chin, so that it looks as if he is suddenly wearing a beard. Charlie looks in the camera lens with increasing anger.

✳ Hall never graduated beyond his "bit" player status. Most of his appearances are fleeting. In *The Music Box*, as the postman who directs the Boys to the house "right on top of the stoop", his appearance lasts barely fifteen seconds.

✳ Charlie Hall appeared in more Laurel and Hardy films than any other supporting player – forty-seven in all.

✳ In 1935 he married Wilda. They had no children.

✳ Only once did Charlie Hall return to England. That was in 1935, shortly after his father died. Charlie's nephew, Ron Hall, described his first meeting with his famous uncle Charlie in hospital in Birmingham:

I was a little boy having an operation on my ear and feeling really miserable. Suddenly this man walked down the ward, wearing a blazer, flannels, two-tone shoes and a colourful cravat – quite a sight in the 1930s when everyone else was wearing drab clothes. It was Uncle Charlie.[34]

✳ Charlie took his mother on vacation to Los Angeles and introduced her to Laurel and Hardy.

✳ Eventually there was less and less employment on the Hal Roach lot so he went to other studios where, because of his accent, he played in films with a British background such as the Sherlock Holmes movie *Dressed to Kill* (1946).

✳ Charlie Hall once appeared in Groucho Marx's television show *You Bet Your Life*. On seeing the show, Stan Laurel wrote to Charlie with congratulations.

✳ Charlie Hall died in 1959.

---

[34] *Sunday Mercury* (31.7.94.)

Landlord Charlie threatens Stan and Ollie in Leave 'Em Laughing

BILLY GILBERT

✳ William Gilbert Baron was born in the dressing-room of an opera house in Louisville, Kentucky on 12th September, 1894. His mother and father were successful operatic stars.

✳ He developed into a "Dutch Comedian" – a type with grotesque gestures, with not very delicate humour. Gilbert prided himself on the fact that he made his accent into a conglomeration of German, Greek and Italian, so that he would not offend one nation in particular and that his accent lended itself so well to fits of rage.

✳ In 1929 or 1930 in Los Angeles he had the good fortune that Stan Laurel was in the audience when Gilbert played the leading part in a revue. Laurel suspected a talent among the scriptwriters and when the performance was over asked Billy who was responsible for the sketches. Gilbert had devised them all himself. This led to a five year contract with Hal Roach's studio.

✳ *Katz's Film Encyclopedia* describes Billy Gilbert as "tall and heavy (280 lbs)" and says, "he appeared in some two hundred feature films and shorts."

✳ Of the comedians alone he supported Thelma Todd and ZaSu Pitts, Clark and McCullough, Wheeler and Woolsey, The Three Stooges, Olsen and Johnson, The Marx Brothers, Our Gang, Thelma Todd and Patsy Kelly, W C Fields, Harry Langdon, Charlie Chaplin, Buster Keaton and particularly Charley Chase. Billy became Charley's closest friend. He starred with Ben Blue in the easily forgettable Taxi Boys two-reelers.

✳ Billy Gilbert appeared in seven films with Laurel and Hardy and provided a voice-over in *Sons of the Desert*.

✳ He married Ella McKenzie (formerly of Our Gang) in 1938.

✳ He died in Hollywood of a stroke on 23rd September, 1971.

Great artiste Billy Gilbert drawn by great artist Tony Bagley

ANITA GARVIN

✳ Anita Frances Garvin was born on 11th February, 1907 in New York.

✳ She was ambitious and convinced of her comic talent. At the age of twelve Anita successfully added four years onto her age and was engaged for a revue in which she had to be sixteen. That same day she was on the stage as one of Mack Sennett's Bathing Beauties who were performing live on the stages of cinemas and theatres.

✳ During a period of freelancing, Anita Garvin met Stan Laurel for the first time in 1925 at Universal Studios. He was making a series of film parodies for the independent producer Joe Rock. Anita recalled, "I still remember that I thought, 'How clever Stan is that he can write, direct and play the leading part; and all that so well too.' " She won a role with Mabel Normand in *Raggedy Rose* (1927), directed by Stan Laurel, who personally introduced her to Hal Roach.

✳ Her debut with the Boys was in *Why Girls Love Sailors*, as the feisty wife of the ship's captain.

✳ *With Love and Hisses* marked her second film with Laurel and Hardy. In it she played the girlfriend of James Finlayson.

✳ In *The Battle of the Century* Anita Garvin had a heavy fall that would gain her a place in movie history. At the end of this two-reeler, while the pies are flying all over the place, she finds herself with her behind in a pie. Anita does not lose her self-control. She gets up and, before walking along pertly, she shakes her leg for just a moment as if to remove some clots of dough from somewhere under her stylish black skirt. Once Anita told an interviewer that it was her own idea to give something extra to the short scene, which was her only appearance in the film. Anita recalled that she wasn't paid for her appearance. She did it as a favour to Stan, during her lunch break.

In Sailors Beware! *Anita Garvin played an international jewel thief who was married to a midget, disguised as a baby*

✳ Anita had a brief pairing with Marion Byron, in *A Pair of Tights* (1928) and two other films. This was Hal Roach's unsuccessful attempt to create a female Laurel and Hardy team in the silent era.

✳ She developed the style of the elegant but stern woman with a poker-face and sparkling eyes, used to perfection when she eventually appeared as Stan's wife in *Blotto* and *Be Big!*

✳ Anita estimated that she appeared in two hundred films, but the tally is probably less than half that. She appeared in eleven films with Laurel and Hardy, her last one being *A Chump at Oxford*, in which she had a small part.

✳ In the 1920s she was married to Jerry Drew, who starred in several silent comedies. In 1930 she married bandleader Red Stanley and they had two children. At the age of thirty-five she decided to end her career and to become a housewife. She was widowed in 1980.

✳ Anita Garvin died on 7th July, 1994.

CHARLEY CHASE

✳ Charley Chase was born in Baltimore, Maryland on 20th October, 1893.

✳ He was six feet tall, had brown hair and blue eyes.

✳ He became the star of a series of Hal Roach one-reelers, the first of which was (appropriately) *At First Sight*, in 1924.

"Charley Chase, comic ace –
handsome face, style and grace."
Drawing and ditty by Tony Bagley

✳ He was also a very successful director, using his real name, Charles Parrott.

✳ He liked horseback riding, flying, hunting and fishing. He played various musical instruments, frequently accompanying himself in his films. One of his most successful numbers was *Smile When the Raindrops Fall*, which became a perennial in Roach comedies. He invented most of the crazy gadgets used in his films.

✳ *Fluttering Hearts* (1927) has a memorable sequence in which Charley brings a female mannequin to life to seduce drunken Oliver Hardy to lure a document from him. Charley made a guest appearance in the Max Davidson comedy *Call of the Cuckoos* (1927). Other guests in the film were Laurel and Hardy and James Finlayson.

✳ Producer Jules White applauded the fact that Charley was always word-perfect on screen and seldom required more than one take.

✳ Author Leonard Maltin said, "It's rather sad to think that a man who appeared in over two hundred short subjects and directed at least one hundred should be almost forgotten today."

✳ Charley Chase described thus the character he portrayed in *Sons of the Desert*:
> There's at least one at every party, club meeting or convention ever held. He's known as "Goodtime Charley" and he is easily recognised by his peculiar characteristics and mannerisms. He is the fellow who slaps you so hard on the back that your false teeth are jarred loose. He slips up behind you and slips ice down your neck. His voice is the loudest – his clothes, likewise. His practical joking includes a varied line of tricks, the most popular number being the one where he pulls the chair from under you just as you are about to sit down. That's me to a tee in *Sons of the Desert*.

✳ Laurel and Hardy returned the compliment of Chase's cameo role in *Sons of the Desert* with their even shorter appearance in his penultimate film for Roach, *On the Wrong Trek*.

✳ He was married to Bebe Eltinge and had two daughters, Polly and June.

✳ Charley Chase died in 1940.

EDGAR KENNEDY

* Edgar Livingstone Kennedy was born in Monterey, California on 26th April, 1890.

* He had several years in travelling revue companies before starting his film career at Mack Sennett's studio in 1912 and progressing to become a Keystone Kop.

* He was also a boxer and was very proud of the fact that he had held out for fourteen rounds against Jack Dempsey, a rising young boxer.

* In 1928 Kennedy was contracted by Hal Roach who used him in various comedies. His trademark became the "slow burn" – slowly oncoming excesses of anger.

* He appeared in nine Laurel and Hardy films and in four was a policeman who tries to correct the Boys. In his first Laurel and Hardy film, *Leave 'Em Laughing*, he loses his trousers in the middle of a busy street. In *Night Owls* the roles are initially reversed when he presses Stan and Ollie to burgle the Chief Commissioner's house. In *The Finishing Touch* he is set upon when glue and roofing slide from the house the Boys are trying to build and in *Unaccustomed As We Are* he's the policeman married to Thelma Todd, whose dress catches fire. So there is plenty of reason for fits of temper, the first stage announcing itself when Kennedy pushes back the police-cap on his balding head as if the revenge brewing needs cooling.

* In the silent *Should Married Men Go Home?* Kennedy is a golfer who tries to play on the same green as Stan and Ollie and that leads to the loss of his toupee (and its replacement by a sod with daisies).

Edgar in the mud with Stan and Ollie in Should Married Men Go Home?

* Less known nowadays are Edgar Kennedy's achievements as a director (under the name E Livingstone Kennedy). He directed two of the best Laurel and Hardy silent films, *From Soup to Nuts* and *You're Darn Tootin'*.

* From 1931 Kennedy appeared in his own series of two-reelers and in all contributed to around five hundred shorts and feature films.

* Kennedy was teased by Laurel and Hardy for the last time in 1943 in the MGM production *Air Raid Wardens*. He was the remover Joe Bledsoe who refused to shut off the lights when asked by Stan and Ollie to do so.

* He died of cancer on 9th November, 1948.

CHARLIE ROGERS

✳ Charles A Rogers was born on 15th January, 1890 in Manchester.

✳ He was a gifted comedy writer; he sold sketches and gags to the great Karno before going to America. Soon after arriving in America around 1913, he discovered that he could make more money writing sketches and gags for vaudeville comics than performing.

✳ Hal Roach signed him as a writer and gagman in 1926 and he went on to become a director. For his contributions in helping to create Laurel and Hardy films he deserves much greater recognition than he has been given.

✳ He appeared in nine Laurel and Hardy films and directed several, including *Fra Diavolo* and *The Bohemian Girl*.

✳ Rogers was the only writer to remain on the Roach staff during the entire Laurel and Hardy era.

✳ Like most successful comedy writers, Rogers was content to take the money and let the comics take credit for his work. It never bothered Rogers that Stan took credit for his work, but it certainly bothers some of the Rogers family who are still alive today. They feel Stan deliberately waited until it was too late for Rogers to get the credit due him.

✳ When Hal Roach Jr and Stan came up with the idea of a series of Laurel and Hardy comedies for television, they planned on using Rogers as their script writer and director, but he had become too successful and they could not afford him. The project was dropped.

Charlie Rogers's most familiar on-screen appearance is as the Prime Minister in Double Whoopee

OTHERS

✻ **Harry Bernard**

Harry Bernard's was a familiar face in twenty-six Laurel and Hardy films. Employed as a bit player at the Hal Roach studios, he can also be seen in the Our Gang, Charley Chase and Thelma Todd/ZaSu Pitts/Patsy Kelly comedies. His appearances may have been brief, but they were effective and he deserves greater recognition. In *Any Old Port*, where he appears as the boxing promoter seated at the counter of the lunch wagon, Ollie addresses him by his real name:

Harry: Hey there!
Ollie: Hello, Harry!
Harry: Well, Ollie. Gee, I haven't seen you in ages.
Ollie: No. My friend Mr Laurel, Mr Bernard.
Harry: How do you do?

✻ **Baldwin Cooke**

Baldy Cooke, with his wife and Stan Laurel, was part of the Stan Jefferson Trio in Stan's vaudeville days. He went on to appear in thirty Laurel and Hardy films.

✻ **Jack Hill**

Jack Hill appeared in thirty-four films with Laurel and Hardy, as a silent, background extra.

✻ **Arthur Housman**

The wonderfully portrayed drunk in *Scram!* etc was Arthur Housman. Stan Laurel said that he had never seen Housman sober, but not drunk in the way he was in the movies. In silent films he had many straight roles before his inebriated typecasting. He had appearances in five Laurel and Hardy films.

Housman befriends the Boys in Our Relations

✻ **Rosina Lawrence**

Rosina Lawrence appeared in three films with Laurel and Hardy and is best remembered as Mary Roberts in *Way Out West*. Born in Westboro in Canada in 1912, she became a child actress, singer and dancer and worked with stars who included Maurice Chevalier, Rita Hayworth and Alice Faye. She died in 1997, one of the longest survivors of the "Laurel and Hardy Stock Company" – always delighted to discuss her experiences at the Hal Roach studios.

Jack Hill is standing behind Stan in Below Zero

* **Walter Long**

We are told that Walter Long liked the "scoundrel" roles he had to portray for they called for a good deal of dramatic ability. He was in five Laurel and Hardy films, his most memorable part being a convict in *Pardon Us*. A report in *Picture Show* (1.8.25.) read:

> There are a few occasions, however, when he does not like being the bad man of the screen. This is when he has to scare children. He happens to be very fond of kiddies and he hates to see them running away from him in terror when he has donned his villainous make-up. He doesn't like having to chase women around either. "I get sick and tired of smashing down doors and attacking helpless women," he will say. "My idea of a really good part is one where I have an honest-to-goodness fight, without any favour shown."

* **Sam Lufkin**

Sam Lufkin appeared in a staggering thirty-nine films with Laurel and Hardy, but rarely had more than a small part. You can spot him as the referee in *The Battle of the Century*.

Sam Lufkin advises Laurel and Hardy to leave town in Going Bye-Bye!

* **Viola Richard**

Viola Richard appeared in six silent shorts with Laurel and Hardy between February 1927 and March 1928. She was also reportedly a passerby in *Tit For Tat*. William K Everson wrote in *The Films of Laurel and Hardy*:

> Viola Richard, one of the two leading ladies in *Should Married Men Go Home?*, is a quite undeservedly forgotten comedienne. Attractive, pert and vivacious, with a fine sense of comedy timing, she should have gone much further than she did – and probably would have, had not a striking resemblance to Clara Bow, then at her peak, held her back from important roles.

* **Stanley Sandford**

"Tiny" Sandford was six feet five inches tall. He was in twenty-three films with Laurel and Hardy, typical roles being the policeman in *Big Business* and *Double Whoopee*.

Tiny Sandford is the rice-spattered warden, between Laurel and Hardy in The Hoose-Gow

* **Thelma Todd**

Thelma Todd starred in comedy shorts with Charley Chase, Laurel and Hardy and eventually in her own comedy series, with ZaSu Pitts and then with Patsy Kelly. Following her death in December, 1935, from carbon monoxide poisoning in her car, her appearance in *The Bohemian Girl* was truncated. The thread of tragedy weaving through the narrative of Thelma's thirty years is a stirring contrast to the comedy and fun at the Hal Roach studios. Her appearances with Stan and Ollie included *Another Fine Mess* and *Fra Diavolo*.

CHAPTER 28:
LAUREL WITHOUT HARDY

✱ Laurel appeared in around seventy films without Hardy. The relegation of these "solo" films to a lower rank of cinema history is partially explained by their limited availability for viewing. Tracking down Stan and Babe's solo films is an on-going, daunting task, but elusive titles continue to surface. In embryonic form there are gags that Stan perfected in the "team" films. With Stan often a brash and cocky comic character (quite unlike the Laurel of later years) and the basically slapstick situations, a closer look reveals brilliant timing, surreal touches and connections with the team films. We offer some examples to give the flavour.

✱ *Just Rambling Along* (1918)
Enticed into a cafeteria, loafer Stan turns the system to his advantage but ends up with a check that he cannot pay. Ten years later in *Should Married Men Go Home?* he has the same problem. A highlight is the beautifully timed hats on/hats off routine.

*Advertising artwork
for* Zeb vs Paprika *(1924)*

✱ *Under Two Jags* (1923)
Variety said:
> Broad gesture at burlesque on the film version of *Under Two Flags*, exhibited two or three years ago. Satire attempted on all outstanding details of the original picture is hard for those who missed it to figure out, the mimicry being poorly handled. Old reliable slapstick gets the laughs. Stan Laurel, in front of the camera eleven and a half minutes of the film's twelve minutes' running time, always manages to be funny.

As for connections with the Laurel and Hardy team films, this is a prime example. Stan joins the Foreign Legion long before *Beau Hunks* and *The Flying Deuces*. Mae Laurel is in the cast.

✱ *The Noon Whistle* (1923)
In these early comedies Stan and James Finlayson have equal roles and the on-screen hostility between them emerges as a recurrent theme. They seem like preliminary warm-ups for the fully-fledged antagonism of *Big Business*. Fin, as foreman at a timber mill, has a workforce of slackers, "all ears rolled back, waiting for the noon whistle". The boss calls him into the office to complain that "the men are so lazy, they lean against each other when they loaf." Fin's attempts to keep track of Stan amid the piles of timber give rise to a succession of splendid knockabout gags, distinguished by impeccable timing. The "impossible" long plank gag used in *The Finishing Touch* and reprised in *Great Guns* has its forerunner here, with Stan at both ends and Fin providing the astonished reaction. Fin's pursuit of Stan in and out of adjacent doors, a supreme example of precision timing, is reworked with a trio in and out of the kitchen cupboard in *Swiss Miss* and a bag of cement hoisted by block and tackle points the way to the piano in *The Music Box* and the mule in *Way Out West*.

* *White Wings* (1923)
When Stan comes up behind a policeman and prepares to kick him, he spares the time to dance two triumphant jigs. It is pure music hall and far removed from Mr Hardy's friend Mr Laurel. Another sequence has Stan leaning against a fire hydrant, with one leg tucked underneath him, tricking a passer-by – a blueprint for *Block-Heads*.

* *Pick and Shovel* (1923)
While digging for coal, miner Stan is constantly at loggerheads with his foreman, Fin. The timing of their inter-play (circling the coal truck, for example) is finely tuned and the pick, shovel and candle gags are samplers for those coming later in *The Second Hundred Years* and *The Hoose-Gow*.

* *Oranges and Lemons* (1923)
Fruit picker Stan and his foreman engage in a running slapstick battle in the fields and the packing station. The devastation is a small foretaste of the scenes of chaos to come in the team films.

* *Save the Ship* (1923)
The opening scene is reminiscent of the opening scene of *Leave 'Em Laughing*.

* *A Man About Town* (1923)
Notable incidents are Stan helping Fin onto a streetcar, little knowing that he is stalking him, and the final scene when Stan cheekily waves his straw hat at Fin – hilarious when we realise that Fin has the last laugh. Fin was in so many of Stan's early films that their appearances together almost seem to be practice runs for Ollie.

* *Roughest Africa* (1923)
During the 1920s Stan made a speciality of parodying currently popular films. Those spoofs that have survived contain examples of Stan's quirky humour and mastery of a gag. Big game hunter Stanislaus Laurello kisses his wife (Katherine Grant) goodbye in Hollywood ("last outpost of civilisation") and sets off on safari with film cameraman Hans Downe (Fin). The surrealist element surfaces from the start: the native porters carry a piano, a double bass and a bath while Fin follows in a car, Stan in a taxi. The African jungle (actually Catalina Island off the Californian coast) provides the setting for a series of animal gags among which the highlight is a "flying elephant". As the tempo increases, Stan is chased by an ostrich and lions, and Fin by a bear. These are, one might say, predecessors to the deleted ostrich scene in *Any Old Port*, the lions in *The Chimp* and *Hollywood Party* and the bear in *The Rogue Song*.

* *Scorching Sands* (1923)
This is a parody of the 1922 Paramount feature *Burning Sands*. Desert travellers Stan, Fin and Katherine Grant are briefly captured by Arabs. Much is compressed into this briskly paced one-reeler: slapstick, sight gags, anachronistic humour (a lift and a swimming pool beneath the sands), a macabre touch (a postponed execution) and two minor but significant bits of business from Stan comprising Ollie mannerisms: he gestures his own priority to Fin and does a rudimentary tie twiddle. *Should Tall Men Marry?*, a late solo film, has hitherto seemed unusual in not casting Stan and Fin as adversaries – somewhat surprisingly, *Scorching Sands* reveals them similarly portrayed as working in unison.

* *The Soilers* (1923)
In this parody of *The Spoilers*, villainous Fin covets gold prospector Stan's claim. Stan does his "scissors skip" and in the film's wrap-up gag is flung into a garbage cart just as Ollie was to be twelve years later at the end of *The Fixer-Uppers*.

✳ *Near Dublin* (1924)

The opening title, "A resident of the Irish village of Trenchcoat always maintained a peaceful disposition until the moment when a brick came into contact with his head," sets the tone for a brisk comic fling in which postman Stan and brick merchant Fin battle it out over the same girl. There's a brief glimpse of Mae Laurel among the village dancers.

✳ *Brothers under the Chin* (1924)

The title derives from the 1922 feature *Brothers under the Skin*. Stan and Fin are twins (!) left in an orphanage for adoption by different parents. Twenty years elapse and Stan is shanghaied on a ship (predating *The Live Ghost*!) whose captain turns out to be (you've guessed it!) Fin. Identical marks under the chin reunite the long-lost brothers. Comments from trade journals provide an inkling of where the humour lies:

> With the aid of cleverly constructed furniture [long before *Brats*!], Stan and Jim are made to look very diminutive as twin babies. Their antics in baby clothes [long before *Wild Poses*!] and in a big clothes basket are particularly comical.

✳ *Short Kilts* (1924)

The surrealist overtones to be found in Stan's solo work surface in the Scotland depicted in this film where, against a background of clan feuding, Stan and Fin battle it out during a frenzied game of musical chairs! After a partial reconciliation, the final free-for-all has them crowning each other with plaques inscribed with the mottoes "Let brotherly love continue" and "Ours is a happy home" – a gag reworked in *They Go Boom* with the motto "Smile all the while" contrasting with Ollie's predicament. Caption to savour: "How much can a Scotsman drink?" "Any *given* amount."

✳ *Twins* (1925)

When Joe Rock became a producer, he signed Stan to make twelve two-reel comedies. Filmed on the Universal lot and using existing sets, they were called "Stan Laurel Comedies". Although Stan did not direct them, good use was made of his talent for improvisation, pantomime and the well-timed execution of a gag. Quality was variable, attributable perhaps to hasty production as the twelve films were completed three months ahead of schedule. *Twins* is noteworthy for using the same theme of mistaken identity that was to be expanded with more subtlety in *Our Relations*. The opening titles, with a joking reference to matrimony, could have come straight from a later Roach film: "Twins like other troubles never come singly. Speaking of troubles we open our story with a married man –". Here, as in *Swiss Miss*, a craving for liquor leads on to a sequence of comic inebriation. Stan gets an off-screen black eye as in *Towed in a Hole* and five years before preparing to leave home in *Blotto*, an overbearing wife reproachfully asks (via a titlecard), "Didn't you forget something?" The wrap-up gag has the surreal overtones frequently found in Stan's solos: rather than run or hide, a pane of glass is painted over to avoid detection.

* *The Snow Hawk* (1925)
  This film reveals Stan at an interesting stage of his development as a solo comedian. Influences of other comedians are apparent, but his screen persona is still very different from that of the team films – though he does cry in one scene.

* *Navy Blue Days* (1925)
  This is a typical Laurel "string of gags" film based on the merest suggestion of a storyline: Stan, a sailor on shore leave in a South American port, follows his petty officer around in the hope of obtaining an invitation to meet the locals.

* *The Sleuth* (1925)
  Detective Stan is hired by a married woman to check on her husband. Stan's investigative technique is to disguise himself first as a maid and then as a vamp, roles he was to reprise two years later in *Duck Soup* and *Why Girls Love Sailors* respectively.

* *Raggedy Rose* (1926)
  Anita Garvin is directed by Stan Laurel in this Mabel Normand film for Hal Roach. Anita plays Janice, the upper class fiancée of the eligible bachelor hero but loses out to working class girl Rose (Mabel Normand) in a reworking of the Cinderella story. In a slapstick sequence Anita is propelled into a bath of water – a foretaste of the Boys' mishap in *Them Thar Hills*.

* *Get 'Em Young* (1926)
  With Laurel taking over Hardy's role due to Hardy burning his arm while cooking a leg of lamb, this film has acquired significance as a stepping stone towards the teaming. Stan is the unwilling bride of a would-be millionaire who has to show up with a spouse at short notice in order to collect a million dollar legacy. The laughs come mainly from the would-be inheritor's valet – played by Stan in knockabout style. There is some funny Karnoesque slapstick as beds slide in the ship's cabin shared by seasick Stan and his employer. Laughs come too as Stan attempts to maintain the dignity of his office despite a running gag which knocks him down. He is unwillingly dragged in to substitute for an absent bride. The combined drag and drunk act develops into a rollicking performance which eclipses Stan's subsequent female impersonations in *Duck Soup* and *Why Girls Love Sailors*. Stan recalled *Get 'Em Young* as the film in which he first used his trademark cry, but earlier examples can be seen in other films. *Get 'Em Young* with Babe Hardy would have produced some very different images. Considerable imagination is required to visualise them, the only clues being his roles in *Slipping Wives* and *Sugar Daddies*.

* *Seeing the World* (1927)
  This curio of fakery and optical effects was filmed mostly in Europe. Our Gang's and Stan's brief contributions were shot in the USA and inserted to give the impression of the whole film having been filmed in Europe. *Variety* reported:

  When Bob McGowan was abroad making shots for future Our Gang comedies with Jimmy Finlayson, he inveigled a number of prominent Europeans to pose with the actor. Unconsciously they posed for scenes which are to be inserted into future Our Gang comedies and the significance of this fact will be pointed out in the sub-titles of these pictures. Those whom McGowan was able to get before his camera were Mussolini, the President of France and the Sultan of Morocco.

CHAPTER 29:
HARDY WITHOUT LAUREL

❋ Hardy appeared in around three hundred films without Laurel. During his early solo film career, prior to his being teamed with Stan Laurel, Oliver Hardy did some writing and directing films besides acting in them. It has been said that no-one ever in films understood the camera as well as he did and he was often asked by producers and directors to give his opinion on their films. Here we look at a few of the films in which he appeared on screen without Laurel.

❋ *Something In Her Eye* (1915)
Babe is one of three paramours of a lady whose eye movements are mistaken for winks. A collapsing chimney gag looks familiar and hindsight reveals a draft for the "crab in the pants" gag from *Liberty*. Two puzzles persist: the identity of the actress (not Billie Rhodes as was at first thought) and the significance of the question mark under her left eye? The lady with something in her eye may well be a female impersonator in view of the large feet, the walk more male than female, the painted eyebrows and apparently a wig.

❋ *A Lucky Strike* (1915)
This Lubin film has Babe in the leading role, striking it rich and looking for a wife. Some bits of business point the way to his later characterisations and his appearance when dressed up to go visiting is not so far removed from that of the "colonel" in *Jitterbugs* twenty-eight years later.

❋ Only three years into his film career, Babe Hardy was teamed with Billy Ruge in the Plump and Runt series. These films were one-reel comedies with 265 pound Babe playing Plump. The Vim film company turned out one a week between February and October 1916. Alas, only five of the thirty-five films produced are known to have survived: *A Battle Royal* (hillbilly Plump joins in family feuding), *The Candy Trail*, *Hungry Hearts*, *Love and Duty* (Private Plump faces a court martial) and *One Too Many* (bachelor Plump requires a temporary wife).

❋ *The Candy Trail* (1916)
Babe, as Plump, rescues his girl from the heavies by following a trail of sweets she has dropped. At the climax there is a hilarious fight scene with Babe disposing of the villains one by one down a trap door, in the style of *The Live Ghost*.

❋ *Hungry Hearts* (1916)
Artist Plump is in love with his model. There are few gags, a shallow plot and some ham acting. What makes it interesting is watching how in Babe's performance he is beginning to develop some of his pantomimic business: the knowing nod, the clenching of fists when realisation dawns, the fastidious gesture and even a fleeting camera look are all in evidence in rudimentary form.

❋ *The Sawmill* (1922)
Among the several films in which Hardy appeared with Larry Semon while working for the Vitagraph and Chadwick companies, this is perhaps the best-known. Semon knew only too well that Hardy was a scene stealer. Semon was sensitive in the extreme about what he considered scene stealing and would not tolerate it in others. But since he applied a perfectionist's touch to his films and knew that Hardy was the best comic heavy available, he seems to have accepted Hardy's proximity. Watch for the typical Hardy "bull run" during the chases and the gags, as in the team films, where he suffers as a result of his own folly: a bullied workman drops a plank on his foot and, in attempting to use his whip on a "dumb bell" lumberjack (Semon), he succeeds in striking himself. Keep in mind *The Hoose-Gow* during the *al fresco* meal which becomes a disaster when a bucket of paint falls on his head – a forerunner of a similar gag in *Towed in a Hole*.

✳ *Golf* (1922)

An introductory title says, "The girl upstairs was prettier than she was cracked up to be," followed by a shot of her face in a mirror, reflected by a crack and distorted. When Hardy enters, he is credited, "With murder in his eye, revenge in his heart and dandruff in his moustache." He proposes to the girl. Another suitor is Vernon Dent, better known as a bit-player in the Three Stooges films. Larry Semon is introduced as "Her brother, who was learning to play on the piano" – he is taking a practice swing as the camera reveals him to be standing on a piano, holding a full set of golf clubs. There are some really clever gags.

✳ *Kid Speed* (1924)

Hardy's role (Dan McGraw, the racing driver rival of the Speed Kid) is pivotal as a foil for Semon and he is on screen sufficiently to steal quite a few scenes. Three years later in *Sailors Beware!* Babe tries to chat up Viola Richard in the same overpowering way as he does here with Dorothy Dwan.

✳ *The Wizard of Oz* (1925)

Larry Semon is the Scarecrow and Oliver Hardy is the Tin Woodman. The costumes are lavish, the trick effects excellent, and there are slapstick gags galore, but most of the original book went "somewhere over the rainbow". It isn't a bad film, just a lost opportunity. Dorothy (in reality Semon's wife, Dorothy Dwan), lives with her aunt

and uncle on their farm. Babe and Larry are farmhands and rivals for the hand of Dorothy, but Dorothy is the rightful heiress to the throne of Oz. Semon's stereotypical black man (credited as G Howe Black!) is scared stiff by a lion and runs frantically with his feet glued firmly to the spot.

✳ *Stick Around* (1925)

Babe was again part of a team, this time with Bobby Ray. *Stick Around* has a two-man firm of interior decorators and a mix-up of wallpaper and circus posters leading to scenes of chaos at a sanatorium. This film contains more pointers to the future Ollie character, the most noticeable being his adoption of a pompous supervisory attitude towards his team mate with the contrast in size being used to comic effect. The "liquor in the water" gag is one of several which are cloned for later Laurel and Hardy films.

✳ *The Perfect Clown* (1925)

Larry Ladd works with Rosie at a broker's office, where business has been good – the brokers are as happy as "a flock of stray cats in a creamery". The boss sends Larry to the bank with a bag containing $10,000. Babe awaits him. There is a chase and a love story, with a twist at the end.

✳ *A Bankrupt Honeymoon* (1926)

Freelancing activities brought Hardy to the Fox Studios where he acted in two films. His days as a heavy were over though the heavy's aggressive streak persists. This two-reeler has him as a taxi driver for an impecunious bridegroom who has an idea for a mobile restaurant. He has to pursue his client for payment of the mounting fare, a situation he reprised the same year in Charley Chase's *Bromo and Juliet*. There are some ingenious gags, pratfalls and a climactic sequence of the runaway "Eat while you ride" bus through the streets of San Francisco. The technical handling is superior to parallel climaxes in *County Hospital* and *The Dancing Masters*.

✳ *Thundering Fleas* (1926)
An encounter with a flea circus (an idea later used in *The Chimp*) leads to a search for one of its escaped members, rendered visible by animation. Attending a society wedding, Our Gang cause disruption by inadvertently letting loose their eponymous companions. The resulting scenes of mass chaos, though less violent, are not far removed from those to come in *You're Darn Tootin'*. Among the afflicted wedding guests are Fin (officiating JP), Charlie Hall (musician), Charley Chase (guest) and Martha Sleeper (bride). An earlier victim is a cop first seen leaning on a fence; as he turns round, lo and behold, it is none other than Oliver Hardy.

✳ *Baby Brother* (1927)
In this Hal Roach Our Gang comedy, Anita Garvin has only a brief scene as a nursemaid for Joe Cobb. She also has a coy boyfriend – Babe Hardy in derby and full moustache!

✳ *Barnum and Ringling, Inc* (1928)
Our Gang stage their own circus in a plush hotel with their motley collection of dressed pets, which run wild. An ostrich enters a room and surprises an inebriated resident – Oliver Hardy! He reacts with a nicely executed double take followed by a backwards faint. Only this brief contribution remains in the film, but an existing production still suggests that Babe originally played in other scenes. This was Babe's last solo film before appearing with Stan in the All Star series. However, his Our Gang contributions extended into the sound era with the use of his voice in *Choo-Choo!* (1932) to provide the yells of the salesman.

✳ The three sound feature films which Hardy made without Laurel strikingly show Hardy's great ability as a talented character actor in his own right and proved that he could have survived as a solo star. . . .

✳ *Zenobia* (1939)
In this low budget Hal Roach film Hardy plays the straight role of a country doctor who becomes embarrassingly involved with Harry Langdon's sick elephant, Zenobia. "Ollie" characteristics such as camera glances and double takes are much in evidence. There is a squashed hat gag, a skit on his size and he even shakes hands unintentionally with his wife. There are statements like, "No levity in this courtroom" and "This is a fine state of affairs" and Hardy sings part of *I Dreamt I Dwelt in Marble Halls* (familiar from *The Bohemian Girl*). Laurel was not in this film, due to contractual squabbles, Hardy's teammate this time being Harry Langdon.[35]

✳ *The Fighting Kentuckian* (1949)
Hardy is cast as a comic sidekick to John Wayne, in the Andy Clyde/William Boyd tradition of "B" westerns but "Ollie" holds our attention: he gives a coy wave with his fingers, hurts his nose, fastidiously removes a speck of dirt from his hat and manages to fall into water.[36]

✳ *Riding High* (1950)
In this Frank Capra film starring Bing Crosby, Babe's cameo appearance is woefully short, but brilliantly funny and at the same time touching. He is a gullible and desperate punter at a racetrack (familiar ground in real life). His name was not listed in the film's credits, for it was the policy of the studio (Paramount) not to give any billing to cameo appearances. Those named though included Rand Brooks (Stan Laurel's son-in-law) and Jackie Gleason (who coined the phrase "the ever-popular Mae Busch").

---

[35] The film's British title is *Elephants Never Forget*.

[36] Wayne offered Hardy a contract as his sidekick in future films, but this was not to be.

Margaret Chute, in Royal Pictorial Magazine *in the early 1930s, said, "Hardy is an expert pianist and he often gets good ideas for pictures and gags when he's playing the piano."*

Stan claimed no musical talent

CHAPTER 30: APOCRYPHAL ANECDOTES?

✳ The world of Laurel and Hardy is a fertile one for questionable stories where printing the legend rather than the facts often took precedence. We advise treating with extra caution the pages of this chapter, especially when the source is a pressbook, a fanzine or a newspaper!

✳ Leo Brooks challenges the story of Oliver Hardy as a child having had a black "mammy". During Brooks's many trips to Georgia he was unable to find anyone who had ever heard of her. There was complete agreement among those whom he interviewed that Mrs Hardy was never in a position during Babe's childhood to be able to afford a servant or a "mammy". All the stories told to Brooks were that she let her children run wild. The US census records of that period listed servants and no servant shows on any of these records as living in the Hardy household. One of Hardy's favourite films was *Gone With the Wind* and the "mammy" was possibly lifted from that film.

✳ Oliver Hardy claimed that, as a child, he toured the South with the Coburn Minstrels; his family said it never happened. He told interviewers that he studied law at the University of Georgia. In fact he never even finished high school. He said his father had been a lawyer, but he was a farmer, railroad construction supervisor and a hotel manager.

✳ Hollywood studio publicists latched onto the Hardy family's belief that they were in some way descended from Sir Thomas Masterman Hardy (1769-1839), made famous at Trafalgar in 1805 by Nelson's supposed last words, "Kiss me, Hardy." Subsequent studies have been unable to find evidence of truth in this claim.

✳ A 1933 pressbook claimed of Stan Laurel:
He is an accomplished athlete.

✳ Some publicity in *Variety*, (5.10.27.) read:
Hal Roach has organised the Hal Roach Studio Orchestra, composed of studio employees, and is personally directing. Roach is a bug on music and wields a mean bow across the fiddle. The first public appearance will be a concert at the Veterans' Hospital in San Fernando, October 2. Personnel of the combo include Hal Roach, director and violin, Oscar Sandberg, assistant director and violin, and Leonard Stevens, manager and trombone.[37]

✳ Billy Gilbert told interviewers that he had to direct *The Music Box*, but could not find anyone suitable for the part of the house owner to whom the piano should be delivered. When he played it to a misunderstanding actor he came across so convincingly that it was decided to give the role of the professor to Gilbert himself. The story can scarcely be true. Gilbert may have helped with the script, but the director was almost certainly James Parrott.

✳ Hal Roach related that Stan and Babe stormed into his office complaining about the script for *The Chimp*. "Who the hell says we have to work a scene with a lion?" Roach calmed them by saying, "Take it easy, boys. This lion will have a trainer to keep it under control." On the set, the trainer instructed the cast and crew not to panic unless he exclaimed, "The lion is out of control!" As the scene went along, the lights and noises confused the lion which, although not enraged, would not obey the trainer. As the director stopped the shooting, he asked what went wrong. The trainer made the mistake of saying that the lion was out of control (meaning that it would not obey orders) but the crew mistook it as a warning that the lion was on the rampage. Everyone went screaming out of the studio. By now the lion "was cranky and refused to go back into its cage on the set." Stan took matters into his own hands (or feet) by walking up to the lion, kicking it square on the behind. He pointed out the cage to the lion and told it to get back in, which the lion slowly did.

In the film "MGM" is always seen in cutaway shots, anyway.

---

[37] The article itself is dated October 4th, *after* the "forthcoming" event.

✳ In the *Old Boys' Cinema Annual of 1933* there is a chapter on Laurel and Hardy along with a story from one of their fans of that time:

> A spinster in Pottsville, Pennsylvania, wrote to Stan and stated that she had been going to picture houses for years and had never missed a Laurel and Hardy comedy. She also claimed that they were so funny that she often laughed until she cried. In fact, the tears and general strain on her eyes from watching their antics had impaired her sight to the extent that she would have to wear glasses. Stan's outgoing mail included a cheque to the spinster for a pair of specs.

At least it squares with Stan's known generosity.

✳ Dorothy Hope wrote in *Film Pictorial* (29.12.34.):

> Dinner with the Laurels at their delightful house "The Laurels" is an adventure. It's also spirited and jolly. The faces of his friends smiled down from their places on the knotty pine walls. Pictures of all your old favourites are there, including Charlie Chaplin, Dan Leno, George Robey and a host of others. Led by Stan Laurel, we all tiptoed out of the den and across the garden, under the deep starlight sky, to where a greenhouse lay gleaming whitely in the mysterious light. . . . In we crept. Stan produced a flashlight. What were we to see? Before us stood only a row of pots, containing

soil and small sprouting leaves. Then, in a reverent whisper, Stan explained, "I have grafted an onion with a tomato so that your salads of the future will be delicately flavoured. In that pot lies a potato grafted with mint, so that your lamb will need no sauce, though the taste will all be there."

Another report said that Stan once crossed a potato with an onion, but even his partner wouldn't risk eating it. Readers loved the personal insights into the lives of the stars. The magazines responded accordingly.

✳ The *Sunday Mercury* (31.7.94.) quoted a story from Ron Hall, nephew of Charlie Hall. Ron recalled a holiday in Blackpool:

> All dressed up, he [Charlie] walked along the edge of a huge outdoor pool, pretending to be drunk. He wobbled up the diving board steps, several lifeguards in pursuit. It was just like a scene from one of his films. Just before he was caught, he teetered on the edge of the board and fell off, creating a huge splash. The lifeguards panicked and fished him out, but it was all a joke. We kids couldn't stop laughing, but he got a right telling off from our grandmother.

✳ Ron told the unlikely story of how his uncle was sacked from Laurel and Hardy films by Hal Roach:

> Once, in the middle of filming, Uncle Charlie, Laurel and Hardy were given time off for a fishing weekend. They must have been having a good time, because they didn't come back for five days. Hal Roach was furious and blamed Uncle Charlie – well he could hardly blame Laurel or Hardy, could he? Uncle Charlie was sacked, virtually ending his career.[38] He never worked with Laurel and Hardy again and only had tiny parts in other films.

---

[38] Hardly. After leaving Roach, in 1940, Charlie continued playing in films until 1956.

Big Business *havoc*

✱ Hal Roach told the story that in making *Big Business* Laurel and Hardy wrecked the wrong house while its owners were on vacation. Stan said adamantly that the story was "a lot of baloney – ridiculous." The owner of the house was an employee of Hal Roach studios and in fact worked on the film as it was being shot, between December 19th and 26th, 1928. He was well reimbursed for the devastation. Note that this actually was Christmas week, disproving Hal Roach's assertion that the film depicts "Laurel and Hardy selling Christmas trees in the Summertime," although that sounds apt work for Laurel and Hardy. A classic case of the legend prevailing – but who can resist a good story?

✱ The *Daily Express* in 1989 said:

Bowler hatted clown Stan Laurel was in another fine mess last night – with Dirty Harry himself. The tough San Francisco cop, alias macho Clint Eastwood, is gunning for British gossips over a bizarre rumour that skinny Stan was his father. The yarn is spreading like wildfire through pubs and clubs all over Britain and no-one knows how it started.[39]

✱ A pressbook for *Pack Up Your Troubles* claimed:

In the cast are more than one thousand veterans of the World War, used in the scenes of the front line trenches.

✱ Publicity material printed at the time of the release of *Babes in Toyland* made the following claim:

Live ferocious crocodiles, from six to nine feet in length, were used. Armed guards stood ready to protect the swimmers.

Watch the film. Crocodiles, yes, swimmers, no!

✱ It also maintained:

Wig makers enjoyed great prosperity during filming. Three thousand different wigs were used in one scene!

✱ An item in a *Saps at Sea* pressbook focussed on Narcissus, the goat in the film. Oliver Hardy allegedly kept a respectable distance from the goat's horns. . . .

He wouldn't accept the trainer's assurances that the goat was not the butting type. All morning and afternoon scenes with the goat were shot and, although Hardy got a crick in his neck from looking over his shoulder, Narcissus never even nudged him. When the sun was dropping, director Gordon Douglas told the hefty actor that he wouldn't be needed any more. Sighing with relief at having concluded the day without any mishaps, Hardy started back for land, pushing past the goat without a second glance. Suddenly there was a shout. There was a splash. There was Oliver Hardy, looking at the goat he had butted into San Pedro Bay.

---

[39] The rumour started five years earlier!

The parody was parodied

✳ One day during the making of *Saps at Sea*, Lucille tripped and fell on a rolled up carpet and hit her head against one of the cameras. She was taken to hospital. Hardy sent her a box of roses and their relationship took off from there. Hardy proposed to her at the Roach studio, even though they had never been on a date, and she accepted. A real-life fairy tale? Leo Brooks says, "I have read many interviews that Lucille gave, including a couple that were never published. I interviewed her twice myself. There is more than enough evidence to make us wonder if their relationship did not begin much earlier than they would have us believe. There was no public announcement of their engagement. In fact Hardy continued to see Viola Morse right up to the marriage. The first Viola and Hollywood knew of the romance was when they read of the marriage in the papers."

✳ While *Sons of the Desert* was being shot, stars and members of the production team themselves organised a fraternal lodge called the Sons of the Desert. Stan was elected "High Factotum" and Babe was voted "Good Night". Director William Seiter was called "Sergeant without Arms".

✳ During Laurel and Hardy's visit to Dudley in 1952 it was stated that Oliver Hardy intended writing the story of their amazing comedy partnership. It was also said that in 1951 he turned down a magazine offer of $35,000 to sell the rights for such a story.

CHAPTER 31: ON TELEVISION

LAUREL AND HARDY FILMS

＊ It is sobering to realise that more people have seen Laurel and Hardy on television than in cinemas.

＊ *Sons of the Desert* was the only feature film on British television during the week 7th till 13th January, 1951. During the same week in 1984, *The Fighting Kentuckian* (with Hardy but without Laurel) attracted an audience of 3.1 millions, making it the tenth most viewed Channel 4 programme of the week.

＊ Among Barry Norman's top three choices for best video of the month in *Film '86* was *Way Out West*.

＊ BBC Television's tribute to Laurel during his centenary in 1990 consisted of two Laurel shorts (*Somewhere In Wrong* and *Roughest Africa*) and two Laurel and Hardy features. It was all most disappointing considering the extensive tributes to Charlie Chaplin during his centenary. There were a few quick words from Barry Norman: "An all-too-short tribute since Stan was grossly superior in all aspects to anything Chaplin could do." Norman's piece featured *White Wings* (a Laurel solo film), *County Hospital* and a couple of shots of Stan in the sixties in his apartment in Santa Monica. But even this tribute was staged to publicise the concurrent release of Virgin Video's *Stan Laurel Centenary Collection*.

＊ As far as we know, Hardy's centenary in 1992 didn't even have a mention on British television!

＊ In the 1990s television screenings of Laurel and Hardy films have been more plentiful in the USA than in the UK. American Movie Classics ran a cable TV "Laughathon" with thirty hours of continuous Laurel and Hardy films in 1995.

DOCUMENTARIES

＊ Mrs Hardy (Gertrude Astor) said to Ollie, "I believe you're going cuckoo" in *Come Clean* in 1931. Forty-three years later *Cuckoo* was the title of a documentary on the Boys, in the BBC's series *Omnibus*.

＊ Granada TV's *Another Fine Mess*, the film of the 1984 International Convention of the Sons of the Desert, was jinxed. An industrial fracas, then a legal dispute over the rights to show Laurel and Hardy films on British television, meant that the programme was not televised until 1989. Overloading the film with extracts of Laurel and Hardy films (40% of the running time of 40 minutes) distorted the balance but a sympathetic and respectful portrait emerged. Granada was the only channel that televised the film.

* *Hollywood Goes to War* (1987) was a two hour documentary devoted to the films shown during the Second World War. The many stars included Laurel and Hardy.

* *The Movies Go To War* (1991), a documentary on Hollywood's contribution to the war effort, seemed to pass off Laurel and Hardy's contribution with the sole mention that Stan "took to the roster with Alfred Hitchcock". Then, as the credits rolled, viewers were rewarded with a glimpse of the rare footage referred to simply as *The Autobiography of a Jeep* (mentioned in Chapter 26).

* On the *South-Bank Show* in 1991 comedian Steve Martin expressed his love for Laurel and Hardy to the accompaniment of an excerpt from *The Stolen Jools*.

Clive James in Fame in the Twentieth Century *(1993) gave timely recognition of Stan and Ollie in* Bonnie Scotland

COMEDY

* A 1974 episode of *The Goodies* had the zany trio involved in some old-time film making with some excellent impersonations of Laurel and Hardy. Although never seen in extreme close-up, the likenesses were impressive, especially "Ollie", but the action was untypical of the Boys. Many of the gags were taken from Buster Keaton's *Sherlock Jr* and *Steamboat Bill Jr*.

* In the *Hancock* episode entitled *Lord Byron Lived Here* from the 1950s, Tony Hancock reprimanded Sid James after a failed ploy, "That's another fine mess you've got me into." Hancock's comparability with Laurel and Hardy was noted in the *Omnibus* tribute to Hancock in 1986.

* In Steptoe and Son's *Seance in a Wet Rag and Bone Yard* from the 1960s, a medium claimed to be able to contact Stan Laurel. Albert Steptoe did a passable impersonation of Stan crying.

* In *Blackadder Goes Forth* (1990) one was struck by Officer Darling's resemblance to Fin – actor Tim McInnery's squint and leer were delightful.

* In one sequence in the 1980s series *'Allo 'Allo*, Rene and his wife Edith were flown to London by the RAF. They were told to report to Churchill and the only clothes that could be found were dark suits and bowler hats. "Churchill" noted that they "looked like Laurel and Hardy."

* In *Cool Head* (1991), impressionist Phil Cool had "Prince Charles", among others, singing *The Trail of the Lonesome Pine*.

* The strangest "appearances" of the Boys were revived (in 1991) in *The Best of Tommy Cooper*, when an Ollie lookalike walked on and off the stage unexplained. It happened on two separate programmes.

✻ On Alexei Sayle's *Stuff* (1991), Alexei pointed to a large picture of Stan and Ollie and called them two of his heroes.

✻ *The Morecambe and Wise Show* in 1993 had Jack Jones doing an impersonation of Laurel and Hardy.

✻ In *One Foot in the Grave* (1993) Victor Meldrew described having his accident prone brother stay with him as like "living with Stan Laurel for a fortnight".

✻ *Funny Business* in 1992 had Rowan Atkinson analysing comedy. He threw in clips of Laurel and Hardy in *Towed in a Hole, The Music Box* etc.

✻ In 1994 *Benny Hill – Unseen* offered the very last comic sketches Benny recorded before his death in 1992. During a lengthy sketch there were seen, very clearly and several times, string puppets of Stan and Ollie hanging on a wall.

✻ *Red Dwarf* (1994) had an episode in which Stan Laurel appeared as a character in a kind of theme park, in which "good" characters (including Stan) competed against "bad" characters (led by Adolf Hitler).

✻ In Britain's longest-running comedy series *Last of the Summer Wine*, when Clegg and Compo were being lectured by their pompous friend, Foggy, in 1992, they looked at each other, Compo scratched his head and Clegg twiddled his tie, in true Stan and Ollie fashion. In an episode in 1995, when Nora Batty was proudly wearing a new hat and another lady appeared wearing an identical hat, *The Dance of the Cuckoos* was played. Lois Laurel was making a cameo appearance as the other lady. The moment was fleeting and easily missed were it not for the music.[40]

✻ In a kitchen in an episode of *Friends* (1996) there was a poster of Stan and Ollie.

---

[40] Lois's dialogue was, "Come on, let's go", words also spoken to the Boys by warder Tiny Sandford in *Pardon Us*.

✻ There have been several references to Laurel and Hardy in *The Two Ronnies*. And Ronnie Barker and Roy Castle (as Stan and Ollie lookalikes Sid and Harry) were in *Another Fine Mess*, part of a series called *Seven of One* in the 1980s. There was a sketch with a floozie, straight from *Come Clean*. Many modern variations on Laurel and Hardy lines added to the charm. For example Sid told Harry that he did not like oranges, so Harry asked him why he bought oranges. Sid replied, "What do you expect me to do, starve to death?"

CARTOONS

✻ Kenny Everett's animated space parody called *Captain Kremmen* (1978) had Laurel and Hardy lookalikes.

✻ Some were surprised to see *Birds of a Feather* in 1988 next to the names Laurel and Hardy in programme listings, but then discovered this was the title of a Laurel and Hardy cartoon. Was Larry Harmon, who made the cartoon, aware that the Boys performed a stage sketch with that title?

✻ Stan and Ollie appeared as puppets in 1990 on *Spitting Image*, digging the British side of the Channel Tunnel. There were several bits of Laurel and Hardy "business" – Stan lighting his thumb, bricks falling on Ollie's head, Stan crying and, "Here's another fine mess you've gotten us into." Another *Spitting Image* show in 1991 used the Stan and Ollie puppets to demonstrate inefficiency in airport security.

Spitting Image

✳ Dan Castellaneta, who provides Homer's voice in the 1990s cartoon series *The Simpsons*, says that Homer's "Doh!" was copied from James Finlayson.

DRAMA

✳ *Another Fine Mess* was the title of a 1983 episode of the detective series *Matt Houston*. Larry Harmon and Chuck McCann played Laurel and Hardy impersonators who had fallen on hard times. They took a job as henchmen for, believe it or not, a Charlie Chaplin impersonator. Harmon and McCann impersonated Laurel and Hardy only once or twice in the show, while performing in a comedy club.

✳ ITV's *Minder* film shown at Christmas in 1985 had some Laurel and Hardy pots in a living room.

✳ An episode of *Columbo* in 1991 had a pair of dogs named Laurel and Hardy as the villains in a murder case!

✳ *X-Files* (1996) had a fellow who dreamed of his body decaying to a skeleton. Towards the end of the programme a television set showed the freak skeleton ending with Stan and Ollie in *The Bullfighters*. One cult meeting another!

✳ In the mini series *Mussolini* (1987) Mussolini was seen wearing a bowler hat. He looked in a mirror and laughed, saying, "The only people still wearing bowler hats are the American comedians Laurel and Hardy." This was supposed to have taken place before October 1926 so its accuracy is questionable.

QUIZZES AND GAME SHOWS

✳ In 1984 *Film Buff of the Year* set, as one of its speciality subjects, the films of Laurel and Hardy. The twosome were always included in the animated titles at the beginning of the programme.

✳ *Looks Familiar*, revived in 1984, had a generous clip from *Below Zero* as the "advert-bridger".

✳ In *Odd One Out* in 1985 one of the coveted prizes on offer was a set of Laurel and Hardy storage jars.

✳ In *Pop The Question* in 1986, more by accident than otherwise, the contestants discovered that there was a connection between *The Trail of the Lonesome Pine* and *The Equals*.[41]

✳ The game show *3-2-1* in 1987 had a Laurel and Hardy routine performed by two dwarfs called the Minitones.

✳ A runaway winner on *Mastermind* in 1988 was Tom King, a freelance writer from Essex. His chosen subject was The Lives and Films of Laurel and Hardy. There was a tie for first place in the semi-final, Tom losing only on passes.

✳ In 1990 Howard Parker took part in a television quiz show entitled *The 64,000 Dollar Question*, hosted by Bob Monkhouse. His chosen specialist subject was Laurel and Hardy. On another game show, *Gag Tag* in 1996, host Monkhouse wore a Laurel and Hardy tie.

✳ Wendy Fairie distinguished herself on *You Bet!* in 1991 by identifying five Laurel and Hardy Roach films from a snippet of dialogue. Wendy correctly identified all the films and gave the year, without a moment's hesitation. Off camera, host Matthew Kelly revealed that she had answered all fifteen questions correctly during rehearsals.

---

[41] The Equals had a hit record in 1968 called *Laurel and Hardy* and, of course, *The Trail of the Lonesome Pine* was a hit for Laurel and Hardy in 1975. The Equals' record peaked at number 35 in the charts, but Stan and Ollie reached number 2.

SOAPS

✳ In 1986, behind the bar of the Queen Vic pub in *EastEnders*, could be seen a beer mat with Stan Laurel on it. Later in the year the milkman whistled *The Dance of the Cuckoos*. In 1995 the heads of Laurel and Hardy were seen quite clearly on the wall of one of the houses.

✳ In *Brookside* in 1986 Sandra had a postcard of Laurel and Hardy on her wall. Stan Slade filmed with *Brookside* in 1996, dressed as Stan Laurel, in a line dance competition when everyone else was dressed as cowboys.

✳ In *Emmerdale* in 1992 Mr Turner, played by Richard Thorpe, dressed as Ollie at a fancy dress party. He said, "You attend to your work and I'll attend to mine," and, "I have nothing to say," as well as, "Here's another fine mess." Someone had obviously been watching *Dirty Work*.

✳ In *Prisoner: Cell Block H* a poster of Laurel and Hardy appeared for months in 1995 in the recreation room. In one episode that year two inmates were compared with Laurel and Hardy because they were always arguing.

CASUAL APPEARANCES

✳ A photograph of Stan and Ollie adorned the setting of the *Bob Monkhouse Show* in 1984.

✳ On the programme *Television* (1985) Ken Russell was interviewed, for no obvious reason, against a background of Stan and Ollie in *Towed in a Hole*.

✳ On *The Southbank Show* in 1985 profiling Michael Crawford, Michael sported a Laurel and Hardy T-shirt.

✳ *TV-AM*'s Giles Brandreth appeared in 1986 wearing a yellow and black Laurel and Hardy jersey.

✳ Over Christmas 1984 Laurel and Hardy were in *A Century of Stars* (an affectionate look at the Water Rats).

✳ During the televised wedding of Prince Andrew and Sarah in 1986, as an army of police went past the thousands of spectators, *The Dance of the Cuckoos* could be heard from the crowd.

✳ The video of Alison Moyet singing *Love Letters* on *The Chart Show* and elsewhere in 1987 showed models of Laurel and Hardy on a shelf.

ENDPIECES

✳ A 1985 celebration show for VE Day made reference to Laurel and Hardy via one of the fifties singers.

✳ A Stan Laurel competition on *Saturday Superstore* in 1985 was set up by Roy Castle.

✳ On *Surprise Surprise* a woman's ambition came true in 1986 when she lived out her fantasy of being in the middle of a custard pie fight in Laurel and Hardy style. The biggest cringe came in 1984 when Cilla Black and Christopher Biggins sang *The Trail of the Lonesome Pine* on the show.

✳ The Sons of the Desert appeared on *Harty Goes to Edinburgh* in 1986. Russell Harty kept them firmly in the background as nine years previously, live on television, he had received an unexpected custard pie in the face from the Sons of the Desert. Once splattered can only mean twice pie-shy.

✳ The crying scenes from *Big Business* were used as advertisements for part of the Water Board shares sale in 1989.

From the flicks to the "Happy Editor's" desk

CHAPTER 32: FILM FUN

❊ The *Film Fun* comic without Laurel and Hardy is difficult to imagine, but the weekly comic started publication in 1920 and ran ten years before Stan and Ollie appeared. Initially they occupied the centre spread, but in 1934 they were moved to the front and back pages.

❊ In the *Yorkshire Evening Post* dated November 1993 John Morgan recalled Laurel and Hardy's roles in *Film Fun*:

> Laurel and Hardy were always hard up. They used to stand outside the Hotel de Posh and stare like a couple of Bisto kids at diners, in dinner jackets, tucking into mounds of mashed potatoes from which sausages stuck out like chapel hat pegs. Corks flew from bottles marked "pop" and showered swells who held ribboned boxes with "chocs" printed on the lids. You could fairly see our heroes drooling at the mouth as they gazed at the sumptuous scene.

❊ In 1934 *Film Fun* contained the story of *Fraternally Yours*, which was the title in the UK of *Sons of the Desert*. The opening paragraphs were an account of a meeting of Oasis Number 13, the oldest lodge in the great order known as the Sons of the Desert. It was in special session and the Grand Exalted Ruler was addressing the assembly, "Every one of whom wore a red Turkish fez and a gold-and-purple sash over one shoulder."

❊ *Film Fun* never paid for the right to use a comedian's name or character. According to the book *The Wonderful World of Film Fun*, when Laurel and Hardy visited England on one occasion, Bill Wakefield, who drew their strip, was expressly forbidden to go near them in case they asked for money.

❊ In 1937 a special supplement entitled *The Laurel and Hardy Book of Wisecracks* was given away in a bumper edition of *Film Fun*. The supplement contained the first fourteen drawings of Laurel and Hardy by Bill Wakefield's son, Terry. The supplement has since become a near legendary collector's piece and is so scarce that only four copies are known to exist in the world today. Terry Wakefield recalled, "It was mid-afternoon when I was summoned to editor Fred Cordwell's office to find him a trifle put out that he had to have the fourteen thumbnail illustrations the next day. The offer was £7, with ideas supplied, which was excellent money in those days and I jumped at it."

When the Film Funsters, the now defunct London outpost of the Sons of the Desert, was established in 1976, it was Terry Wakefield who drew the crest on their membership card

❊ Denis Gifford wrote obituaries to Terry Wakefield in *The Guardian* and *The Independent* on 30th September, 1989:

> He was the son of Billy Wakefield, who himself was one of the leading comic artists of the day. He left school at the age of 14 to become his father's assistant. On leaving the army in November 1945, Terry was asked to take over Laurel and Hardy for *Film Fun*. It was a series Wakefield had frequently helped out on, and he was now to continue Stan and Ollie's adventures right to their final appearance in the issue dated 15th November, 1957.

Holding Stan's birth certificate in the Laurel and Hardy Museum is Bill Cubin

Just one of the hundreds of photographs in the Museum shows Stan, Lucille and Babe relaxing outside the Roach "Lot of Fun"

CHAPTER 33:
ULVERSTON AND THE MUSEUM

✳ *Loaded* magazine in January 1998 said:
Ulverston in Cumbria could be any other town, really. There is a Woolies, an Oxfam shop and a bookies. But then it all gets a bit odd. For some reason there's a lighthouse, even though the town is almost five miles from any coastline. There's also a bypass that goes right through the centre of town. A café in the centre closes for lunch and, until recently, the place had the most pubs per person in England.

✳ The Laurel and Hardy Museum in Ulverston consists of a couple of rooms of seventeenth century origin. It was the brain-child of the late Bill Cubin, who, as mayor, had a plaque placed on the house where Stan Laurel was born, at 3 Argyle Street in Ulverston. Bill managed to save some of the furniture from the house before it was modernised and this started an ever-expanding collection of memorabilia, which includes hundreds of pictures and letters. When wall space ran out, Bill simply papered the ceiling! First opened in 1976, the Museum had several "official" openings, one by Jeffrey Holland, "Spike" of television's *Hi-Di-Hi*, and another by Bella Emberg.

✳ One visitor captured the atmosphere perfectly:
While I was visiting the museum in Ulverston, a family with young children came into the museum's miniature cinema. Bill suddenly donned a mortar board and gown, made us practise *Good Morning To You* and then, while showing the corresponding clip from *Pardon Us* in the cinema, kept his "class" in order with a timely tap of his cane. So began our enjoyable lesson. Those young persons sure listened and, who knows, thanks to "Sir" they may well take up Laurel and Hardy as their chosen subject.

✳ Bill's wife Lucy recalled her visit to the first Sons of the Desert convention in Chicago in 1978. "Bill stood up at the front, told everybody about Ulverston's connection with Stan Laurel and invited all four hundred delegates back to Ulverston to stay with us. I could have killed him."

✳ When Her Majesty the Queen visited Ulverston in May 1985, Mayor Bill Cubin presented her with a copy of the book *Laurel Before Hardy*. The Queen's expressed interest doubtlessly stems from her father, King George VI, who was an avowed Laurel and Hardy fanatic. *Putting Pants on Philip* was not shown!

✳ Not content with his world-famous Laurel and Hardy Museum, in 1986 Bill Cubin bought a double decker bus which he started to convert into a travelling Stan and Ollie showcase. Putting a new meaning to "Laurel and Hardy on Tour", Bill planned to tour Britain, but his plans did not materialise.

✳ In 1991 Bill was seen using a wooden toilet seat, which had once belonged to Stan Laurel's grandmother, as a drinks tray in Ulverston's Rose and Crown pub. The *Daily Star* (22.10.92.) reported: "A loo used by comedian Stan Laurel is to be moved from his former home in Ulverston to the town's Laurel and Hardy Museum."

✳ In 1985 a lengthy feature article on the Laurel and Hardy Museum appeared – believe it or not – in the *South China Star*!

✳ In 1990 the population of Ulverston was swelled by an estimated five thousand visitors, intent on commemorating Stan Laurel's centenary. There were tours of Ulverston, taking in locations associated with Stan's childhood, and Laurel and Hardy films in the town's cinema. It was estimated that the Sons of the Desert Grand Parade involved more than 1,500 members. It remains the largest massed gathering of the Sons of the Desert.

✳ It is sometimes suggested that, because of the propensity for macabre movie closings in Laurel and Hardy films, Laurel had a dark sense of humour. He told a reporter, "You should see the lighthouse in the graveyard at Ulverston . . . where I was born. They put it up when I was a kid – a tombstone with a light on top. It was the Eighth Wonder of the World to me. Ever since then it's been my ambition to have a tombstone like that!"

✳ Born in Ulverston, Harry Ingle became a fan as a young boy. Years later, during the 1939-45 World War, Harry contacted Stan Laurel. "I was in the navy in San Diego and I telephoned Stan in Hollywood," Harry explained. "When he heard I was from Ulverston he wanted to visit me but I was in port for only twenty-four hours." Harry did meet the great man four years later, when Laurel and Hardy visited Ulverston. Harry proudly declares that he attended Lightburn School in Ulverston in the 1920s. The school was built on the site of Spencer's Gaff, where Stan Laurel's father and mother, Arthur (AJ) and Madge, acted out melodramas on the stage.

Ulverston's most famous son

CHAPTER 34: SONS OF THE DESERT

BLESSED FREEDOM

✳ John McCabe, founding father of the Sons of the Desert, explained, "I conceived the idea of a Laurel and Hardy appreciation society that was specifically not a fan club but a group of buffs. Fanatics are fans and vice versa and buffs are discriminating in the things they like and dislike. Laurel and Hardy made some rather dreadful films. Rare, but they made them. So we have this group which is not a social organisation in the usual sense of the word, but it is an act of satire of social organisations. Stan approved it for that reason and we had a deliberately nonsensical constitution, to which he added." The first meeting of the Sons was in New York in May 1965.

✳ Says McCabe, "The Sons of the Desert was founded in the same spirit as the namesake Laurel and Hardy film it honors: to kid regular social organisations, to satirise such things as officers and offices and boards of directors and taking oneself solemnly in the midst of all that fraternal whoop-tee-do. The Sons of the Desert's structure is that it has no structure. That is the blessed freedom of it. That is the key point of the fun of it."

✳ Stan Laurel had another choice of name initially for the international appreciation society about to be formed. He favoured "Boobs in the Woods".

✳ Worldwide there are around a hundred and fifty "tents" (branches) of the Sons of the Desert, almost all named after a Laurel and Hardy film.[42]

---

[42] Send a SAE to the publisher of this book for a current listing of UK tents.

TENT TRIVIA

✳ At one of the Sons' earliest gatherings in Britain, the Hull Film Theatre announced "An Evening with Laurel and Hardy" on 14th and 15th December, 1972. The first two films, *The Lucky Dog* and *Two Tars*, had a piano accompaniment from a seventy-seven year old lady called Cora Acum, who had played the piano for thirty hours at a Buster Keaton festival earlier in the year!

✳ Denis Gifford's Film Funsters were an early tent – London's "All Star Outpost". Honorary Officers in the club included Bob Monkhouse as Vice Sheik (that is to say, the sheik in charge of vice), Eric Morecambe as an Honorary Stan and Ernie Wise as an Ollie. Syd Little was a Stan and Eddie Large an Ollie; Roy Castle was a Stan and Ronnie Barker an Ollie; Harry Secombe was an Ollie, while Peter Cushing, the only member who actually played in a Laurel and Hardy movie (*A Chump at Oxford*), was a Stan.

✳ Which tent has the oldest age group of members? In 1992 the Why Girls Love Sailors Tent in Joliet, Illinois had over one hundred members and the average age was 84 years. One of the members used to play the organ in a large movie palace, as a young girl, and remembered playing for the old Laurel and Hardy silent films when they came to Chicago theatres.

✳ Ian Richardson, a teacher at a large comprehensive school in the suburbs of Hull, started to show a Laurel and Hardy two-reeler every second Friday, to an audience of some thirty pupils and a good few staff! In 1990 they formed a tent. Dougie Brown did something similar in Stranraer in 1997.

✳ At one time the Sons of the Desert converged annually on Clitheroe for a civic reception and film show. So great was the laughter at the film show one year that one member lost his teeth!

✳ At a Liverpool meeting the projectionist told the audience that the film would be followed by a written quiz, with valuable prizes, so that they would all have to pay attention. The audience were relieved when the projector halted after only a few frames. In true Laurel and Hardy fashion, it was a vacuum cleaner that eventually saved the day when testing the electrical circuits!

✳ The Laughing Gravy Tent in Yorkshire had a waiting list for would-be members! They went eight years with no vacancies.

✳ The Leave 'Em Laughing Tent entered a Laurel and Hardy float on the Liverpool Mayor's Parade and on several occasions won trophies. They also won first prize, for the best float, at the Liverpool Festival Garden Parade in 1984.

✳ Part of one tent's constitution said, "We do not object to teetotallers. We just don't understand them."

✳ Dave Beecroft had a regular spot on the radio, discussing beer etc. He suggested the formation of a tent and in May 1979 the tent was launched in the main studio at Radio Leeds as part of a *What's Brewing* transmission. Around forty Laurel and Hardy followers were in the studio and the atmosphere was electrifying.

✳ At one Sons of the Desert meeting four members produced the sound effects (water, walking, glass breaking, dog noises, etc) for the film *Early to Bed*.

✳ The Beau Hunks Tent of Seattle meet in the Beau Hunks Bijou, a six-car garage that has been converted into a mini theatre.

✳ Atop the letterhead of the Dancing Cuckoos Tent of Detroit once stood the great seal of the Unicorn Hunters, a group founded by Bill Rabe at Lake Superior State College as "an excuse to do any silly thing that crosses his mind".

✳ The Constitution of the Sons of the Desert states that officers "shall have absolutely no authority whatever". Officers have various titles, the leader of each tent being known as Grand Sheik.

✳ When the Laughing Gravy Tent of Birmingham held an evening during which members were invited to bring along their favourite bits of memorabilia, items on show included Laurel and Hardy sculptured in soap, a salt and pepper set, a pair of mugs, money boxes, glove puppets, autographs and even a pair of Stan Laurel's socks! Proud owner Grand Sheik John Ullah had won the socks in a raffle.

✳ In the Doris Day Pet Foundation's Newsletter Doris expressed her thrill at being presented with a Laughing Gravy Award. A framed and matted still was presented to the foundation, featuring Laughing Gravy, the celebrated canine which was banished by the heartless landlord in the film which bears the dog's name.

✳ One issue of the tent newsletter *The Spooktator* had a map of the London Underground, but with names like Thicker Than Bayswater, The Battle of the Sudbury, Lord Paddington, Shepherd's Mae Busch, A Chump at Oxford Circus and Way Out Westminster.

✳ Grand Sheik John Burton was travelling by train from Doncaster to Berwick, wearing a *Fra Diavolo* T-shirt. An old lady who was seated across from him kept looking at him without saying a word. As the train approached Newcastle she rose to leave and said, "I've been wanting to do this since you got on the train. . . ." She performed the kneesie-earsie-nosie routine[43] and left!

---

[43] Kneesie-earsie-nosie was a game played by Laurel in *Fra Diavolo*. It involved slapping his knees, touching his ears and pulling his nose in sequence – a tricky piece of co-ordination. Many Sons of the Desert can do it well.

* The Beau Chumps Tent of Sunderland made a home movie called *Chumps at Blackpool*, which clocked up forty-eight laughs during its nine minutes.

* Spied on the menu at a Sons gathering at the Beech Hill Hotel in Bowness on Windermere: "McLaurel's Mackerel – grilled fillets cooked on bed springs and served with tomato and anchovy butter."

* When Sons showed some Laurel and Hardy films at a residential home one of the residents uttered, "Oh poor Stan," at one of the scenes. The lady had not been known to speak a word for several months before this!

* Grand Sheik Brian Clarry made a 4,387 kilometre round-trip from Durack in Australia to meet some of his Melbourne members.

SCHOLARLY SONS

* In 1986 a large plaque was unveiled on the King James 1st Grammar School in Bishop Auckland, where Stan was a boarder and pupil. The church where Stan was christened was the setting for a special service for Stan. The Sons of the Desert nominated Stan Laurel for a Cinema 100 plaque, which resulted in another ceremony in Bishop Auckland in 1996 for the unveiling of a plaque at King James School.

* Australian Sons of the Desert had a memorial plaque placed on the site of Mae Busch's birth, in Melbourne, Australia. The plaque is fixed to the fence at 56 Page Street, Albert Park. The house was offered for sale in 1994 and the fact that Mae Busch was born there was included in sales notices.

* In a poll Sons were asked if they preferred Laurel and Hardy sound or silent films? 41 said, "sound", 2 said, "silent" and 46 had no preference. When asked if they preferred Laurel and Hardy shorts or feature films, 37 voted for shorts, 1 for features and 51 had no preference.

* The Way Out West Tent of Los Angeles have an on-going survey of favourite Laurel and Hardy films, with votes from their members and from surfers of the Internet. At a count in 1998 the favourite feature was *Sons of the Desert* (with 38% of the votes), the favourite sound short was *Helpmates* (36%) and the favourite silent short was *Big Business* (41%).

SONS ON SHOW

* The Sons of the Desert occasionally have trouble with their image in the media and are pictured as mindless freaks with funny hats, cracking up as soon as a pie flies through the air. The silliest television misrepresentation was in *Walk Me Home*, a British-German production. It had fans screaming and dancing in the light of a projector's beam on their night out!

* *The Herald*'s Jack McLean tried to analyse the Sons of the Desert, attesting:
    It is not hard to see why Stan and Ollie have their own society. They were simply the best. People, otherwise thought sensible, do ridiculous things when it comes to Laurel and Hardy.

* The *Blackpool Evening Gazette* (3.5.86.) reported on a Sons of the Desert convention in Blackpool in 1986:
    "It's all very silly," chuckled a rather plump and chirpie chappie, bedecked in a bright, red fez, as he fiddled with a TV set.

✳ At a gathering in 1987 a *Sun* reporter sensed a sensational angle and interviewed one of the participants. "I see you had dwarf-throwing this morning. Did you have any protesters and did the dwarf get hurt?" The reporter was reassured, "There were no protesters and the dwarf never even cried out when the fiftieth competitor swung him violently around her head and threw him forty yards, whereupon his right arm fell off." The reporter scribbled enthusiastically, then stormed off angrily when introduced to the dwarf – a three foot rag doll!

✳ *Network* is the quarterly magazine of the Inland Revenue. The January 1990 edition ran an article beginning thus:

> The latest affliction to strike staff in tax offices in the North West is L&H syndrome. Sufferers can now attend a therapy unit (or tent) that meets regularly in Manchester.

✳ The Sons of the Desert have a Laurel and Hardy Charity Fund, to which tents and individuals make voluntary donations. Causes to have benefited range from Age Concern and Children in Need to Motor Neurone Disease and Cancer Relief. Part of the satisfaction lies in the enjoyment of staging special Laurel and Hardy film shows and other events as fund-raisers. The Fund is administered by Nancy Wardell, who is Stan Laurel's cousin.

✳ In addition to the Charity Fund many tents and individuals make donations directly to many causes.

✳ The first Internet tent, based in the USA, was the Hog Wild Tent, so called because, like Stan and Ollie in *Hog Wild*, the organisers had "the hardest time putting up a simple line of communication!" They report, "Membership is unofficial. As in *Atoll K*, there are no laws, no passports and no taxes! Meetings run twenty-four hours a day, seven days a week. Members are urged to view Laurel and Hardy films at their leisure, alone or in groups and to share their thoughts and opinions with others visiting the tent." They aim to "turn the information highway into the finale from *Two Tars!*" The Laurel and Hardy Website was rated among the top five percent of all sites on the Internet by Point Survey (a service which rates and reviews only the *crème de la crème* of Cyberspace).

CONVENTIONS

✳ At a convention in 1986 in the USA Sons passed out coupons for "free" breakfasts, which they typed in advance on hotel stationery. The hotel honoured them!

✳ During a convention in Sunderland the most common complaint heard by the hotel manager was, "I ordered a room with a southern explosion!" [44]

✳ At a conclave in Saint Paul in 1988 the programme notes sounded intriguing: "Frustrated by childhood piano lessons? Or just envious of Billy Gilbert's *Music Box* tirade? Here's your chance to make Another Fine Mess." Standing by a piano was the reincarnation of Professor Theodore von Schwarzenhoffen, bellowing at Stan and Ollie to move it away. Then came a magnificent display of piano wrecking and Sons were invited to take a whack at an upright.

---

[44] The line was used by Stan Laurel in *Any Old Port*.

* At another convention, one child's mother, curious at seeing Stan and Ollie lookalikes, inquired, "I hope you don't mind me asking, but are you accountants?"

* Silly[45] games are fixtures at conventions, examples being Swiss Miss Cheese Rolling, Any Old Port Pool Ball Game, Helpmates Plant Pot Throwing and Call of the Cuckoos Wheelbarrow Race. Pee Wee[46] is a perennial.

* At a 1996 convention nearly all five hundred of the delegates met on the upper deck of a cruise ship to pose for a group photo. They all wore sailor outfits and this was the first time so many Sons had been together identically dressed.

---

[45] The word "silly" in Old English means "blessed".

[46] The game of Pee Wee was played by Stan in *Babes in Toyland* and involved hitting a piece of wood with a stick, the object being to make the wooden piece travel as far as possible.

EUROPE

* Laurel and Hardy Club enthusiasts from Belgium, Czechoslovakia, France, Netherlands and Spain travelled to Paris for their first convention in 1936. These pioneers were the first to pay corporate homage to their screen idols on European soil. MGM not only sponsored the event (to publicise the European release of *The Bohemian Girl*) but also paid the expenses of the conventioneers. World War 2 terminated the Laurel and Hardy Club and nearly six decades would elapse before their successors, the European tents of the Sons of the Desert participated in a second such celebration.

* In fact the Sons of the Desert held two conventions (in 1993 and 1995) in a disused monastery in Rolduc, Kerkrade, Netherlands, attended by hundreds of international guests from Belgium, Czechoslovakia, England, Germany, Italy, the Netherlands, Scotland and the USA. But where were the French, long professed admirers of *Loréléardi*?

* The calm of the cloisters contrasted with the conviviality in the former wine cellar now converted into a bar, appropriately named The Prodigal Son. Lines from one of Laurel and Hardy's stage sketches came to life thanks to a lively recreation by Ray Saunders and Simon Wooff: "I'm sorry, sir, but you see, he can write but he can't read." And the stain glassed windows survived the threat of a Pee Wee contest.

* The location for a public film show in Valkenburg was billed in the programme notes as a "Romantic Open-air Theatre". A steadily increasing downpour drenched the five metres high screen and the spirits of all but a few hardy souls willing to sit through *Sons of the Desert* to the end title. The audience identified with the dilemma of the rain-drenched Stan and Ollie on the roof and claimed a new record for dedication in the watching of Laurel and Hardy films.

✳ In 1968 the Laurel and Hardy Foundation was established in the Netherlands. Its principal aim was to maintain and enlarge the possibilities for the screening of the films of Stan and Ollie in the Netherlands. Three years later the Laurel and Hardy Foundation joined the Sons of the Desert, under its new name of The Perfect Day Tent. It became the first overseas tent.

✳ Peter Mikkelsen reports one of the truly big moments of his membership of the Sons of the Desert was finding a copy of *Why Girls Love Sailors*: "I had for years been interested in finding this once lost film. I got in touch with MGM here in Denmark, with a negative result. I tried the American Film Institute. Again nothing came out of it. Local advertisements did not do any good either. One day an American Son was kind enough to give me the address of a European collector. Since *Duck Soup* had been found (in 35mm) in Belgium, I had a hunch that Europe might be a good place to look for these films. The European collector turned out to be a very dedicated and cooperative man. Yes, he did have a 16mm print of *Why Girls Love Sailors*. If I would like a video copy, I had only to mention it to him. I don't think that I have ever written a letter so fast in my life."

✳ A professional cartoonist known as "Merho", Robert Merhottein contributes a comic strip to a daily Belgian newspaper and features the adventures of a cartoon character called Kiekeboe who bears more than a passing resemblance to James Finlayson. What is more, Stan and Ollie are in one of his albums. Also involved is a Laurel and Hardy film buff who provides a mouthpiece for Sons of the Desert publicity.

Robert Merhottein drew a cartoon strip depicting his visit to a Sons of the Desert UK Convention in 1989

CHAPTER 35: BONNIE SCOTLAND

✳ There are plenty of Scottish connections: two films with Stan but without Ollie, *Hoots Mon* (1919) and *Short Kilts* (1924), two Laurel and Hardy films *Putting Pants on Philip* (1927) and *Bonnie Scotland* (1935), four visits to Scotland (1932, 1947, 1952 and 1954), the presence of Fin, that dour Scot, in many outstanding Laurel and Hardy moments and with Stan in many Roach silent comedies. And there is a Scottish piper among the immigrants to *Atoll K* (1951).

✳ Stan Laurel's father, Arthur Jefferson, is listed in a Post Office directory of 1905 as Managing Director of the Metropole Theatre in Glasgow.

✳ The Jeffersons lived in Glasgow in Prince Edward Street, off Victoria Road; 17 Craigmillar Road, Battlefield; 42 Buchanan Drive, Rutherglen and 185 Stonelaw Road, Rutherglen. Queen's Park in Glasgow was the local secondary school for Stan, then Rutherglen High School, also known as Stonelaw School.

✳ The Panopticon Theatre in the Trongate, Glasgow was where Stan made his first public appearance in 1906. The theatre had a varied history until it closed in 1938. Today the building is Grade B listed and plans are underway to re-open the theatre as a museum. Fred Lawrence Guiles writes:

> A small, working-class audience is gathered in the Panopticon, a tavern-sized auditorium in Pickard's Museum, watching indulgently as a skinny, coat-tail-flapping youth bounces on stage from the wings. He has the baggy pants, red nose and knotty cane umbrella of the popular music hall hayseed comic. The entire act was squirrelled from months of watching others, one chestnut after another. Stan Jefferson is eager to please and the all-male audience is generous. They smile and even laugh. A few men in the adjoining penny arcade, looking for at least a glimpse of ankle in the penny flickers, hear the laughter and leave the machines. The boy's smile widens with innocent joy. Stan will not project total confusion until he is more sure of himself.

✳ Stan Laurel's mother, Madge Metcalfe, died in Glasgow on 1st December, 1908 at the age of fifty. She was buried at Cathcart Cemetery in Glasgow. An obituary read:

> Prior to her marriage, she was not in any way theatrically connected and it speaks volumes for her abilities and energy to find that she soon afterwards played the leading "heavy" roles in her husband's plays. Her most important part was Olga Snake in *Bootblack*, in which she excelled. In addition to acting she proved an invaluable aid to her husband in the decoration schemes for his various theatres and play staging and he attributes much of his early success to her artistic taste in that affection as well as to her business tact.

✳ The Scottish village built for *The Little Minister*, a Katherine Hepburn movie, was also used in *Bonnie Scotland*. Mary Gordon was in both films. When Stan and Ollie ask her to give them a room and a bath she retorts, "I can give you the room, but you'll have to take the bath yourself." Mary Gordon was born in Scotland in 1882 and also appeared in *Pick a Star* and *Way Out West*.

✳ A lady died while watching *Bonnie Scotland* in Aberdeen. She laughed so much that she choked on a piece of popcorn.

✳ Scottish Television got hold of the completely erroneous story that, when Stan Laurel died, his body was returned to Scotland.

✳ When the Edinburgh Playhouse reopened
as Scotland's new international theatre in
September 1993, the lead item in a
commemorative publication recalled the
appeal of the theatre in its early days and
read:

> Laurel and Hardy provided a milestone
> when, in 1932, they appeared in person
> to launch their latest lark, *Laughing Gravy*.
> Police reserves were called out to deal
> with the crowds. Not content with
> appearing on stage, the twosome insisted
> on getting a panoramic view of the city
> from the roof.

*Per head of population, Scotland
has more tents of the Sons of the Desert
than any other country*

"Now there's a panoramic vista!"

CHAPTER 36:
INFLUENCES AND CONNECTIONS

✳ Buster Keaton used the same bus in *The Cameraman* (1928) that Piedmont Mumblethunder and Philip boarded in *Putting Pants on Philip*. The number (501) can be clearly seen in both films on the side of the bus.

✳ In Harold Lloyd's *Feet First* (1930) was a sequence which was obviously inspired by Stan's altercation with a rope in *Liberty*, which was made a year earlier. The difference here was that Lloyd used a fire hose which was cut; Stan's rope merely ran out. In the cast were Laurel and Hardy perennials James Finlayson, Arthur Housman and Noah Young.

✳ Thelma Todd became a comic foil for Groucho Marx in the tango scene of *Monkey Business* (1931) and the boating scene of *Horse Feathers* (1932). Leo McCarey directed the Marx Brothers' *Duck Soup* (1933), the title of which was taken from the earlier Laurel and Hardy short and in it Harpo and Chico did Laurel and Hardy's hat switching routine with Edgar Kennedy. In another scene, there was a revamped version of the door gag as used in *Early to Bed*. William Seiter (director of *Sons of the Desert*) also directed the Marx Brothers' *Room Service* (1938). Who would have expected to see

Was Marilyn Monroe's famous scene in The Seven Year Itch *(1955) homage to* Putting Pants on Philip *(1927)?*

Walter Woolf King, the composer of operettas in *Swiss Miss*, cast or perhaps miscast, as a "baddie" in *The Marx Brothers Go West* (1940), which was inspired by *Way Out West*?

✳ Two items in Mae West films sounded like reprises from Laurel and Hardy films: *Belle of the Nineties* and *Sons of the Desert* (both 1934) used the "all of me" gag[47], while *Every Day's a Holiday* and *Way Out West* (both 1938) included the sale of the Brooklyn Bridge to the gullible.

✳ In the Olsen and Johnson film *All Over Town* (1937), James Finlayson was MacDougal and Stanley Fields (the sheriff in *Way Out West*) played "Slug". The director was James Horne, who directed twelve Laurel and Hardy films.

✳ In the Will Hay film *Hey! Hey! USA* (1938), the spoiled brat was played by Tommy "Butch" Bond, who played a similar part in *Block-Heads*, as the kid with the football which was booted down the stairs.

✳ Will Hay's *Old Bones of the River* (1938) had a sequence in which the revolting natives were subdued by spreading tacks over the ground of the fort as in *Beau Hunks*.

✳ The Walt Disney cartoon *Pinocchio* (1940) had the vocal talents of Dick Jones (child extra in *Babes in Toyland*) as Pinocchio and Charles Judels (cheese shop owner in *Swiss Miss*) as Stromboli.

✳ When Disney remade *Babes in Toyland* in 1961, there was little resemblance to the Laurel and Hardy film. Disney's Silas Barnaby was hardly menacing and his singing and dancing were difficult to accept compared to Henry Brandon's odious leer and melodramatic laugh. The pair who mimicked Stan and Ollie were this time Barnaby's assistants.

---

47 "I'm from . . ." "What part?" "All of me!" The gag was still going strong when Spike Milligan used it on television in 1996.

* The Abbott and Costello film *Lost in a Harem* (1944) featured a large body of Arabs, who had the nerve to call themselves Sons of the Desert – one of whom was Adia Kuznetzoff (the chef from *Swiss Miss*). A sentry was played by Eddie Dunn (a convict in *Pardon Us*).

* *Way Out West* was reflected in a 1952 Columbia short, mentioned in the trade magazine *Exhibitor*:

   Rootin' Tootin' Tenderfeet: Max Baer and Slapsie Maxie Rosenbloom are seen in a sort of brief western burlesque with emphasis on slapstick. The boys are out west looking for an heiress to whom they have to deliver a deed. A saloonkeeper, to whom the heiress is a slave, gets his wife to pose as the heiress, and the boys hand her the papers. The rest of the footage is taken up with their efforts to get them back and into the hands of the rightful person. Fair.

* In the Henry Fonda film *Twelve Angry Men* (1957) a juror was explaining why he decided the young man was not guilty when one of the other men in the room started to whistle the Laurel and Hardy theme tune.

* Incidents in *A Shot in the Dark* (1964) had blueprint moments in Laurel and Hardy films. . . .

   Police car draws up, Inspector Jacques Clouseau (Peter Sellers) steps out and trips into the fountain in front of the house. Echoes *The Midnight Patrol*.

   Clouseau puts a key into a drawer, forgets to remove it and rips his trousers. Echoes *Twice Two* and others.

   A suit sleeve is ripped off. Echoes many Laurel and Hardy films.

   Playing billiards, Clouseau rips the playing cloth. Echoes *Brats*.

   Benjamin Ballon (George Saunders) miss-cues on hearing Clouseau's name. Echoes *Any Old Port*.

   Clouseau and Ballon have cues which get mixed up under each other's arms, like the guns in *Beau Hunks*.

   Clouseau opens door, makes statement and proceeds to walk into wall behind door. Echoes *Blotto* and others.

Man riding bicycle is forced off the road and into a pond. Echoes *Men o' War*.

   Clouseau rips his trousers as he bends down to do Russian dance and has to walk out with Maria Gambrelli (Elke Sommers) doubled in one pair of trousers. Echoes *You're Darn Tootin'*.

   After Kato (his little yellow friend) attacks him, Clouseau is left sitting in an open doorway, but is hit in the back by the returning door. Echoes *Perfect Day*.

   Clouseau and Ballon hit their heads together as they bend down. Echoes many Laurel and Hardy films.

   In the finale, when Clouseau as about to name the killer, in the mayhem he looks straight into the camera, pleading to the director for sanity, as Ollie did in many films.

* Peter Sellers visited Stan Laurel for tea during Stan's retirement years. Because of his admiration for Stan, Peter based the character Chance in the film *Being There* (1979) on a mixture of his own real-life gardener and Stan.

* In the 1966 version of *Stagecoach* the sound engineer mentioned in the credits was Elmer Raguse, a name frequently featured in the titles of Laurel and Hardy films.

* Beryl Reid is remembered as an Ollie lookalike in the film *The Killing of Sister George* (1969).

With Suzannah York as Stan

✱ *The Comic* (1969) was superficially based on Stan's life. Carl Reiner, who made the film, had asked Stan for permission to film his life, but had been refused. After Stan's death, Reiner made the film with Dick Van Dyke in the star role, about the sadness of an aged comedian's last days. He cashed in on a widely held misconception of Laurel's last days.

✱ *Myra Breckinridge* (1970) was one of the "turkeys" of the cinema. This tawdry concoction exploited old Hollywood favourites through film clips and scattered throughout the film were fleeting, but totally irrelevant, glimpses of Laurel and Hardy in *Great Guns*.

✱ *A Clockwork Orange* (1971) prominently used bowler hats.

✱ Bill Forsyth's first film, *That Sinking Feeling* (1979), had some very Laurel-like pantomime and pathos and there was one scene where a warehouse night watch-man was kept occupied by the hero, who led a spirited song and dance of *At The Ball, That's All* from *Way Out West*.

✱ The Clint Eastwood film *City Heat* (1984) with Burt Reynolds had continual "Stan and Ollie" name calling sequences – Eastwood was nicknamed "Ollie" and Reynolds was "Stanley".

✱ Steve Martin and John Candy in *Planes, Trains and Automobiles* (1987) employed a classic partnership like Stan and Ollie with continuous comic disaster, including the wrecking of a car.

✱ Ray Bradbury's affectionately poignant short story, *The Laurel* and *Hardy Love Affair* (1987), told of a romance built on affection for Stan and Ollie. A real-life relationship was blended with Stan and Ollie connections, including tie twiddling and frequent visits to the steps used in *The Music Box*.

✱ *Midnight Run* (1988) starred Robert De Niro and Charles Crodin as a wisecracking duo in another love-hate relationship of non-stop fighting and making up, in Laurel and Hardy style.

✱ In the film *Parenthood* (1989) starring Steve Martin there was a close-up of a man's hand apparently joining together two halves of a thumb, an obvious copying of Stan's hand trick in *The Bohemian Girl*.

✱ The end of the film *Copycat* (1995), starring Sigourney Weaver and Holly Hunter, had to be refilmed because the stars looked like Laurel and Hardy!

✱ *The Nutty Professor* (1996) was a remake of the Jerry Lewis 1963 film. There were plenty of "fat man" jokes and the professor (Eddie Murphy) did an embarrassed tie fumble. His adversary Reggie did a spectacular "scissors jump" which would have made Stan proud.

✱ The *Daily Mail* (7.3.97.) reported that Tom Cruise and John Travolta were planning to star in a film homage to Laurel and Hardy. Not a remake of one of the Boys' films, it was described as having the essence of their style and featuring two bumbling American cab drivers.

Men about town – on vacation?

CHAPTER 37: ON TOUR

1932

✳ On completing filming of *Pack Up Your Troubles*, by late spring, 1932 Laurel and Hardy decided it was time for a holiday. Stan wanted to visit his native England and Babe fancied the golf courses of Britain, so they arranged their first visit together to these shores. The response they received altered all holiday plans and their visit became a whistle-stop tour.

✳ "We came here on vacation," said Laurel, "but it's turned out to be the hardest work we've ever had in our lives." Hardy added, "We don't mind that. We'd do anything to show our gratitude to filmgoers over here. We never expected all this enthusiasm."

✳ On a visit to the New Oxford cinema in Manchester, where inevitably there were large crowds, they managed to enter comparatively freely, leaving their taxi before the onlookers realised who were in it. Their exit, however, was not so easy and they were mobbed in the aisle. As they emerged into the street a surging mass forced them back inside.

✳ The throng in front of the Metropole Hotel in Blackpool refused to disperse until they saw Laurel and Hardy on the balcony. Once the pair showed their faces, there was a cheer and the crowd grew even bigger. Later nine thousand people packed the Baronial Hall of the Winter Gardens.

✳ In Leeds Stan had a family reunion as he met his aunt and uncle, Mr and Mrs John Shaw, and their daughter Mary. At the city's Majestic cinema, which was overflowing with around a thousand people, Stan and Ollie's appearance on stage was the signal for a deafening roar and continuous applause. Unable to make themselves heard, the comedians began to go through some of their familiar mannerisms, which brought increased laughter from the delighted audience.

✳ Following a week in which he had not found time to take so much as a practice swing, Hardy's golfing ambition was finally fulfilled when the duo visited Scotland. On being requested to demonstrate his prowess with a golf club, Hardy gave a reporter a few tips. Most people of eighteen stone would be severely hampered by their size, but Babe seemed blissfully unaware of his bulk – which is confirmed by his eight handicap. Hardy always took his golf seriously and, as well as dressing immaculately, prepared for the game by bandaging his fingers, rather like a boxer does before putting on his gloves.

✳ As the comedians' train pulled into Glasgow's Central Station, the whole place was a mass of screaming, hysterical fans. Stan and Babe were led by the police down an alleyway, heading for the safety of the Central Hotel. With the fans in pursuit, the situation became more frightening and several people received severe injuries as a heavy stone balustrade gave way under the weight of the crowds. People were crushed by the débris and one person fell under a passing train. Another fell down an open manhole.

✳ After newspaper coverage of the incident in which Laurel and Hardy barely escaped with their lives, on their arrival in Glasgow, one unimpressed reader wrote, "Sir, I read with amazement the accounts in several papers of what took place at the arrival of two film stars. I am led to believe that thousands of people took part in a huge scrimmage to see the passing of two men and that some eight people were injured, fortunately with no very serious results. Surely there are other things for people to think about than two film stars?"

✳ Some people insist that they saw the Boys on stage in Aberdeen. Their contention has been strengthened by the existence of a signed photo of the two which was once on show at His Majesty's Theatre in the city. In the thirties the manager, J J Donald, was a big fan of Laurel and Hardy. While on holiday in Hollywood, he was invited to a star-studded party by Paulette Goddard. She told him that among the guests would be her husband, Charlie Chaplin, as well as Stan Laurel and Oliver Hardy. Mr Donald armed himself with a picture of his two heroes and got them to sign it that evening. It later took pride of place in his theatre, where it confused many.

✳ When Laurel and Hardy left Britain for France, they thought things would be quieter, but once again their fans were waiting. As soon as they arrived in France they were mobbed and the crowds even followed them into the customs office, where an indignant official tried unsuccessfully to stop photographs being taken.

✳ During their trip to the British Isles, Laurel and Hardy's reception was intense everywhere they went. For the first time they realised that they were big time movie stars. In many ways the Boys were as naïve as the characters they played on the screen. They returned from their trip and went straight back to work as if nothing had happened. As the world's greatest comedy team, the Boys had tremendous leverage to do whatever they wanted, yet neither of them nor their agent Ben Shipman appeared to know how to use that leverage. They even meekly let Henry Ginsberg dock their pay for the period they were gone.

1947

✳ It was through Lord (Bernard) Delfont that the Boys were given the chance to come over to the British Isles and play the music halls in 1947. Stan Laurel, his wife Ida and Oliver Hardy sailed on the Queen Elizabeth. Ida was seasick all the way, but Stan enjoyed the journey. Lucille Hardy was recovering in California from a minor operation, but recovered sufficiently to join her husband on tour.

✳ *Pathé News* interviewed Laurel and Hardy when they arrived in England.
Interviewer: Now you're over here again, what are you going to do?
Hardy: Well we're going to do some personal appearances and also a picture.
I: What's the picture going to be called?
Laurel: *Robin Hood* I think.
I: Are you going to see any relatives over here?
L: I'm going to visit my dad, my sister and a few cousins.
I: Anything special you want to do over here, Oliver?
H: Nothing, but . . . try . . . and make the people happy and . . . [to Stan] will you keep quiet a minute . . . have a good time and have everyone else have a good time. [To Stan] I'm talking to the gentleman. Will you be quiet just a moment. . . . Now I think that after a couple of weeks we might. . . . [To Stan] What is it?
L: You're standing on my foot!

✳ There was a commotion in Leamington town centre when Laurel and Hardy strolled into Woolworth's in search of some "real English shopping". They were mobbed by fans, who brought the store to a standstill. Stan and Ollie were told, in a good-humoured parting shot from the manager, never to return.

✳ In June Laurel and Hardy were back in Blackpool. Hardy rested himself against a balcony railing. "Don't lean on that railing," quipped Laurel, "or we'll all be on the promenade! Can't you see the headlines? 'Hardy falls off balcony at Blackpool – crushes twenty!' "

✳ The press announced, "After a few more appearances at provincial theatres, they plan to tour the Continent, visit South Africa and perhaps Australia. Next year they will be returning to this country to play in pantomime." They didn't!

✳ Leo Robson recalled that there was a toilet that the artists used and many had etched messages and graffiti on the walls. Newly etched on the door was a message from Stan, who had been there the week before.

✳ On their way to see Laurel's eighty-six-year-old father at Barkston, they took the opportunity after lunch at the Red Lion Hotel of practising at darts. First, however, they sought instruction from Willie Gillison, a local sportsman, who obliged with one throw which hit fifty. Hardy turned to leave but Laurel stared at the board and eventually persuaded his partner to accompany him with a throw – which they made from about two feet!

✳ Also on the agenda was a tour of the Standard Motor Company's works at Canley, during which Hardy downed two giant mugs of canteen tea.

✳ It was during the 1947 tour that the Boys became members of The Grand Order of Water Rats. Fred Russell proposed Laurel and Will Hay proposed Hardy.

✳ Norman Wisdom tells how Laurel and Hardy came to watch his show and Stan offered to step in for Norman's injured partner. But the theatre manager wouldn't allow it. Norman also recalls appearing on a charity show at the Victoria Palace when Stan and Ollie topped the bill. The friendship with Stan endured, with Norman visiting him in Hollywood.

✳ When the Boys reached Glasgow, Hardy had lost forty-three pounds. This he put down to the physical effort required in doing thirteen shows per week.

Laurel and Hardy were invited to Lauder Ha' in Lanarkshire and met the great Scots entertainer Sir Harry Lauder

✳ During one performance, however, Hardy jokingly inferred that his weight loss was due to the severe rationing – still in force following the Second World War. This outraged one member of the audience, who wrote to the local newspaper berating this American visitor who had the audacity to demean the food the British were offering him. The complainant went on at length to describe the comfort of the hotels in which the duo stayed, compared to the war-time conditions in which most of the British public were still living. He pointed out that the British had endured these conditions for seven years, whereas Hardy had been here for only four months. The remark was immediately dropped from the act, and some weeks later when the subject of Hardy's weight loss again came up, Babe commented, "It's all due to hard work. Rationing doesn't worry me. I'm a light eater anyway."

✳ Stan White had the pleasure of serving Laurel and Hardy and their wives at the Grand Hotel in Manchester when they were appearing at the Palace Theatre. He recalled that a taxi arrived at the front entrance to take Laurel and Hardy to the Palace, Hardy stood outside the taxi and the whole street erupted with cries of "Ollie, Ollie". The big man just waved in appreciation.

✳ On 13th September Laurel and Hardy were taken to the Poolstock Motorcycle Raceway in Wigan, where they were driven round the track, waving to more than eight thousand spectators. They presented a trophy to speedway aces Ronnie and Oliver Hart.

✳ A gala reopening of the smallest public railway in the world, a fifteen-inch gauge track across the Romney Marshes in Kent, was combined with the railway's twenty-first birthday. Laurel and Hardy agreed to come down to perform the opening ceremony and ride on the train. No expenses were required. All they asked was to be fetched from London and returned in two hired cars in case one broke down, as they could not risk missing "curtain up" at the theatre. The spontaneous acts of comedy were well received. The cars were not needed as Stan and Ollie returned in the General Manager's saloon on what was then the Southern Railway.

✳ On 3rd November the Royal Variety Performance at the Palladium in London featured Laurel and Hardy with a piece especially written for the night. The King opined, "We haven't laughed so much for years."

1952

On board the
Queen Mary

*With Jack Ritchie,
Assistant Picture
Editor of the*
Glasgow Herald
*during the Boys'
appearances at the
Glasgow Empire*

✳ A reporter had this to say about an appearance in Liverpool:

The Empire was packed, people standing five deep at the back and down both sides of the theatre. The lights dimmed and the building was as black as the inside of a bowler hat in a cellar. A spotlight lit one corner of the stage; just five notes of a signature tune; the top of the bill act hadn't appeared yet, but the ovation was thunderous. Then "They" walked onto the stage and the theatre trembled with the clapping and the cheering. Stanley smiled and scratched his head. Oliver wiggled his tie. They could have finished on that. Never before or since have I known an audience show such love and affection. It was too much for Ollie. He cried. A memory to be placed in a golden box.

✳ Another reporter said:

Stan Laurel and Oliver Hardy strike a familiar, but still amusing, note in a sketch which incorporates all the familiar gestures and situations. Mr Laurel and Mr Hardy favour American humour and the supporting programme may, perhaps, have been designed to maintain balance. But there appears to be a preponderance of acts in which, though the names are not familiar, the material is.

✳ Peter Morris recalled:

At the end, Babe stepped into the footlights and said, "Stan and I hope you enjoyed our little bit of nonsense and we thank you kindly." They thanked us!

*A hat from the local Odeon and fish and chips
from the local "chippy" kept Stan happy when
they visited Cardiff*

✻ "Compere" in *The Sunderland Echo* said: To have emulated the style of Danny Kaye, or even the brisker and less ingenious slapstick of Abbott and Costello, would have been a betrayal of their reputation. The material they use seems like a chunk of film script; if people nowadays find it feeble and unfunny it is only because the funniest things about Laurel and Hardy films have always been Laurel and Hardy. Nobody cared then what the films were about and those enthusiasts who learned to recognise and appreciate their particular brand of humour won't fail to miss it in their stage appearance now.

✻ A Manchester reporter interviewed Ida and Lucille to find out what it was like to be married to two of the world's greatest funny men. "Lots of headaches," said Ida. "Lots of fun," said Lucille and continued, "Bossy? Impatient? Why he's so thoughtful and considerate. He taught me to cook. Babe gets up first every morning to make the coffee. He grows our own fruit and vegetables and is a lot of help with preserving and canning." The reporter observed that Mrs Laurel and Mrs Hardy were fans of British fish and chips, "in a newspaper of course – much better." Mrs Laurel continued, "Life with Stan is not lugubrious. He, the one who has been pushed and bullied around the screen all our lives, is quite bossy at home and he's good at getting his own way! He won't even let me sing opera. You see, he likes jazz!"

Lucille, Babe, Ida and Stan

✻ In Coventry Hardy told reporters that he and his wife were thinking of settling down in Warwickshire. It never happened – Hardy often used this line when on tour!

Left and top of page on stage in A Spot of Trouble

1953/54

✳ On national radio in 1987 Lord Delfont explained, "The first place I booked them for was the Newcastle Empire. I remember I paid them £1000 a week, which in those days appeared to be an astronomical salary and they wondered if I could make it pay. But the place was packed from top to bottom. Wherever they went, they were packed out."

✳ Lord Delfont continued, "Stan loved talking about comedy. Oliver was a serious, thinking man. He was quite religious. He used to read the Bible every morning in bed. They were quite different in character.

✳ Laurel and Hardy arrived in Ireland on 9th September, 1953. As they pulled into Cobh harbour, just outside Cork, the four of them, Stan, Babe, Ida and Lucille were on deck, leaning over the railing. Suddenly they noticed tiny boats all around, blowing whistles, and people shouting, "Laurel and Hardy! Laurel and Hardy! Laurel and Hardy!" They waved at the crowd and all the boats in the harbour blew their whistles. The entire children's population of Cobh played truant from school. They blocked all the traffic and, despite the presence of amused policemen, they clung onto Laurel and Hardy.

Arriving in Cobh

✳ The carillon bells of St Coleman's Cathedral played *The Dance of the Cuckoos*. Laurel and Hardy looked at each other and wept.

✳ Later they set off to kiss the Blarney Stone. The walk up the many steps in the castle was too much for Babe and only Stan was willing to be held by the guide and lowered over the parapet to kiss the stone. Hardy said, "Nobody would hold me. I'm too big."

✳ Hardy argued with Harry Deane, who was one of Cobh's most famous personalities, about who was the heavier. They struck a bet and went to be weighed. Babe was always one for a wager; he lost by a few ounces.

✳ Harry Worth appeared on their bill in 1953. He recalled Hardy sitting in his dressing room rolling his own cigarettes. "They took an interest in all acts and they took an interest in me particularly because they liked my style. By the time I was appearing on those bills, I'd introduced two or three minutes of patter before I brought on my ventriloquist dolls. I used to talk about myself and what I was going to do. It struck them as funny and Hardy said, 'Now, you develop that style. The vent is OK, but comedy might get you somewhere.' Eventually it turned out that it did!"

✳ Steve King attended a dinner in Hull, held in honour of Laurel and Hardy in December. He recalled, "I remember that Stan was a diabetic and was drinking only water. Babe suffered badly with circulation trouble in his legs, but I found him to be the perfect gentleman. He was easier to approach than Stan, simply because you were somehow made aware that Stan was the genius and the brains behind the team and you respected him for it. I was amazed that Stan replied to all his letters in person. He had thousands. He told me that he wouldn't have been where he was without his fans and if they took the trouble to write, the least he could do was reply in person, if only to write once."

✳ King continued, "On the last night at the Palace Theatre in Hull Babe climbed to a dressing room which was six floors up, to ask the dancers to sign their autograph books. 'We always like to get the signatures of everyone that Stan and I have worked for.' Note that he did not refer to them as working for Stan and Ollie, but rather Stan and Ollie working for them, as if it was their show! When Babe descended the stairs, the stage manager, Ted Hunter, said to Babe, 'Mr Hardy, you shouldn't have climbed those stairs with your bad legs.' To which came the reply, 'But Stanley and I wanted the young ladies' autographs.' 'They would gladly have come to you, or one of my men could have asked them for you,' replied the stage manager. Babe looked a little shocked. 'Oh, no. I was asking the favour, therefore it was up to me to approach them.' I think that sums up the wonderful people that Stan and Babe were."

✳ In view of his earlier links with Glasgow, Stan Laurel must have felt neglected when the only newspaper coverage was an interview with Hardy. The article contained some very dubious "facts". Ramsden Greig, of the *Evening Citizen*, on asking Hardy what he had been doing since his last visit to Glasgow, claimed he replied, "The Babe is preparing to make a millionaire of himself. So is Stan Laurel. It all depends on the result of a court action we have set going in America. Our earlier pictures are making a fortune for a group of business men who bought them from our producer, Hal Roach. Roach paid us a flat fee to make these films. There was no such thing as working on a percentage of the takings in those days. Roach sold the films when he went broke. Now these oldies are being shown in Continental cinemas and on Continental television and we don't get a dollar from the profits. If we win our case we will get several million dollars in back fees." [48]

✳ Elizabeth Stephenson met Laurel and Hardy when they were on stage at Her Majesty's Theatre in Carlisle in April. She says simply that they were "fantastic." She recalls that Babe had a sore throat and that his trousers were fastened by a safety pin!

---

[48] The most important point of this case is that, at the time of making their films, Laurel and Hardy did not negotiate television residuals, as this medium was very much in the future. This is probably the reason for the action failing.

Alf Ellsworth MBE was a good friend of the manager of the Glasgow Empire and had his photograph taken with Laurel and Hardy when they played there in 1954

✳ Laurel and Hardy visited Hull's docks. Two dockers working in the hold of a ship have spoken of seeing the Boys looking down at them from the bridge. One said to the other, "Hey, look, there's Laurel and Hardy." They both waved. With that Stan laughed down at them and did that famous scratch of the head.

✳ Laurel and Hardy called at the Bull Inn in the Nottingham village of Bottesford. The landlady was Stan's sister, Olga Healy. They found time to have Christmas dinner at the Bull and even served behind the bar. There is a story that Stan and Ollie gave a brief performance at the Bull, in a back room, for a few patrons. It is also erroneously claimed that Laurel and Hardy slept in the Bull Inn.

Programmes from the Edinburgh Empire

─── PROGRAMME ───
for week commencing MONDAY, APR. 28th, 1952

1. OVERTURE   -   - *The Empire Orchestra*

2. MERLE & MARIE -   -   - *Open the Show*

3. LORRAINE   -   - *Singing Cartoonist*

4. THE KENWAYS -   -   -   - *Aerialists*

5. "DAISY MAY"
The Captivating Starlet
Assisted by SAVEEN

6. NEWMAN TWINS   - *Novelty Contortionists*

INTERMISSION
THE EMPIRE ORCHESTRA
Under the direction of BOBBY DOWDS

FULLY LICENSED BARS
in all parts of the Theatre
FAVOURITE PROPRIETARY BRANDS
at POPULAR PRICES
WHISKY   GIN   PORT & SHERRY
2/-   1/9   2/-
BEERS & MINERALS AT MODERATE PRICES

7. MERLE & MARIE   -   - *Frivolous Feet*

8. THE SKATING SAYERS   - *Thrills on Wheels*

9. JIMMIE ELLIOTT   -   - *Animal Mimic*

10. MACKENZIE REID & DOROTHY
Scottish Accordionists

11. Bernard Delfont presents
**STAN   OLIVER
L A U R E L and H A R D Y**
in "A SPOT OF TROUBLE" .
A Comedy Sketch in Two Scenes
Locale: A Small Town in the U.S.A.
Scene 1: Waiting Room at the Railway Station
Scene 2: The Chief of Police's living-room
Officer (a small town cop with a mind smaller
than the town) .... Leslie Spurling
The Chief of Police (a fiery blustering type)
Kenneth Henry
Two Gentlemen en route   STAN   OLIVER
LAUREL and HARDY

The Management reserves the right to refuse admission to the Theatre, and to change, vary or omit, without previous notice, any item of the programme

PROGRAMME
for week commencing MONDAY, 12th APRIL, 1954
(Usual Performances on Good Friday)

1. OVERTURE   -   - *The Empire Orchestra*

2. JILL, JILL & JILL   -   - *Dance Time*

3. ALAN ROWE -   - *Born to Impress*

4. URSULA & GUS   - *Continental Jugglers*

5. BOBBIE KIMBER
Compere from T.V.'s "Music Hall"
with Augustus Peabody

6. DEREK ROSAIRE
presents his Wonder Horse
"TONY"

INTERMISSION
THE EMPIRE ORCHESTRA
Under the direction of GORDON L. ROLFE

7. JILL, JILL & JILL   -   - *More Rhythm*

8. DUNN & GRANT   - *Acrobatically Funny*

9. DOROTHY REID & MACK   - *Accordionists*

10.
BERNARD DELFONT
presents
**STAN   OLIVER
LAUREL & HARDY**
Assisted by
GORDON CRAIG, LESLIE SPURLING
and JOHN SULLIVAN
In their latest comedy entitled
"BIRDS OF A FEATHER"
In Two Scenes
Note: There is a lapse of several hours between
Scenes 1 and 2
Manager and Stage Director......Jack Whitmore (for Bernard Delfont)

11. BETTY KAYES and her PEKINESE PETS

The Management reserve the right to refuse admission to this theatre, and to change, vary or omit, without previous notice, any item of the programme

Drawing by Tony Bagley

CHAPTER 38: EPILOGUE

✻ The characters Laurel and Hardy portrayed had as many layers as an artichoke. First they were bumbling, accident-prone incompetents, upon whom havoc settled at the simplest act. Beneath this were layers of dauntless dignity, hopeless heroism and wistful sadness with, deepest of all, a dash of the devil. Now the fiddle and the bow can play no more. Time has ended the concert. And the world is beginning to realise how much it loved fat Oliver and skinny Stan.[49]

---

[49] Robert Youngson in his compilation film *When Comedy Was King* (1960).

✻ In a book on US radio and television personality Joe Franklin, Sandra Andacht says, "Stan once told me that he wanted to write a book about Laurel and Hardy called *Two Minds Without a Single Thought*. Unfortunately he never did." But the title lives on in the Latin motto inscribed on the Sons of the Desert escutcheon.

✻ The Hal Roach studios went bankrupt in 1959. They were demolished in 1964.

✻ In 1961, at the insistence of many Hollywood comedians, Stan Laurel alone was awarded an honorary Oscar. While appreciating the tribute, he regretted that it came four years after Hardy's death. It would have gladdened him more if the two could have shared the halo.

The Boys in
A Spot of Trouble

APPENDIX 1:
CHRONOLOGICAL LISTING
OF LAUREL AND HARDY FILMS

Listed here is the title used in the original American release, followed by the date of the first release in America and a description. All feature and featurette films have sound.

Lucky Dog, The	1921	Silent short
Forty-five Minutes from Hollywood		
	1926	Silent short
Duck Soup	1927	Silent short
Slipping Wives	1927	Silent short
Love 'Em and Weep	1927	Silent short
Why Girls Love Sailors	1927	Silent short
With Love and Hisses	1927	Silent short
Sugar Daddies	1927	Silent short
Sailors Beware!	1927	Silent short
Second Hundred Years, The	1927	Silent short
Now I'll Tell One	1927	Silent short
Call of the Cuckoos	1927	Silent short
Hats Off	1927	Silent short
Do Detectives Think?	1927	Silent short
Putting Pants on Philip	1927	Silent short
Battle of the Century, The	1927	Silent short
Leave 'Em Laughing	1928	Silent short
Flying Elephants	1928	Silent short
Finishing Touch, The	1928	Silent short
From Soup to Nuts	1928	Silent short
You're Darn Tootin'	1928	Silent short
Their Purple Moment	1928	Silent short
Should Married Men Go Home?		
	1928	Silent short
Early to Bed	1928	Silent short
Two Tars	1928	Silent short
Habeas Corpus	1928	Silent short
We Faw Down	1928	Silent short
Liberty	1929	Silent short
Wrong Again	1929	Silent short
That's My Wife	1929	Silent short
Big Business	1929	Silent short
Unaccustomed As We Are	1929	Sound short
Double Whoopee	1929	Silent short
Berth Marks	1929	Sound short
Men o' War	1929	Sound short
Perfect Day	1929	Sound short

They Go Boom	1929	Sound short
Bacon Grabbers	1929	Silent short
Hoose-Gow, The	1929	Sound short
Hollywood Revue of 1929, The		
	1929	Feature
Angora Love	1929	Silent short
Night Owls	1930	Sound short
Blotto	1930	Sound short
Brats	1930	Sound short
Below Zero	1930	Sound short
Rogue Song, The	1930	Feature (colour)
Hog Wild	1930	Sound short
Laurel-Hardy Murder Case, The		
	1930	Sound short
Another Fine Mess	1930	Sound short
Be Big!	1931	Sound short
Chickens Come Home	1931	Sound short
Stolen Jools, The	1931	Sound short
Laughing Gravy	1931	Sound short
Our Wife	1931	Sound short
Pardon Us	1931	Feature
Come Clean	1931	Sound short
One Good Turn	1931	Sound short
Beau Hunks	1931	Featurette
On the Loose	1931	Sound short
Helpmates	1932	Sound short
Any Old Port	1932	Sound short
Music Box, The	1932	Sound short
Chimp, The	1932	Sound short
County Hospital	1932	Sound short
Scram!	1932	Sound short
Pack Up Your Troubles	1932	Feature
Towed in a Hole	1932	Sound short
Their First Mistake	1932	Sound short
Twice Two	1933	Sound short
Me and My Pal	1933	Sound short
Fra Diavolo	1933	Feature

185

Midnight Patrol, The	1933	Sound short	Way Out West	1937		Feature
Busy Bodies	1933	Sound short	Pick a Star	1937		Feature
Wild Poses	1933	Sound short	Swiss Miss	1938		Feature
Dirty Work	1933	Sound short	Block-Heads	1938		Feature
Sons of the Desert	1933	Feature	Flying Deuces, The	1939		Feature
Oliver the Eighth	1934	Sound short	Chump at Oxford, A	1940		Feature
Hollywood Party	1934	Feature	Saps at Sea	1940		Feature
Going Bye-Bye!	1934	Sound short	Great Guns	1941		Feature
Them Thar Hills	1934	Sound short	A-Haunting We Will Go	1942		Feature
Babes in Toyland	1934	Feature	Tree in a Test Tube, The	1943		Sound short (colour)
Live Ghost, The	1934	Sound short				
Tit for Tat	1935	Sound short	Air Raid Wardens	1943		Feature
Fixer-Uppers, The	1935	Sound short	Jitterbugs	1943		Feature
Thicker Than Water	1935	Sound short	Dancing Masters, The	1943		Feature
Bonnie Scotland	1935	Feature	Big Noise, The	1944		Feature
Bohemian Girl, The	1936	Feature	Nothing But Trouble	1945		Feature
On the Wrong Trek	1936	Sound short	Bullfighters, The	1945		Feature
Our Relations	1936	Feature	Atoll K	1951		Feature

APPENDIX 2:
LAUREL AND HARDY'S FOREIGN FILMS

Night Owls 2 reels
   Italian: *Ladroni* 4 reels
✔ Spanish: *Ladrones* 4 reels

Blotto 3 reels
✔ French: *Une Nuit Extravagante* 4 reels
✔ Spanish: *La Vida Nocturna* 4 reels

Brats 2 reels
   German: *Glückliche Kindheit*

Below Zero 2 reels
✔ Spanish: *Titemba Y Titubea* 3 reels

Hog Wild 2 reels
   French: *Pêle-Mêle*
   Spanish: *Radio-Mania*

Pardon Us 6 reels
   French: *Sous Les Verrous*
   German: *Hinter Schloss Und Riegel*
   Italian: *Muraglie*
✔ Spanish: *De Bote En Bote* 7 reels

Be Big! and *Laughing Gravy* 3 reels each
✔ French: *Les Carottiers* 6 reels
✔ Spanish: *Los Calaveras* 6 reels

Chickens Come Home 3 reels
✔ Spanish: *Politiquerias* 6 reels

The Laurel-Hardy Murder Case 3 reels
   with added scenes from *Berth Marks*
   2 reels
   French: *Feu Mon Oncle*
   German: *Der Spuk Um Mitternacht*
✔ Spanish: *Noche de Duendes* 5 reels

✔ indicates that the film has survived.

187

APPENDIX 3:
RECOMMENDED READING

Laurel and Hardy live on in *Bowler Dessert*, the twice yearly magazine established in 1976 for Laurel and Hardy buffs. Some items in this book originated there. For subscription details, send a SAE to the publisher of this book.

INDEX

Abbott and Costello: 170, 178, see also Costello, Lou

Academy Awards: 70, 71, 74, 116, see also Oscars

Adrian, Iris: 23

A-Haunting We Will Go: 50, 75, 97, 98

Air Raid Wardens: 34, 98, 135

Angora Love: 98

Another Fine Mess: 64, 69, 89, 138

Any Old Port: 30, 83, 84, 90, 99, 137, 140, 164, 170

apocryphal anecdotes: 147-150

Arbuckle, Roscoe "Fatty": 39

Atoll K: 35, 40, 44, 65, 99, 120, 167

Autobiography of a Jeep: 124, 152

Babes in Toyland: 32, 49, 65, 75, 77, 78, 80, 94, 114, 149, 165, 169

Baby Brother: 145

Bacon Grabbers: 11, 37

Balloonland: 116

Bankrupt Honeymoon, A: 144

Banks, Monty: 112

Barker, Ronnie: 45, 57, 153, 161

Barnum and Ringling, Inc: 145

Battle of the Century, The: 11, 27, 37, 55, 73, 87, 99, 131, 133, 138

Battling Bosko: 115

Beau Hunks: 12, 29, 31, 64, 75, 90, 106, 139, 169, 170

Be Big!: 67, 133

Below Zero: 29, 37, 63, 75, 88, 137, 154

Bernard, Harry: 137

Berth Marks: 49, 63, 64, 85, 87, 99

Big Business: 28, 64, 73, 77, 127, 138, 139, 149, 155, 163

Big House, The: 31, 78

Big Noise, The: 35, 50, 77, 95, 99, 102

Big Snooze, The: 116

Bishop Auckland: 7, 15, 41, 163

Block-Heads: 34, 50, 51, 83, 95, 98, 103, 127, 140, 169

Block-Heads (musical): 67

Blotto: 29, 85, 105, 133, 141, 170

Blotto (magazine): 24

Bohemian Girl, The: 23, 32, 37, 52, 75, 77, 84, 94, 101, 136, 138, 145, 165, 171

Bonnie Scotland: 32, 47, 49, 63, 64, 77, 79, 84, 94, 101, 127, 152, 167

Bosko's Garage: 116

Bosko's Knight-Mare: 115

Bosko's Picture Show: 116

Bowler Dessert: 17, 23, 188

bowler hat: 27, 47-49, 54, 58, 65, 67, 113, 116, 117, 152, 154, 171

Brats: 29, 43, 88, 90, 141, 170

Brave Tin Soldier, The: 116

Brooks, Leo: 16, 22, 23, 28, 38, 55, 74, 79, 80, 147, 150

Brothers under the Chin: 141

Buddy's Adventures: 115

Bullfighters, The: 35, 99, 154

Busch, Mae: 40, 77, 80, 83, 89, 93, 94, 101, 125, 129, 130, 145, 162, 163

Busy Bodies: 62

Call of the Cuckoos: 47, 64, 80, 134, 165

Campbell, Eric: 40

Candy Trail, The: 143

Cannon and Ball: 58

Cardiff: 177

cars: 28, 47, 87-89, 93, 95, 105, 140, 171

cartoon films: 18, 29, 115-117, 153, 154, 169

Case of the Stuttering Pig, The: 115, 117

Castle, Roy: 38, 44, 68, 153, 155, 161

centenaries: 43, 125, 151, 159

Chaplin, Charlie: 9, 16, 18, 40, 47, 58, 68, 69, 72, 74, 112, 132, 148, 151, 174

Chase, Charley: 22, 30, 40, 49, 71, 77, 80, 93, 95, 98, 109, 123, 125, 132, 134, 137, 138, 144, 145

Chickens Come Home: 49, 63, 64, 76, 89, 98, 126, 129

Chimp, The: 43, 51, 89, 90, 140, 145, 147

Choo-Choo!: 145

chronological listing of Laurel and Hardy films: 185

Chump at Oxford, A: 11, 34, 53, 95, 102, 121, 133, 161

Circus, The: 117

Classic Images: 61

clothes: 22, 47-48, 152

Clyde, Andy: 126, 145

Cobh: 179

Color Rhapsodies: 116

colour: 31, 35, 71, 73, 81, 82, 94, 113, 114, 119

Come Clean: 29, 75, 80, 83, 84, 90, 105, 151, 153

Comic, The: 171

compilation films: 5, 55, 74, 120, 121, 183

Concealed Bed, The: 126

connections: 154, 169-171, 181

continuity errors: 87-96

Coo-Coo Nut Grove: 115

Cooke, Baldwin: 137

Cork: 179

Costello, Lou: 11

County Hospital: 30, 43, 90, 99, 106, 144, 151

Cuckoo Song The, see *Dance of the Cuckoos*

Culver City: 30, 64

Cushing, Peter: 11, 53, 161

Dahlberg, Mae: 7, 16, see also Laurel, Mae

Daily Express: 10, 61, 149

Daily Mail: 171

Daily Mirror: 12

Daily Star: 45, 61, 159

Daily Telegraph: 71

Dance of the Cuckoos, The: 43, 64, 65, 113, 115-117, 153, 155, 179

Dancing Masters, The: 11, 95, 99, 144

deletions: 31, 83-85, 94

Delfont, Lord (Bernard): 174, 179

Dent, Vernon: 144

derby: 47, 145, see also bowler hat

Dick + Doof: 60

Dirty Work: 47, 65, 75, 80, 83, 99, 155

Doctor Bluebird: 116

Do Detectives Think?: 27, 87, 120

Don Quixote: 85

Double Whoopee: 11, 28, 99, 131, 136, 138

Driver's Licence Sketch, The: 38, 113

Duck Soup: 69, 142, 166, 169

Early to Bed: 73, 162, 169

Eastwood, Clint: 149, 171

Empire Theatre, Edinburgh: 181

Empire Theatre, Glasgow: 177, 180

Empire Theatre, Liverpool: 54, 177

Empire Theatre, London: 127

Empire Theatre, Newcastle: 40, 179

epilogue: 183

Everson, William K: 55, 84, 138

Exhibitor: 170

factfile: 7

fandom: 43-45 etc

favourite films: 16, 23, 79, 147

Fighting Kentuckian, The: 23, 145, 151

film collecting: 119-121

Filmfax: 72, 97

Film Fun: 157-158

film 107 and beyond: 123-124

Films in Review: 62

films listing: 185

Film Weekly: 59, 60, 84

Finishing Touch, The: 37, 98, 135, 139

Finlayson, James: 28, 34, 43, 50, 53, 75, 76, 80, 88, 95, 101, 102, 111, 125-128, 131, 133, 134, 139, 142, 154, 166, 169

Fixer-Uppers, The: 94, 99, 129, 140

Flying Deuces, The: 13, 34, 63, 75, 78, 79, 98, 111, 121, 139

Flying Elephants: 117, 120

foreign language films: 28, 31, 85-86, 187

Foreign Legion: 61, 75, 106, 139

Fort Laurel: 17, 18

Fra Diavolo (Devil's Brother, The): 23, 31, 53, 75, 77, 91, 101, 127, 136, 138, 162

Fraternally Yours: 157, see also *Sons of the Desert*

freak endings: 27, 35, 75, 98, 115, 154

From Soup to Nuts: 27, 37, 49, 84, 99, 135

Garvin, Anita: 10, 27, 37, 53, 125, 133, 142, 145

Gehring, Wes: 17

Get 'Em Young: 124, 142

Gilbert, Billy: 40, 64, 75, 80, 90, 125, 132, 147, 164

Going Bye-Bye!: 75, 99, 138

Golf: 144

golf: 7, 25, 40, 87, 128, 135, 173

Gombell, Minna: 50, 51

Great Guns: 11, 34, 38, 97, 98, 112, 139, 171

Great Race, The: 9

Guardian, The: 54, 157

Habeas Corpus: 73, 75, 77, 80

Hall, Charlie: 80, 89, 90, 93, 125, 130, 131, 145, 148

Halliwell, Leslie: 9, 44

Hall, Ron: 131, 148

Hancock, Tony: 57, 152

Hardy, Lucille: 21-25, 55, 70, 74, 79, 174, 178, 179

Hardy, Oliver: 7, 21-25 etc

Hardy without Laurel: 43, 73, 95, 123, 143-145 etc

Harlow, Jean: 11, 29, 38, 40

Harmon, Larry: 117, 153, 154

Harper, Alan: 120

Harris, Georgie: 51

Hatley, T Marvin: 55, 64, 74, 84

Hats Off: 27, 48, 53, 73, 117

Hay, Will: 41, 169, 175

Helpmates: 44, 69, 84, 113, 163

Hill, Jack: 137

Hog Wild: 89, 120, 164

Holiday For Shoestrings: 116

Hollywood Canine Canteen: 116

Hollywood Party: 11, 32, 37, 99, 140

Hollywood Picnic: 116

Hollywood Revue of 1929, The: 11, 74, 86

Hollywood Steps Out: 116

Hoose-Gow, The: 88, 138, 140, 143

Hoots Mon: 167

Hop, Skip and a Chump: 116

Horne, James: 106, 169

horses: 37, 65, 75, 84, 87, 115

Housman, Arthur: 99, 125, 137, 169

Hungry Hearts: 143

Independent on Sunday, The: 62

Independent, The: 157

influences: 57, 67, 97, 142, 169-171

Internet: 163, 164

Jefferson, Arthur (Snr): 15, 41, 45, 107, 126, 167

Jefferson, Arthur Stanley: 7, 11, 15-19, 51, 126, 137, 167, see also Laurel, Stan

Jitterbugs: 23, 98, 143

Jones, Virginia Lucille: 7, 21, 24, 150 see also Hardy, Lucille

Just Rambling Along: 49, 139

Karloff, Boris: 11

Karno, Fred: 7, 16, 17, 41, 68, 69, 72, 136, 142

Keaton, Buster: 9, 11, 19, 62, 74, 132, 152, 169

Kelly, Patsy: 40, 54, 77, 132, 137, 138

Kennedy, Edgar: 40, 41, 78, 98, 125, 135, 169

Keystone Kops: 30, 135

Kid Speed: 144

Langdon, Harry: 34, 40, 111, 132, 145

Lantz, Walter: 116, 117

later films: 97, 99, etc

Lauder, Sir Harry: 126, 175

Laughing Gravy: 36, 37, 44, 65, 89, 168

Laughing Gravy (dog): 37, 89, 162

Laurel and Hardy Charity Fund: 164

Laurel and Hardy Club: 165

Laurel and Hardy Foundation: 166

Laurel and Hardy (play): 11, 67

Laurel-Hardy Murder Case, The: 62, 85

Laurel, Lois: 7, 15, 18, 30, 51, 113, 153

Laurel, Mae: 139, 141

Laurel, Ruth: 7, 16, 25, 79

Laurel, Stan: 7, 15-19 etc

Laurel without Hardy: 31, 49, 96, 123, 139-142, 151 etc

Lawrence, Rosina: 10, 137

Leave 'Em Laughing: 75, 98, 131, 135, 140

Leno, Dan: 69, 148

Lewis, Jerry: 19, 171

Liberty: 11, 120, 143, 169

Lind, Della: 49, 95, 110, 114

Little and Large: 65

Live Ghost, The: 75, 94, 141, 143

Lloyd, Harold: 9, 19, 57, 169

Lollipop film: 124

London, Babe: 29

Long, Walter: 89, 125, 138

Looney Tunes: 115, 116

Los Angeles Times: 28, 81, 104, 128

Love 'Em and Weep: 87, 126, 129, 131

Lucky Dog, The: 161

Lucky Strike, A: 143

Lufkin, Sam: 138

Lyn, Jacquie: 31, 108

Man About Town, A: 140

March of the Wooden Soldiers: 32, 45, see also *Babes in Toyland*

Marian, Edna: 49

Marshall, George: 40, 79, 91

Marx Brothers, The: 126, 132, 169

Mastermind: 154

McCabe, John: 9, 21, 22, 67, 72, 161

McCarey, Leo: 16, 64, 71, 117, 169

McGrath, Tom: 11, 67

Me and My Pal: 64, 98

Me and My Shadow: 98

Men o' War: 47, 88, 170

Merho: 166

Merry Mutineers: 116

Metcalfe, Madge: 15, 41, 160, 167

Metropole Theatre, Glasgow: 15, 126, 167

MGM: 11, 28, 31, 34, 74, 75, 78, 81, 82, 97, 135, 147, 165, 166

Mickey's Gala Premiere: 115

Mickey's Polo Team: 115

Midnight Patrol, The: 75, 84, 92, 93, 170

Milledgeville: 22

Monkhouse, Bob: 57, 154, 161

Morse, Viola: 150

Mother Goose Goes Hollywood: 116

Movie Mad: 116

Movie Struck: 116

Murphy, Jimmy: 10, 38, 72

Museum, Ulverston: 44, 159

music: 19, 32, 33, 55, 63-66, 74, 81, 84, 85, 89, 94, 101, 115, 153, see also musicals

musicals: 67, 101, 102, 114

Music Box, The: 30, 44, 47, 57, 62, 64, 70, 74, 75, 80, 90, 131, 139, 147, 153, 164, 171

Navy Blue Days: 142

Near Dublin: 141

Neilson, Lois: 7

Night in an English Music Hall, A: 16

Night Owls: 28, 85, 88, 135

Noon Whistle, The: 139

Norman, Barry: 57, 151

North Shields: 15, 19, 39

Nothing But Trouble: 74, 99, 112

Novelty Shop, The: 115

Now I'll Tell One: 73, 123

Oliver the Eighth: 30, 47, 80, 93, 99

Omnibus: Cuckoo: 25, 113, 151

One Good Turn: 30, 98

On the Wrong Trek: 10, 30, 64, 95, 134

Oranges and Lemons: 140

Organ Grinder, The: 115

Oscars: 30, 64, 183, see also Academy Awards

Our Gang: 70, 74, 77, 102, 132, 137, 142, 145

Our Relations: 23, 33, 76, 77, 99, 121, 127, 137, 141

Our Wife: 29, 47, 89

Pack Up Your Troubles: 31, 51, 69, 91, 108, 119, 149, 173

Pair of Tights, A: 133

Palace Theatre, Hull: 180

Palace Theatre, Manchester: 176

Panopticon Theatre, Glasgow: 15, 167

Pardon Us: 11, 31, 37, 63, 77, 78, 83, 86, 89, 119, 138, 153, 159, 170

Parker, Jean: 13, 40, 96

Parrott, Charles, see Chase, Charley

Perfect Clown, The: 144

Perfect Day: 28, 76, 98, 105, 121, 170

Pet Store, The: 116

Photoplay: 17, 21, 60

pianos: 12, 13, 47, 49, 64, 66, 80, 90, 139, 140, 144, 146, 147, 161, 164

Pick and Shovel: 140

Pick a Star: 10, 63, 117, 167

Picturegoer, The: 59

Pitts, ZaSu: 40, 132, 137, 138

plays: 11, 15, 67, 68

Plump and Runt: 143

Pollard, Daphne: 94

Pollard, Snub: 37, 40

polls: 44, see also favourite films

Porky's Five and Ten: 116

Pratfall: 47

pressbooks: 29, 30, 79, 97, 101, 105, 107, 109, 111, 147, 149

print, in: 59-62

props: 38, 47-48 etc

Putting on the Act: 116

Putting Pants on Philip: 16, 27, 37, 73, 87, 159, 167, 169

radio: 23, 37-39, 43, 64, 65, 67, 84, 111, 162, 179

Raggedy Rose: 133, 142

Raphael, Ida Kitaeva: 7, 17, 174, 178 etc

recollections: 27, 51-55, 72, 114, 126, 133, 142, 148, 157, 168 etc

Reeves, Myrtle Lee: 7, 22, 23

reviews: 15, 31, 32, 34, 37, 67, 68, 101-104 etc

Richard, Viola: 138, 144

Riding High: 145

Roach, Hal: 28, 30, 33, 34, 40, 51, 70, 71, 73, 75, 77-82, 104, 113, 114, 127, 133, 135, 136, 142, 147-149, 180 etc

Roach studios: 16, 22, 27, 28, 37, 38, 41, 47, 51, 60, 64, 70, 71, 74, 97, 105, 107, 109, 110, 117, 126, 127, 131, 132, 136-138, 150, 183 etc

Rock, Joe: 10, 133, 141

Rogers, Charlie: 136

Rogers, Virginia Ruth: 7, 79, see also Laurel, Ruth

Rogue Song, The: 31, 74, 81, 82, 104, 113, 140

Romney, Hythe and Dymchurch Railway: 120, 176

Roughest Africa: 124, 140, 151

Royal Pictorial Magazine: 22, 52, 59, 85, 146

Sailors Beware!: 133, 144

Saloshin, Madelyn: 7, 22

Sandford, Stanley "Tiny": 83, 125, 138, 153

Saps at Sea: 50, 63, 76, 80, 95, 111, 128, 149, 150

Save the Ship: 140

Sawmill, The: 143

Scorching Sands: 140

Scram!: 90, 137

Scrappy's Party: 116

Screen Snapshots: 123

Secombe, Harry: 38, 161

Second Hundred Years, The: 73, 140

Seeing the World: 142

Sellers, Peter: 170

Semon, Larry: 23, 123, 143, 144

Sennett, Mack: 19, 61, 112, 126, 129, 133, 135

sequels: 77

Shield, Le Roy: 64, 101

Shipman, Ben: 97, 174

Ship's Reporter: 120

Short Kilts: 141, 167

Shot in the Dark, A: 170

Should Married Men Go Home?: 37, 87, 135, 138, 139

Should Tall Men Marry?: 140

Shuvalova, Vera Ivanova ("Illeana"): 7

Silly Symphonies: 29, 116

singing: 21, 32, 53, 63, 81-82, 91, 93, 101, 103, 126, 129, 145

64,000 Dollar Question, The: 154

Skinner, Frank: 12

Skretvedt, Randy: 45, 76, 83, 123

Slade, Stan: 155

Sleuth, The: 142

Slippery Pearls, The, see *Stolen Jools, The*

Slipping Wives: 142

slips: 62, 87-96

Snow Hawk, The: 142

Soda Squirt: 115

Soilers, The: 140

solo films, see Laurel without Hardy and see Hardy without Laurel

Something In Her Eye: 49, 120, 143

Sons of the Desert: 31, 43, 44, 48, 49, 64, 76, 79, 83, 85, 93, 109, 132, 134, 150, 151, 163, 165, 169

Sons of the Desert (club): 12, 13, 44, 54, 67, 114, 129, 151, 155, 157, 159, 161-166, 168, 170, 183

stamps: 38

Stan and Ollie (musical): 67

Stan Visits Ollie: 113

star quotes: 57-58 etc

Stevens, George: 37, 40, 58

Stick Around: 144

Stock Company: 74, 125-138 etc

Stolen Jools, The: 11, 29, 74, 152

Sugar Daddies: 142, 126, 127

Sunday Mail: 48, 61

supporting players: 74, 125-138 etc

Swiss Miss: 23, 33, 48-51, 63, 64, 95, 102, 110, 114, 139, 141, 169, 170

television: 19, 21, 24, 38, 44, 57, 70, 74, 75, 81, 115, 117, 120, 124, 136, 151-155, 180

testimonials: 9-13, 163

That's My Wife: 27

Their First Mistake: 47, 83

Them Thar Hills: 44, 63, 75, 77, 93, 120, 129, 130, 142

They Go Boom: 141

Thicker Than Water: 30, 39, 75, 80, 94, 99, 107

This Is Your Life: 21, 38, 123

Thundering Fleas: 145

tie twiddle: 22, 53, 74, 108, 113, 116, 140, 153, 171, 177

Times, The: 45, 60, 61

Timid Toreador: 116

Tit for Tat: 77, 120, 129, 138

Todd, Thelma: 40, 64, 77, 101, 127, 132, 135, 137, 138, 169

tours, Laurel and Hardy on (British): 13, 18, 48, 52, 53, 54, 64, 97, 120, 121, 123, 173-181

Towed in a Hole: 30, 44, 49, 63, 69, 79, 91, 141, 143, 153, 155

Toyland Premiere: 116

Trail of the Lonesome Pine, The: 43, 54, 63, 65, 75, 103, 152, 154, 155

Tree in a Test Tube, The: 48, 113, 123

Twentieth Century Fox: 23, 50, 51, 85, 97-99, 144

Twice Two: 30, 91, 107, 170

Twins: 141

Two Lazy Crows: 116

Two Tars: 85, 87, 161, 164

Two Tickets to Broadway: 99

Ulverston: 7, 11, 12, 15, 19, 34, 39, 41, 44, 67, 159-160

Unaccustomed As We Are: 28, 98, 135

Under Two Jags: 139

Universal Studios: 16, 70, 82, 133, 141

Untitled Laurel and Hardy: 98

Utopia, see *Atoll K*

Van Dyke, Dick: 38, 40, 57, 171

variations: 83-86

Variety: 34, 79, 80, 101, 139, 142, 147

video: 27, 31, 37, 61, 70, 86, 119-121, 151

Voice of Hollywood, The: 124

Waiting for Godot: 67

Wakefield, Bill: 157

Wakefield, Terry: 157

Wardell, Nancy: 164

Water Rats, Grand Order of: 69, 155, 175

Way Out West: 10, 11, 23, 33, 44, 62-65, 75-77, 84, 95, 103, 113, 127, 137, 139, 151, 167, 169, 170, 171

We Faw Down: 37

What-A-Mess at the Seaside: 117

When Comedy Was King: 5, 183

White Wings: 140, 151

Why Girls Love Sailors: 27, 74, 133, 142, 166

Wilder, Billy: 61

Wild Poses: 74, 75, 141

Wisdom, Norman: 13, 175

With Love and Hisses: 53, 87, 133

Wizard of Oz, The: 23, 73, 144

World Film News: 9, 34, 60, 103

Wrong Again: 64, 65, 87

You Bet!: 12, 154

Youngson, Robert: 55, 74, 183

You Ought to be in Pictures: 116

You're Darn Tootin': 63, 87, 120, 135, 145, 170

Zenobia: 96, 145